OLD TESTAMENT MESSAGE

A Biblical-Theological Commentary

Carroll Stuhlmueller, C.P. and Martin McNamara, M.S.C.

EDITORS

Old Testament Message, Volume 10

JEREMIAH 26-52, HABAKKUK, ZEPHANIAH, NAHUM

Lawrence Boadt, C.S.P.

 Michael Glazier, Inc.
Wilmington, Delaware

ABBREVIATIONS

ANET *Ancient Near Eastern Texts Relating to the Old Testament.*
      James B. Pritchard, editor. 3 ed. with supplement. Princeton University: 1969

ANEP *The Ancient Near East in Pictures Relating to the Old Testament.*
      James B. Pritchard, editor. Princeton University: 1954

First published in 1982 by: MICHAEL GLAZIER, INC.
1723 Delaware Avenue, Wilmington, Delaware 19806

Distributed outside U.S., Canada & Philippines by: GILL & MACMILLAN, LTD., Goldenbridge, Inchicore, Dublin 8 Ireland

Library of Congress Catalog Card Number: 81:85273
International Standard Book Number
  Old Testament Message series: 0-89453-235-9
  JEREMIAH 26-52, HABAKKUK, ZEPHANIAH, NAHUM
  0-89453-244-8 (Michael Glazier, Inc.)
  7171-1174-1 (Gill & Macmillan, Ltd.)

Cover design by Lillian Brulc
Typography by Robert Zerbe/Graphics

Printed in the United States of America

TABLE OF CONTENTS

EDITORS' PREFACE viii

GENERAL INTRODUCTION TO VOLUME TWO . x

Jeremiah 26-52

INTRODUCTION TO JEREMIAH 26-52 3

BOOK I: JEREMIAH 26-36
A Limited Hope Within the Message of Judgment..... 8

  I. Jeremiah 26-29. Jeremiah counters the
      false word of Hope...................... 10
      26:1-24 The Response to the Temple Sermon .. 10
      27:1-22 The Call to Submit to Babylon........ 16
      28:1-17 Prophet Against Prophet 21
      29:1-32 Jeremiah's Letter to the Exiles 26

  II. Jeremiah 30-33. The "Book of Consolation" ... 34
      A Special Word on Chapters 30-31 38
      30:1-31 "Fear Not, O Jacob my Servant!"..... 39
      31:1-40 "I will make a New Covenant" 45
      32:1-15 Investing in the Future 59
      32:16-44 Jeremiah's Prayer 63
      33:1-26 The Promise to Jerusalem and Judah ..67

  III. Jeremiah 34-36. Warnings to Attend to
      the Warning............................ 71
      34:1-22 "Obey the Word of the Lord,
      Zedekiah!" 72
      35:1-19 The Rigorism of the Rechabites 77
      36:1-32 Jehoiakim Rejects Jeremiah's Words ...82

BOOK II: JEREMIAH 37-45
JEREMIAH'S LIFE DURING THE FINAL DAYS
OF JUDAH 91

  I. Jeremiah 37-38. Fainthearted Zedekiah
     Confronts Jeremiah 92
     37:1-21 Jeremiah in Prison 92
     38:1-28 A Second Story of Jeremiah's Arrest ... 95

  II. Jeremiah 39-45. Jeremiah After the Fall 97
     39:1-18 Jeremiah's Release and Freedom 98
     40:1-16 An Upright Governor, Gedeliah 101
     41:1-18 The Abomination of Ishmael 104
     42:1-22 Jeremiah's Warning Against Going
        to Egypt 107
     43:1-13 Jeremiah Taken Into Egypt 109
     44:1—45:5 Jeremiah's Final Warning 111

BOOK III: JEREMIAH 46-51
ORACLES AGAINST FOREIGN NATIONS 117
     46:1-28 Oracles Against Egypt 120
     47:1-7 Oracle Against Philistines 124
     48:1-47 Oracles Against Moab 126
     49:1-22 Oracles Against Ammon and Edom ... 130
     49:23-39 Oracles Against Damascus, Kedar
        and Elam 135
     50:1-32 Warning and Curse of Babylon 138
     50:33-46 The Redeemer Comes in Power 142
     51:1-33 God's Punishment of Babylon........ 143
     51:34-58 Babylon's Fate 146
     51:59-64 Thus Shall Babylon Sink 148

BOOK IV: JEREMIAH 52
APPENDIX FROM 2 KGS. 24:18—25:30 150

The Book of Habakkuk

Introduction 157
    1. The New Testament and Habakkuk 157
    2. Date and Origin of the Book 159

3. History of Interpretation 162
4. Cultic Prophecy and Habakkuk 165
5. Major Themes 167

Habakkuk 1:1—2:5a A Cry for Divine Justice 171

Habakkuk 2:5b-20. Introduction 182
   2:5b-20 Judgment on the Nations........... 183

Habakkuk 3:1-19 The Psalm.................. 189

The Book of Zephaniah

Introduction.................................. 201
   1. The Historical Background 201
   2. The Composition of the Book........... 204
   3. The Structure of the Book 207

Zephaniah 1:1—3:20 208
   1:1—2:3 The Coming Day of Judgment 208
   2:4-15 Judgment Day for the Nations 214
   3:1-20 The Call to Jerusalem to Repent 220

The Book of Nahum

Introduction.................................. 233
   1. Date and Origin 233
   2. The Assyrian Danger 237
   3. Plan of the Book...................... 238
   4. Oracles Against Enemies 238
   5. Nahum and the Cult 240

Chapter One.................................. 242

Chapter Two 250

Chapter Three 259

BIBLIOGRAPHY SUGGESTIONS 274

Editors' Preface

Old Testament Message brings into our life and religion today the ancient word of God to Israel. This word, according to the book of the prophet Isaiah, had soaked the earth like "rain and snow coming gently down from heaven" and had returned to God fruitfully in all forms of human life (Isa 55:10). The authors of this series remain true to this ancient Israelite heritage and draw us into the home, the temple and the market place of God's chosen people. Although they rely upon the tools of modern scholarship to uncover the distant places and culture of the biblical world, yet they also refocus these insights in a language clear and understandable for any interested reader today. They enable us, even if this be our first acquaintance with the Old Testament, to become sister and brother, or at least good neighbor, to our religious ancestors. In this way we begin to hear God's word ever more forcefully in our own times and across our world, within our prayer and worship, in our secular needs and perplexing problems.

Because life is complex and our world includes, at times in a single large city, vastly different styles of living, we have much to learn from the Israelite Scriptures. The Old Testament spans forty-six biblical books and almost nineteen hundred years of life. It extends through desert, agricultural and urban ways of human existence. The literary style embraces a world of literature and human emotions. Its history began with Moses and the birth-pangs of a new people, it came of an age politically and economically under David and Solomon, it reeled under the fiery threats of prophets like Amos and Jeremiah. The people despaired and yet were re-created with new hope during the Babylonian exile. Later reconstruction in the homeland and then the trauma of apocalyptic movements prepared for the revelation of "the mystery hidden for ages in God who created all things" (Eph 3:9).

While the Old Testament telescopes twelve to nineteen hundred years of human existence within the small country of Israel, any single moment of time today witnesses to the reenactment of this entire history across the wide expanse of planet earth. Each verse of the Old Testament is being relived somewhere in our world today. We need, therefore, the *entire* Old Testament and all twenty-three volumes of this new set, in order to be totally a "Bible person" within today's widely diverse society.

The subtitle of this series—"A Biblical-Theological Commentary"—clarifies what these twenty-three volumes intend to do.

Their *purpose* is theological: to feel the pulse of God's word for its *religious* impact and direction.

Their *method* is biblical: to establish the scriptural word firmly within the life and culture of ancient Israel.

Their *style* is commentary: not to explain verse by verse but to follow a presentation of the message that is easily understandable to any serious reader, even if this person is untrained in ancient history and biblical languages.

Old Testament Message—like its predecessor, *New Testament Message*—is aimed at the entire English-speaking world and so is a collaborative effort of an international team. The twenty-one contributors are women and men drawn from North America, Ireland, Britain and Australia. They are scholars who have published in scientific journals, but they have been chosen equally as well for their proven ability to communicate on a popular level. This twenty-three book set comes from Roman Catholic writers, yet, like the Bible itself, it reaches beyond interpretations restricted to an individual church and so enables men and women rooted in biblical faith to unite and so to appreciate their own traditions more fully and more adequately.

Most of all, through the word of God, we seek the blessedness and joy of those

who walk in the law of the Lord!...

who seek God with their whole heart (Ps. 119:1-2).

Carroll Stuhlmueller, C.P.   *Martin McNamara, M.S.C.*

GENERAL INTRODUCTION
TO VOLUME TWO

THIS VOLUME OF *Old Testament Message* treats together the second half of the Book of Jeremiah and three short prophetic collections of the late seventh century, B.C., Zephaniah, Nahum and Habakkuk. All four were contemporaries in the days of Josiah and his son Jehoiakim, from about 630 B.C. down to 600 B.C. Those were exciting days although not always the most peaceful and secure ones. Josiah's break into freedom from the Assyrians thrilled the nation, as did his recapture of many of the lands that had belonged to Israel in earlier days. His religious reform stirred hopes and fears and certainly must have increased tension significantly. Then came his untimely death fighting against Egypt and the resulting loss of Judah's power and freedom. Egypt dethroned one son and placed another in power. Soon, the Babylonians defeated the Egyptians and took control of Palestine. They allowed Jehoiakim to remain on the throne if he could prove loyal, but the spirit of rebellion was too strong for him to control. In two disastrous invasions ten years apart, 598 and 587, Babylon destroyed Israel's status as a national state and dismantled its entire religious structure.

For all of this, we have the valuable testimony of the Second Book of Kings as background to the words of these four prophets who each spoke to one or another aspect of the contemporary situation. The Book of Jeremiah with its wealth of oracles and biographical information about the prophet naturally forms the richest source of our study. The previous volume in this series deals with the profound religious thought found in just the first half of Jeremiah. This volume continues with the traditions preserved about Jeremiah's last days in particular and fills this out with commentary on the three minor prophets of the day.

The advantage of putting these all together in one volume comes from the historical insight we gain from seeing such a period of crisis through many different eyes. Those few years may have been the single most important moment in Israel's history as a political nation and as a religious system. Later out of the exilic responses generated by defeat and by recognition of their former religious blindness came the new foundations of both Jewish and Christian faiths. To understand the developments in Ezekiel and in the Priestly editing of the Pentateuch during the Exile, and to appreciate the great rebuilding efforts made by Second Isaiah (Isa 40-55) at the end of the Exile and other prophets in the early postexile period, we must have a good grasp of the situation before the disaster. Luckily we possess that wealth of reflective interpretation needed to gain a good sense of the religious state of affairs of the time.

Two points are of particular importance in viewing these four prophets side by side. First, it enables us to identify at least two, and possibly three (if we include Zephaniah) prophets who come from the central establishment and speak from professional platforms within the cult or official administration, and compare them with Jeremiah, who challenges the establishment and its traditions. The comparison does not diminish our respect for the importance of Jeremiah but does allow us to see that the central cultic prophets were not always as mechanically uninspired and heedless of social questions as they are frequently made out to be. Nahum shows the most restricted outlook of the three because the book contains only oracles dealing with the Assyrian question. But both Habakkuk and Zephaniah address questions of trust and faith and the problem of God's just punishment of his own people which bear many resemblances to Jeremiah's words.

The second point of comparison bears upon the influence of Isaiah's prophetic message a century earlier. The confident proclamation of Yahweh's love for Zion and his willingness to protect her in time of need clearly draws much from the traditions of Isaiah at the time of the Assyrian siege under Sennacherib. Nahum and Habakkuk both employ Isaianic imagery in their messages, and stand out as witnesses to the widespread belief in the promises of the Davidic covenant in 7th century Judah. This contrasts starkly with the pessimism of Jeremiah who consistently views the destruction of the nation and the kingship as inevitable even to the point where God has actually commanded the prophet not to intercede on behalf of the people (14:11-12; 15:1-2).

As in the other volumes of this commentary, space does not permit the inclusion of the whole text of these prophetic books. A key selection from each major unit heads the section, but the commentary will range across the whole passage to show its overall message. Therefore, the reader may want to look over the whole text of a section in his or her bible and also check the many biblical references in the commentary. Since this is a theological commentary series, the discussion of the text hopefully directs the reader back to the word of the Scripture itself and challenges each person to think more deeply about the quality and meaning of his or her own Christian life today as a result of the encounter with the Word of God.

Jeremiah
26 – 52

INTRODUCTION TO
JEREMIAH 26 – 52

THE SECOND HALF of the Book of Jeremiah has a different flavor from chaps. 1-25. In the first part, the oracles and individual sermons dominated. A reader would have a hard time identifying exactly when many of the prophecies had been spoken. Sometimes it is even difficult to determine where one oracle ends and another begins! Chapters 26-52, on the other hand, contain mostly narratives about the prophet's life and work with a special collection of his words against foreign nations thrown in for good measure. In this brief introduction, only the particular aspects of the last half of the book will be discussed. A more extensive treatment of the background of Jeremiah can be found in the preceding volume in this Commentary series.

The existence of stories about the prophet raises real questions about who preserved and wrote them down. Jeremiah's scribe and right-hand man Baruch plays a leading role in some of these narratives, and many have assumed that he must have produced most of the biographical information, especially in chaps. 37-45 about the last days of his friend and mentor. However, we simply do not know this for certain and it must remain only a pleasing and heartwarming guess. A more probable source for the present theological interpretation of Jeremiah's life and words lies in the teaching and preaching of Israel's religious leaders in exile in Babylon. Recent studies have stressed the importance of the Deuteronomistic teachers (possibly made up of both prophets and levitical priests in developing Israel's interpretation of the catastrophe of defeat and exile in 587). It appears in the Book of Deuteronomy itself, in their historical collection that runs from Joshua through 2 Kings, and in the prose passages in Jeremiah. We have already seen many close connections in thought between Jeremiah and the Deuteronomic school in chaps. 1-25. The ties become more understandable in the second half of the book where it is clear that the stories about Jeremiah serve as models for the exilic communities. His words were proved true by subsequent events, and naturally those exiled far from the homeland would look more to his insights than to the comforting phrases of prophets like Hananiah (chap. 28). E. W. Nicholson has developed arguments for this position in his book, *Preaching to the Exiles*. He argues with considerable force that many of the prose portions of Jeremiah show the results of a number of years of sermons preached upon the words of Jeremiah's oracles. Behind almost every prose unit stands a genuine oracle or basic insight of the prophet, but it has been expanded by exhortations and moral reflections that apply to an audience in exile. Thus words Jeremiah intended for the specific moment of 609 to 587 become reinterpreted as enduring lessons for those left in the land of Israel reeling from disaster, and for her exiles in Babylon, and ultimately for exiles everywhere in all times.

The oracles in chaps. 1-25 contained the basic message of Jeremiah, but they lacked the dramatic personal "story" of the prophet necessary to make his message live on most fully in the lives of later generations. Not only do chaps. 26-52 give us this, but they allow a fine portrait of the true prophet to be drawn up and meditated upon by the exilic community. Jeremiah especially makes a good model for Israel's exilic community because he embodies the rich prophetic traditions established by his predecessors from Amos and Hosea to Isaiah and Micah, as well as by having personally experienced the pain of rejection and defeat that the people suffered. Some commentators compare elements of Jeremiah's work to both the figure of Job and to the suffering servant in Second Isaiah. Jeremiah may have been the model for both, although the connection to Job seems less probable. But we certainly can suggest that the sufferings of Jeremiah played an important part in Israel's post-586 definition of a prophet, at least in Isa 51:13—53:12.

The combination of biographical narrative, comment and exhortatory homilies on Jeremiah's oracles that now constitute the final form of the Book of Jeremiah also allows it to speak in the 20th century. The detailed information about his social ostracism and sense of alienation, his struggles against the institutional thinking of his day, and his open wrestling with God, all appeal to the modern approach to faith that searches for the unique and personal dimensions of our relationship to God. Paradoxically, since Jeremiah had to fight many of his battles in the political and social arena against his fellow citizens, his message supports the current interest in developing an international justice and a new world order that questions whether God always supports a nation or a group of nations just because they honor him and proclaim freedom or democracy as their aim. God can oppose his own people, his own city and temple, his own covenant of old. He cannot be taken for granted, nor can we stop seeking the new directions he is leading us toward now. Many today who anguish over the course of national and international events can find in the message of Jeremiah as strong a support as did Israel in its Babylonian exile.

Another vital contribution of the narratives and oracles against foreign nations in this half of the book comes from the information they reveal about the social setting of

Jeremiah's preaching. The number of officials and priests who cross these chapters represent all shades of opinion. Some, such as the family of Shaphan the Scribe, loyally support Jeremiah to the end. Others, including the kings, sincerely believe that he proposes a disastrous break with true trust in Yahweh and undermines the traditional faith. The entire section within chaps. 26-44 might be called the "Passion of Jeremiah" mostly because it details so much of the political uncertainty and misunderstanding that existed during this time of crisis. Jeremiah seemed to be the only voice in the whole dialogue of what should be done that remained constant in his approach. The context of his oracles in the midst of failing political fortunes and hysteric cries for action illuminates how courageous he was and exactly how challenging his words were to the situation.

Importantly, many of the major themes of his own oracles from chaps. 1-25 are taken up again in chaps. 26-52. The words on false prophecy in chap. 23 become the subject of a narrative about how he dealt with the question in chaps. 27-28. His "Confessions" in chaps. 11-12, 15, 17, 18 and 20 gain in pathos when compared with the story of his sufferings in chaps. 37-39. His famous sermon against the temple in chap. 7 reappears in a slightly different fashion as the initial narrative in chap. 26 to introduce the basic motif of judgment that governs all the passages that follow. Naturally enough, his treatment of sin, the call for repentance, the inevitable judgment of doom, and the role of Babylon as divine agent, all continue through the second half of the book. But above all, these chapters highlight the lonely stance of Jeremiah as the prophet of the Mosaic covenant who intercedes for and mediates God's word to the nation, yet is rejected. This view of the prophet, so dear to the tradition of Hosea and Deuteronomy, came through in the anguished laments of chaps. 1-25, but is now given its proper emphasis by including incidents from his life and their interpretations as an essential part of his message.

The structure of chaps. 26-52 can be broken down into four major sections with a variety of subdivisions:

I. Chaps. 26-36 A limited hope within the Message of Judgment
26-29 Jeremiah counters the False Word of Hope
30-31 Promises of restoration.
32-33 Two signs of hope.
34-36 Further warnings and limits to hope.

II. Chaps. 37-45 Stories of the Last Days of Jeremiah.
37-38 Jeremiah and Zedekiah at the end.
39-45 Jeremiah after the Fall of Jerusalem.

III. Chaps. 46-51 Oracles against Foreign Nations.

IV. Chap. 52 An Historical Appendix about the Fall of Jerusalem.

Each of these will be analyzed in more detail in the comments that follow, for the organization of the material gives valuable clues to the purposes of the editors. It especially helps us to understand how they understood the significance of Jeremiah within Israelite tradition. But we must remember that we do not necessarily receive the first impression that he made on his hearers.

The Septuagint translation, from the pre-Christian period, lacks many passages and obviously stems from a much shorter Hebrew copy than does the usual Masoretic Hebrew text which forms the basis for all modern translations. This fact suggests that at some point the Hebrew collection of Jeremiah's words was carried to Egypt and treasured there until translated into Greek. But meanwhile, editors continued to add more material to the Hebrew text that remained in Babylon or had been taken back from exile to Palestine. In this case, the passages not found in the Septuagint probably represent the latest levels of reflection on Jeremiah, perhaps several decades after his death.

BOOK I

JEREMIAH 26 – 36

A LIMITED HOPE WITHIN THE

MESSAGE OF JUDGMENT

CHAPTERS 26-36 form a loose unity based on the theme of hopefulness. Despite some optimistic—even idealistic— oracles found in chaps. 30-31, the mood of Jeremiah's hopefulness stays muted, almost somber, throughout. God will restore the land and bring the people back from exile in his time, but not quickly. Jeremiah rounds off its predicted length to 70 years, longer than the lifespan of any of the exiles. In the meantime, the proper disposition must be to rediscover the Lord, listen to his Law and to the words of his servants the prophets, and wait.

Chapters 26-29 open the eleven-chapter section with a number of narratives about the prophets who take the opposite position from Jeremiah, promising safety and a speedy release from the power of Babylon. Jeremiah constantly refuses to grant any validity to their false hope. Chapters 30-31 and 32-33 then collect together the major words of hope uttered by the prophet and reworked by his disciples and editors. The central message of these oracles

(30-31) and symbolic actions (32-33) unites the promise of future restoration of the exiles to their homeland with a promised new covenant in the religious sphere. Chapters 34-36 return to warning about the limitations of this hope. In 34, Zedekiah betrays the pledge to free all slaves and so brings the punishment back on his head; in 35, the Rechabites serve as a lesson for Judah about the rigors of fidelity and the cost it requires. In 36, the king tries to kill the prophetic words by burning the scroll on which they have been written, but even such a radical attempt to stop the curse of judgment is doomed since God always preserves the power of the word in his prophets.

Note in the structure of this major division the sandwich effect. It opens with warnings against false prophets who have a mistaken notion of hope, and closes with further examples of wrong-headed ideas about trust in God's protection. Only in the middle section do the editors allow the visionary dreams of restoration to stand free. These are protected on both sides by careful conditions to avoid any repetition of the lies proposed by the false prophets, namely that God *had* to save his people and *could not* let them be destroyed. Beyond this A-B-A pattern that holds the section together, we can note strong similarities between the opening and closing chapters. Chapter 36 seems to echo many of the themes of chap. 26, especially the temple setting and the involvement of all levels of the authorities and people in the discussion of the message.

What might at first appear to be quite a diverse lot of oracles and stories becomes under close observation a tightly knit and purposely ordered unity that allows some message of salvation in Jeremiah's preaching but keeps it far more modest than the flights of imagination found in either Isaiah or Ezekiel. This may be further evidence that the Book of Jeremiah was completely edited while the exile was still on and probably closer to the beginning than to the end.

I. Jeremiah Counters the False Word of Hope
Jeremiah 26 - 29

The major concern of these opening four chapters of the second half of Jeremiah centers on the question of prophetic authority. In some way, all deal directly with the question of the false prophet. In chap. 26, the priests and prophets spearhead the opposition to Jeremiah's most fundamental message: his call to repent or see Jerusalem destroyed. The cases of Micah and Uriah then raise the issue of how a people deals with conflicting prophetic messages. Chapters 27-28 leap ahead to the reign of Zedekiah to present a very difficult example from Jeremiah's own ministry: his confrontation with the prophet Hananiah after delivering his most unwelcome insistence that the whole nation from king to commoner submit wholeheartedly to the rule of Babylon as God's will. His opponent Hananiah, meanwhile, declared the coming end of Babylonian power and indirectly gave support to the movement to fight against Nebuchadnezzar's rule. Finally, in chap. 29, Jeremiah faces a similar situation among the first group of exiles who had been deported to Babylon in 598. He encourages them to accept Babylonian captivity despite the oracles of other prophets on the scene who counsel otherwise.

These chapters, especially 27-29, stand out as a cohesive group with many special features found only here, including the spelling of Nebuchad*rezzar* instead of Nebuchad*nezzar*, the use of formal titles ("*the prophet* Jeremiah"), and unusual spellings for proper names (e.g., Jeconiah for Jehoiachin, Jeremia for Jeremiah).

THE RESPONSE TO THE TEMPLE SERMON
26:1-24

26 In the beginning of the reign of Jehoiakim the son of Josiah, king of Judah, this word came from the

LORD, ²"Thus says the LORD: Stand in the court of the LORD'S house, and speak to all the cities of Judah which come to worship in the house of the LORD all the words that I command you to speak to them; do not hold back a word. ³It may be they will listen, and every one turn from his evil way, that I may repent of the evil which I intend to do to them because of their evil doings. ⁴You shall say to them, 'Thus says the LORD: If you will not listen to me, to walk in my law which I have set before you, ⁵and to heed the words of my servants the prophets whom I send to you urgently, though you have not heeded, ⁶then I will make this house like Shiloh, and I will make this city a curse for all the nations of the earth.'"

26:1-6 seems to cover the same ground as chap. 7 does. The message threatens the destruction of the temple itself if the people do not accept the invitation to repent of their evil and turn back to the ways of God. If they refuse, the temple city of Jerusalem will become like that of the earlier temple city of Shiloh where the ark had remained during the period of the Judges until captured by the Philistines in the battle of Ebenezer (1 Sam 4; Ps 78:60-61). At that time, the Philistines must have moved on to destroy Shiloh itself for the archaeological remains show that it suffered total devastation in the eleventh century.

Since the similarities between the two chapters are striking, chap. 26 must be a shortened version of the earlier sermon. It lacks any of the detailed lists of offenses found in 7:6-9 and contents itself with summing them up under the twofold failure of the nation either to walk in the Law of the Lord or to heed the words of his servants the prophets. It also neglects to mention the pagan idolatry going on in Jerusalem and passes over the proper relation of sacrifice to justice, both of which figure notably in chap. 7. Another difference between the two speeches lies in the almost total focus on Jerusalem in the later chapter, while chap. 7 always speaks to the whole land of Judah as well as to the

capital city. The reason for this shortened account in chap.
26 lies in the overall purpose of the editors. They want to
show the reaction of the various groups of citizens to
Jeremiah's message. This leads them to write down a short
sermon, but a long description of its consequences. Not only
does Jeremiah go on trial immediately but the cases of two
other famous dissenting prophets are brought up to illus-
trate the danger to which he has exposed himself by not
holding back even a word (26:2)!

If we look at the scene in vv. 7-9, we can imagine everyone's rage. Jeremiah stationed himself in the gateway as
people came and went from their sacrifices and prayers.
Many undoubtedly prayed that God would stand by them
for personal needs or desires; meanwhile the priests and
prophets performing the official liturgy may well have been
reciting psalms of confidence that God would never abandon Zion and the temple (*cf.*, Pss 66, 68 or 108 as examples).
All of them, priests, prophets and people, were unprepared
for the threats uttered by Jeremiah. The "curse" pronounced in v. 6 should be understood more as a witness
to all nations that God had abandoned Israel. The ruined
temple would be the evidence that their god had struck
down his own rather than protected them. Said in the
temple itself, it offended the reverence due to God's house,
challenged the promises and the covenantal *hesed*, the "enduring mercy" of Yahweh, and had to be taken as a capital
offense. The formula, "You shall die" occurs in the early
laws of Israel to signify the death sentence. Jeremiah could
well have been stoned to death (see Lev 24:10-16).

Legal custom probably required the official judges to
rule in a case of capital punishment, and so the princes are
called down from the administrative palace to the open
space in front of the gates where trials were normally con-
ducted (Ruth 4:1-12). These "princes" were high officials
in the king's central administration and often served as
his messengers (21:1) and counsellors in matters of policy
(36:12-19). The real issues come out in the trial scenes of

vv. 10-16. The priests and the prophets are determined to stop Jeremiah by bringing charges against him that will end his career once and for all. The princes preside at the hearing, and presumably have the power to carry out a sentence, but they do not seem to have acted alone in deciding the case. Verse 16 shows that the voice of the people had an important role to play in the final judgment, and it is they who turn from the plan of the religious leaders to support Jeremiah's plea. Whether it was because of their respect for the office of prophet and their conviction that Jeremiah was authentic despite his unbelievable predictions, or simply out of fear that God would indeed bring a curse on them all if he was railroaded to death, we cannot know.

Jeremiah defends himself by declaring that these words do not come from him but from the Lord, and if they act against him, they act against God. He only speaks what God sends him to speak, and he himself has no other weapon but the word. They can take his life, but God's word cannot be stopped so easily. Instead of a warning with its invitation to repent and be spared, they would insure judgment by spilling his innocent blood.

The people argue that Jeremiah has spoken in the name of God, which suggests that they recognized in his words the signs of a true prophet. It could not be just the formula, "Thus says the Lord," for Hananiah uses the same words in 28:2. More likely they were moved by his message of doom as the sign of a special commission that placed him outside the ordinary role of prophets in the liturgy, but clearly within another tradition of Israelite prophets who challenged the political order in the name of Yahweh. This seems even more certain when the elders bring up the example of Micah of Moresheth as a parallel to Jeremiah's case. The elders in Israel were the representatives of the local interests of the people, and the decision makers for towns and villages. They often played important roles in issues that affect the traditions of Israel (*cf.*, Exod 17:5-7;

24:1-4; Josh 20:4; 1 Sam 8:4; 11:3; 2 Sam 17:4; 1 Kgs 20:7-9).
So here they reach back a hundred years to note that the
message of Micah did not fall on hostile ears, but caused
Hezekiah and the people to repent and thus be saved from
disaster. Many of Micah's words have been preserved,
including the short sentence in v. 18 (from Mic 3:12), but
nowhere else do we hear that he had such an influence over
royal policy. This passage does confirm for us, however,
the certainty that the oracles of prophets were saved and
written down within a fairly short time after their delivery.

Finally, in vv. 20-23, the editors attach a more recent case
of a prophet who spoke out against the king with far
different results.

> 20There was another man who prophesied in the name
> of the LORD, Uriah the son of Shemaiah from Kiriath-
> jearim. He prophesied against this city and against this
> land in words like those of Jeremiah. 21And when King
> Jehoiakim, with all his warriors and all the princes,
> heard his words, the king sought to put him to death; but
> when Uriah heard of it, he was afraid and fled and
> escaped to Egypt. 22Then King Jehoiakim sent to Egypt
> certain men, Elnathan the son Achbor and others with
> him, 23and they fetched Uriah from Egypt and brought
> him to King Jehoiakim, who slew him with the sword
> and cast his dead body into the burial place of the
> common people.

Uriah had a message similar to Jeremiah's. When the
king sought to execute him he fled to Egypt for safety, the
latest in centuries of refugees from Asia who found a home
in the Northeast corner of Egypt's Delta region nearest the
Sinai. But Jehoiakim had no trouble getting him back from
Egypt as a prisoner when he sent a high-level delegation
headed by one of his princes, Elnathan. Since the pharaoh
Necho had put the king on the throne in 609 in place of his
brother Jehoahaz, he had probably also signed a vassal
treaty with Jehoiakim that guaranteed the extradition of
each other's enemies upon request. The prophet Uriah was
executed as a criminal against the state—killed by a sword

thrust and not permitted burial in a personal tomb. This chilling story of royal violence against a prophet underlines the danger Jeremiah faced during the reign of Jehoiakim. An earlier prophet, Zechariah, met death at the hands of Joash, the king of Judah in the 9th century, for saying much the same thing (2 Chron 24:17-22). The postexilic authors of that account saw the subsequent assassination of Joash as divine punishment for murdering a prophet. Jehoiakim's execution of Uriah could expect a similar divine vengeance to be exacted in turn.

Part of the mixed up nature of the times reveals itself in the role of Elnathan, the prince in charge of the Uriah case. In 26:22, he appears as the willing agent of the king in hunting down the prophet, but in chap. 36, he listens to Baruch's reading of Jeremiah's scroll with reverence and even tries to persuade the king not to destroy it (36:11-13, 25).

THE LEADING FAMILY OF SHAPHAN IN JERUSALEM

SHAPHAN
(2 Kgs 22:3-13;
finds the Book
of the Law in
the temple

AHIKAM	*GEMARIAH*	*ELASAH*
(2 Kgs 22:14-17; goes to Huldah the prophetess; Jer 26:24, saves Jeremiah's life)	(Jer 36:12, 25; He tries to save Jeremiah's scroll)	(Jer 29:3; carries Jeremiah's letter to Exiles)

GEDALIAH	*MICAIAH*
(Jer 39:11-14; 40:1—41:3; made governor of Judah by the Babylonians)	(Jer 36:11; reports Jeremiah's scroll to the leading princes)

Important for Jeremiah's safety was the support he received from the family of Shaphan, the royal scribe who found the Book of the Law in the temple while overseeing its repair for king Josiah (2 Kgs 22:3-14). He had three sons who gave vital support to Jeremiah in crucial moments, and because of their powerful position as a leading family in the government through at least three generations and four kings (Josiah, Jehoahaz, Jehoiakim and Zedekiah), they were able to save his life more than once. One son, Ahikam, both worked with his father Shaphan in consulting the prophetess Huldah about the new Book of the Law (2 Kgs 22:12-17), and years later intervened to save Jeremiah from the priests and prophets at the time of the Temple Sermon (Jer 26:24). A second son, Gemariah, was among the princes who tried to save Jeremiah's scroll from the king's anger (36:25). The last son, Elasah, helped deliver Jeremiah's letter to the exiles (29:3). Among the grandchildren, Micaiah, the son of Gemariah, brought Baruch and the scroll to the princes' attention in the first place, and Gedaliah, the son of Ahikam, became the first governor of the Babylonian province of Judah after the final destruction of Jerusalem in 587 (39:11-14, 40:1—41:3). From the list of their activities, Shaphan's family members must have belonged to the pro-Babylonian faction that supported Josiah's reforms and the kingship of his son Jehoahaz at the expense of the rightful crown prince, Jehoiakim. When the Egyptian army took temporary control of Palestine from 609-605, they deported Jehoahaz as a prisoner to Egypt and installed Jehoiakim as their vassal. Thus Jehoiakim represents the pro-Egyptian party in Judah and undoubtedly tried to check the power of Shaphan as much as possible. But this family still had enough influence to aid Jeremiah in crucial moments.

THE CALL TO SUBMIT TO BABYLON
27:1-22

27 In the beginning of the reign of Zedekiah the son of Josiah, king of Judah, this word came to Jeremiah from the LORD. [2]Thus the LORD said to me: "Make yourself thongs and yoke-bars, and put them on your neck. [3]Send word to the king of Edom, the king of Moab, the king of the sons of Ammon, the king of Tyre, and the king of Sidon by the hand of the envoys who have come to Jerusalem to Zedekiah king of Judah. [4]Give them this charge for their masters: 'Thus says the LORD of hosts, the God of Israel: This is what you shall say to your masters: [5]"It is I who by my great power and my out-stretched arm have made the earth, with the men and animals that are on the earth, and I give it to whomever it seems right to me. [6]Now I have given all these lands into the hand of Nebuchadnezzar, the king of Babylon, my servant, and I have given him also the beasts of the field to serve him. [7]All the nations shall serve him and his son and his grandson, until the time of his own land comes; then many nations and great kings shall make him their slave.

Chapter 27 deals with a very specific message from Jeremiah to both Israel and other nations. They are to submit to the rule of Babylon without rebellion and they are to close their ears to any prophets who preach a quick end to the Babylonian power. The prophet directs this word to three separate parties: (1) the ambassadors of the neighboring small states, (2) the king, Zedekiah, and (3) the priests and people. In this chapter, he does not speak to the prophets because the message is aimed *against* them.

Because the details stand out sharply in these three oracles, historians have been able to pinpoint the time to the year 595-594, based on the remains of the *Chronicles of the Babylonian Kings* from 625 to 594, now in the British Museum. Soon after his conquest of Judah in 598, Nebuchadnezzar faced further attacks in Northern Syria, and then in 596 a war to the East, perhaps in Elam, and in 595 a revolt in his own land plus disturbances to the West. The presence of so many ambassadors from neighboring states of Judah could well mean plans for revolt were in the air.

Quite likely these rumors and hopes were stirred up further by the words reported in chap. 28 from prophets like Hananiah.

Although the chapter opens with a note that it happened in the first year of Jehoiakim, this has to be a mistake. The rest of the chapter definitely identifies the king as Zedekiah, and 28:1 goes on to say that Hananiah prophesied in Zedekiah's 4th year, the same year as the preceding events. Probably a distracted scribe copied the beginning of Jer 26:1 over again by mistake. During this year, Jeremiah begins to appear in public with the wooden yoke of an ox around his neck. Perhaps he said very little at first, since his position was well-known to all, and the symbolic use of a yoke would have been readily understood as a reference to the common metaphor of being under a foreign power. No doubt the presence of so many Moabite, Edomite, Ammonite and Phoenician officials in Jerusalem and the rumored reports about Nebuchadnezzar's problems at home clued Jeremiah into what was being hatched in the palace. In any case, Jeremiah saw this plotting for independence as utter stupidity. He had to oppose it. But we should not think that he had a better military mind or more political insight than the king and princes; his reasons were strictly religious. God had decreed Babylon's victory, and the Lord had given the lands, including Judah, over to Nebuchadnezzar by choice. The Babylonian king was Yahweh's servant (27:6), the instrument of divine will, and human opposition could not win out against him.

The Hebrew word *sheqer*, a "lie" or "falsehood," appears again and again in chaps. 27-29 to label any prophetic messages that challenged this point. The promises of salvation or of a quick end to the exile, or solemn advice to refuse to serve the Babylonians all stem from political hopes that neglect the plan of God which has determined a long period of domination by Babylon. Jeremiah's advice is to settle down, serve the foreign administration obediently, whether in Judah or in exile, and to wait upon the Lord. Babylon will have its day, but it too shall end (27:7).

The first message to the foreign ambassadors in vv. 3-11 presents Israel's God as both creator of the world and divine warrior. He is "Lord of hosts," the commander of all cosmic armies; he does not fear Babylon or its gods. In power, he has created all peoples and structures his creation any way he sees fit, from kings down to the beasts in the wilds. Jeremiah here points back to the faith-tradition of Israel found in Gen 1-2 and in the narratives of Deuteronomy where God leads his people out of Egypt with an "outstretched arm" (Deut 7:19; 4:34; 5:15; 9:29; 11:2; 26:8; *cf.* Exod 6:6). If and when he wills it, deliverance lies in God's power. But at the same time, he can also send punishment in the form of military disaster on those who rebel against Babylon. The "sword, famine and pestilence" might well qualify as Jeremiah's favorite threat, occurring 15 times in the Book (14:12; 21:7,9; 24:10; 27:8,13; 29:19,18; 32:24,36; 34:17; 38:2; 42:17,22; 44:13).

This leads the prophet immediately to a warning against his colleagues who urge rebellion to speed God's deliverance up. The catalog of soothsayers, dream givers, diviners and sorcerers—as well as prophets—in v. 9 suggests that Israel's hopes had reached a fever pitch of excitement with new signs and indications of Babylon's collapse coming in from everywhere and from every kind of "authority." This is the *lie*, because acting on it will mean nothing but further disaster for these small western states. What little freedom the Babylonians had allowed them, would now be lost for good.

The second oracle of Jeremiah follows a short time later (vv. 12-15).

> [12]To Zedekiah king of Judah I spoke in like manner: "Bring your necks under the yoke of the king of Babylon, and serve him and his people, and live. [13]Why will you

and your people die by the sword, by famine, and by pestilence, as the LORD has spoken concerning any nation which will not serve the king of Babylon? [14]Do not listen to the words of the prophets who are saying to you, 'You shall not serve the king of Babylon,' for it is a lie which they are prophesying to you. [15]I have not sent them, says the LORD, but they are prophesying falsely in my name, with the result that I will drive you out and you will perish, you and the prophets who are prophesying to you."

It presupposes that Zedekiah had heard about Jeremiah's message to the foreign ambassadors, and repeats many of the same phrases. Jeremiah did not want the king to get the mistaken notion that his words to Moab and Edom and Ammon, etc. were only the familiar oracle form *against* foreign nations. Such oracles occur elsewhere in Jeremiah (chaps. 25, 46-51) and function indeed as comforting promises to Israel and Judah. But in this case, the prophet includes both Judah and its neighbors in one message because their proposed course of action will affect Judah as much as the other states. Verse 14 does not mention all the soothsayers and dream specialists, which were more typical of pagan religious practices, but Jeremiah certainly knew that many of them found willing clients in Jerusalem itself (*cf.*, 7:17-18; 23:13-14; Ezek 12:24; 13:17-21; Deut 18:9-13). The results of such "false" prophecy would be the same for foreigner and Israelite prophet alike.

The third oracle brings the same message to the priests and people in vv. 16-22, with an added emphasis on the destruction of the temple. 2 Kgs 24:13 records how the Babylonians took all the gold vessels and furnishings in 598-597 after the first siege, but left the bronze instruments and furniture. At the time of the final collapse, 2 Kgs 25:13-17 narrates the immense efforts by the conquerors to break up and cart off even the largest bronze pillars of the temple to Babylon. At the time of this oracle, Jeremiah could not have known for sure that it would end in this manner, but he foresaw it and even challenged the optimistic prophets of hope to prevent it by praying to Yahweh to protect and preserve the temple. The theme of this final address echoes the same ideas as the two Temple Sermons in chaps. 7 and 26, namely that God would not defend the temple while injustice and idolatry controlled the actions of Judah.

Interestingly, the shorter text of chap. 27 in the Septuagint leaves out vv. 17, 18, and 20 which make up a taunt to the false prophets to stop worrying about recovery of the *gold* vessels and instead to intercede with God to prevent the loss of even the *brass* candlesticks in the next fall of the city! These verses may be a later reflection on the basic oracle by Jeremiah's followers in light of the events of 587-586.

PROPHET AGAINST PROPHET
28:1-17

28 In that same year, at the beginning of the reign of Zedekiah king of Judah, in the fifth month of the fourth year, Hananiah the son of Azzur, the prophet from Gibeon, spoke to me in the house of the LORD, in the presence of the priests and all the people, saying, ²"Thus says the LORD of hosts, the God of Israel: I have broken the yoke of the king of Babylon. ³Within two years I will bring back to this place all the vessels of the LORD'S house, which Nebuchadnezzar king of Babylon took away from this place and carried to Babylon. ⁴I will also bring back to this place Jeconiah the son of Jehoiakim, king of Judah, and all the exiles from Judah who went to Babylon, says the LORD, for I will break the yoke of the king of Babylon."

⁵Then the prophet Jeremiah spoke to Hananiah the prophet in the presence of the priests and all the people who were standing in the house of the LORD; ⁶and the prophet Jeremiah said, "Amen! May the LORD do so;

may the LORD make the words which you have prophesied come true, and bring back to this place from Babylon
the vessels of the house of the LORD, and all the exiles.
⁷Yet hear now this word which I speak in your hearing
and in the hearing of all the people. ⁸The prophets who
preceded you and me from ancient times prophesied
war, famine, and pestilence against many countries and
great kingdoms. ⁹As for the prophet who prophesies
peace, when the word of that prophet comes to pass,
then it will be known that the LORD has truly sent
the prophet."

¹⁰Then the prophet Hananiah took the yoke-bars from
the neck of Jeremiah the prophet, and broke them. ¹¹And
Hananiah spoke in the presence of all the people, saying,
"Thus says the LORD: Even so will I break the yoke of
Nebuchadnezzar king of Babylon from the neck of all
the nations within two years." But Jeremiah the prophet
went his way.

Chapter 28 carries the discussion between Jeremiah
and his opponents about the length of the Exile down from
the plane of national policy to a personal encounter with
one man. The story is filled with biographical details that
create a colorful drama between Jeremiah and Hananiah.
No one can miss the lesson and yet the passage lacks the
long moral exhortations so common in the prose speeches
of chaps. 1-25. In many ways the two prophets have much
in common. Both come from outlying suburbs of Jerusalem,
and both preach in the temple grounds, and both use the
same formulas. The scene in chap. 28 pictures the two men
in a kind of duel while the crowd watches. It may even be
an indication that Jeremiah, for all of his opposition to
establishment decisions, normally operated as an oracle-
giver in the same context of temple services as did many
prophets who supported those decisions. Moreover, neither
man seems to be speaking in an ecstatic state or to be over-
whelmed with a sudden inspiration. The dialogue suggests

rather that both men had thought through their words and repeated them a number of times over days and even weeks. In this they differ quite a bit from the type of oracle found in Nahum which has the qualities of a litany and hymnic elements very typical of liturgical ceremonies. One can almost imagine the two men on soapboxes at various points in the temple courtyard much like the orators at Hyde Park Corner in London or in countless downtown parks of American cities.

Hananiah takes the exact opposite position from Jeremiah on every point. He announces the end of Babylonian rule, the return of the temple vessels, the restoration of the king and the end of the exile, and all within two years. To demonstrate the power of this word that he believed came from Yahweh, he breaks Jeremiah's yoke in two (v. 10).

We can presume that Hananiah's predictions would have been generally well-received by his audience, although we can wonder about the reaction of king Zedekiah to the possibility that his predecessor Jehoiachin would be coming back as king. Because of Hananiah's inclusion of the young king in his promise and because of Ezekiel's habit of dating his oracles from the reign of Jehoiachin rather than from that of Zedekiah (Ezek 1:1-2), many commentators have proposed that Zedekiah had been technically appointed to be only the regent while the king was kept prisoner to insure the pacification of Judah. Evidence to support this theory was discovered just before World War II in some Babylonian tablets which listed provisions for the support of king Jaukin (=Jehoiachin) and his five sons in the capital city of Babylon (see ANET 308). 2 Kgs 25:27-30, the final verses of the Deuteronomistic history, end with a note about the release of Jehoiachin from prison during the reign of Nebuchadrezzar's successor about 562, and the privilege granted to him to be supported by the Babylonian royal treasury until his death. Through this brief closing remark, the writers of the Book of Kings signaled a change in the divine plan of punishment and a cause for future hope.

Naturally, Jeremiah wished to see peace and prosperity restored to Judah as much as anyone did, and answers Hananiah with a hopeful *Amen*!, *i.e.*, "let it be so! But . . ." However, in vv. 7-9 he sets out a very definite standard for prophetic oracles. The ancient tradition of prophets has been to warn of war and judgment against the people. A prophet will only rarely proclaim the state of peace and harmony, and if he or she does, then the hearer should be cautious about accepting that word until it comes to pass. Jeremiah clearly separates the prophetic role that he exercises from that of cultic prophets who offer words of healing or blessing in the liturgy. There, *shalom*, the Hebrew word for peace and wholeness, has its proper place. But those who have been commissioned by Yahweh through a special call, and Jeremiah includes predecessors like Amos and Micah, and probably Hananiah, in this, must act as watchmen for Israel. These prophets understand themselves as covenant mediators, who oversee its execution and challenge any who neglect its demands. Their duty is not to pat Israel on the back for its successes but to warn and to summon it to fidelity. The messenger and watchman would not be needed if *shalom* existed. For this reason, a message of peace must be suspect from the start until it can be shown to play a part in the divine plan. The extended remarks on Jer 23 discuss the psychology of the prophet as a spokesperson for the Divine Council and its legal proceedings against an unfaithful people.

Jeremiah insists that the ultimate test of a true prophecy is fulfillment. This follows the command of Deut 18:21-22:

> And if you say in your heart, "How may we know the word which the Lord has not spoken?"—when a prophet speaks in the name of the Lord, if the word does not come to pass or come true, that is a word which the Lord has not spoken.

Such a test, however, does not make it any easier for the hearers of two contradictory oracles to decide which should be followed. Yet Jeremiah's position seems definite enough—if the choice lies between a word of complacency and a word of warning, always take the warning; the comforting outcome will be its own reward if it should prove true.

When Hananiah repeats his word of salvation in vv. 10-11 and dramatizes it with the breaking of Jeremiah's wood yoke, the latter has nothing more to say. His original message was complete, and until God gives him a new word, he will stand by that proclamation. After some time, a new word does come. It builds on the metaphor of the yoke without any major changes in thought, but this time Jeremiah insists that Babylon was more like iron than wood. Did he mull over the humiliation of having his symbolic act ridiculed and outperformed in public and keep asking "Why did you let this happen, O Lord?" We don't know for sure how the further inspired oracle came, but we can guess that it may well have emerged out of an agonizing internal struggle of just this sort. God often works in very human ways to communicate a larger vision to those who pray to him. Out of their own experiences of failure to understand where God is moving in their lives, a thin thread suddenly stands out clearly where we had missed it before and ties together the whole sequence of events we have gone through. In any case, Jeremiah began to understand that the iron yoke represented the unbreakable decision of God, not the fragile wood of human coalitions of kings and armies trying to smash Babylonian domination.

The contest between Jeremiah and Hananiah had gone on for some time, and Jeremiah withheld his final certainty until the vision of the iron yoke left no room for further possibilities of mercy or deliverance. At that moment he must also have realized how dangerous this ongoing debate was, leaving the option to each person to choose one way or the other about which prophet had been more convincing. Hananiah, undoubtedly sincere in his belief, had performed a symbolic action that carried more power than Jeremiah's own. What Jeremiah had proclaimed with the yoke, Hananiah had broken when he broke the yoke. Jeremiah now must have a still stronger sign to undergird his message. He declares flatly that God had not sent Hananiah, nor had he given him a word of hope. What therefore Hananiah proclaimed was a lie. To counter this false hope and to fulfill the rule of Deut 18 that the truth must come to pass, he laid the curse of Deut 18:20 on a false prophet: "He must die!"

Chapter 28 ends with the chilling report that Hananiah did die as Jeremiah had predicted. No one knows what was the cause of his death, but it hardly mattered, God's word had caused it. Once this got around the city, it must have enhanced the authority of Jeremiah considerably. It certainly provided all the explanation needed for why this one incident was singled out for preservation in Jeremiah's biography.

JEREMIAH'S LETTER TO THE EXILES
29:1-32

29 These are the words of the letter which Jeremiah the prophet sent from Jerusalem to the elders of the exiles, and to the priests, the prophets, and all the people, whom Nebuchadnezzar had taken into exile from Jerusalem to Babylon. ²This was after King Jeconiah, and the queen mother, the eunuchs, the princes of Judah and Jerusalem, the craftsmen, and the smiths had departed from Jerusalem. ³The letter was sent by the hand of Elasah the son of Shaphan and Gemariah the son of Hilkiah, whom Zedekiah king of Judah sent to Babylon to Nebuchadnezzar king of Babylon. It said: ⁴"Thus says the LORD of hosts, the God of Israel, to all the exiles whom I have sent into exile from Jerusalem to Babylon: ⁵Build houses and live in them; plant gardens and eat their produce. ⁶Take wives and have sons and daughters; take wives for your sons, and give your daughters in marriage, that they may bear sons and daughters; multiply there, and do not decrease. ⁷But seek the welfare of the city where I have sent you into exile, and pray to the LORD on its behalf, for in its welfare you will find your welfare. ⁸For thus says the LORD of hosts, the God of Israel: Do not let your prophets and your diviners who are among you deceive you, and do not listen to the dreams which they dream, ⁹for it is a lie which they are prophesying to you in my name; I did not send them, says the LORD.

¹⁰"For thus says the LORD: When seventy years are completed for Babylon, I will visit you, and I will fulfil to you my promise and bring you back to this place. ¹¹For I know the plans I have for you, says the LORD, plans for welfare and not for evil, to give you a future and a hope. ¹²Then you will call upon me and come to pray to me, and I will hear you. ¹³You will seek me and find me; when you seek me with all your heart, ¹⁴I will be found by you, says the LORD, and I will restore your fortunes and gather you from all the nations and all the places where I have driven you, says the LORD, and I will bring you back to the place from which I sent you into exile.

Chapter 29 describes a major letter that Jeremiah addressed from his home in Jerusalem to the citizens who had been deported in 597 after Nebuchadnezzar received the surrender of the city during a short siege. King Jehoiakim had died and left his young son Jehoiachin to face the Babylonian army's rapid attack on the capital city. The new king had little choice but to surrender and be deported along with the queen mother, Jehoiakim's wife, and most of the leaders who had supported the anti-Babylonian policies of the previous few years. As v. 3 tells us, this included most of king Jehoiakim's nobles and any skilled craftsmen and artisans that the Babylonians considered useful for work on projects back in Babylon. It also included 7,000 soldiers from the army of Judah, in order to prevent any future military revolt on the part of the conquered Israelites.

One important letter takes up most of the chapter, but we can identify parts of at least three letters or separate messages from Jeremiah, along with a discussion of a fourth letter sent from the prophet Shemaiah, who was in exile, back to the priest Zephaniah in Jerusalem. Thus, the structure of this chapter should be broken down into three parts, each of which addresses a separate source of opposition to Jeremiah's words:

a) vv. 1-15, and 20-23, The letter to the exiles about the false prophets Ahab and Zedekiah;
b) vv. 16-19, a word directed to king Zedekiah and the people of Jerusalem;
c) vv. 24-32, which report the letter of Shemaiah and Jeremiah's return message to the exiles.

Since this chapter is closely tied to the preceding material in chaps. 26-28, we can characterize its overall theme as part of Jeremiah's ongoing battle against the false prophets of hope.

The opening verses clearly talk about a letter that Jeremiah sent by means of two important officials, Elasah and Gemariah, who were traveling to Babylon on official business from king Zedekiah. Written prophecies may have been more common than usually thought. Jeremiah sends another letter to Babylon in 51:59-64, and that letter, if really delivered, would have been written about this same time. Again in chap. 36, Baruch takes down all the words of Jeremiah on a scroll, but the same term is used in Hebrew there for the collection of his sayings as appears here as a "letter." Other prophets, too, are recorded to have written down their words for others to see. Thus Isaiah is told by God to write down his prophecies for his disciples in Isa 8:1, and as a public record for people to read in Isa 30:8. Habakkuk, too, had to inscribe his prophecies for all to see (Hab 2:2). Although prophets and messengers probably relied mostly on the spoken word in their day to day work; in times of great importance, or if addressing the king or other high official, they could put down their message in writing. We don't know whether Jeremiah himself could write or not, but he seemed to have the services of a scribe to take dictation for him in the person of Baruch, son of Neriah. Critics used to insist that few Israelites could read or write and that documents and books must have been restricted to professional leaders such as priests and scribes for both reading and interpretation. But the last fifty years have witnessed an explosion of inscriptions and notes from soldiers and clerks and even common workers turn up in Palestine and so we can better presume today that many, if not most, of the 6th century Israelites could at least read. Note the touching letter from a farmworker to the local commander in the time of king Josiah:

> Let my lord commander hear the case of his servant! As for thy servant, thy servant was harvesting at Hazar-susim (?) . . . While thy servant was finishing the storage of grain with his harvesters, Hoshaiah son of Shobai came and took thy servant's mantle . . . All my companions will testify on my behalf! If I am innocent of gui[lt, let him return] my mantle, and if not, it is the commander's right to take [my case under advisement and to send word] to him [(asking) that he return the] mantle of thy servant . . .

> (ANET 568)

Jeremiah addresses his letter to the elders of Israel first, and then to the priests, prophets and people, as he had done in chap. 26 at the time of his sermon in the Temple. Because v. 1 suggests that many of the elders had died already, it seems best to assume that several years had passed since the exiles had left Judah for Babylon. Indeed, a time close to that of the prophecy of chap. 27 would fit very well. Both in this first letter of Jeremiah and in the warnings to foreign ambassadors in 27:1-11, he opposes any spirit of rebellion or talk of open revolt. Since Nebuchadnezzar had major problems with enemies to the East in 594, that was the year in which hopes of fighting for independence would have been highest. The Babylonian king may have been worried enough about the restless states to the west in that year to demand that Zedekiah send a high level delegation of royal officials to renew his pledge of loyalty.

The two ambassadors that carry Jeremiah's letter both have illustrious names. Elasah is the third son of Shaphan, the influential family friend of Jeremiah, while Gemariah was the son of the former High Priest under king Josiah, Hilkiah (2 Kgs 22:3-14). Both represented the pro-Babylonian faction that fell out of favor during the reign of Jehoiakim and were probably reinstated when the Babylonians put Zedekiah on the throne. However, we do not know if they actually supported Jeremiah's message in his letter or not. They probably had diplomatic status that permitted them to travel and visit places without being searched or stopped by the Babylonian police. Thus Jeremiah took advantage of their official mission to get a special word to the exiles.

The letter starkly opposes the currents of rebellion sweeping Jerusalem and probably the exilic settlements as well. He tells the Jews to settle down and become full, participating members in the Babylonian society. From the list of activities he suggests, it seems that the exiles had few real restrictions on them besides leaving Babylonian territory. They were allowed to set up villages and run themselves much as they had back in Palestine. Jeremiah accents this point by addressing the elders rather than the priests or prophets first. Ezek 8:1 and 14:1 show that these local leaders played the chief role in keeping the Israelite communities together during the exile. Jeremiah even goes so far as to demand that the people pray to Yahweh for the *shalom,* the peace and prosperity, of Babylon.

The theology of Jeremiah draws the line once again between those who will accept God's hand at work in the events of the Fall of Jerusalem and exile, and those who constantly seek only victory and good things from the Lord. In vv. 3-7, Jeremiah's God not only takes credit for exiling the people, but also declares his protection over Babylon and emphasizes that the Israelites must pray that it remains a strong nation if they are ever to see their homeland again. In contrast, the false prophets dream of fast defeat for Babylon and a quick return home from exile. This is the lie, the false truth that Jeremiah so strongly condemns. Of course, Jeremiah is no particular lover of Babylonian culture, as his oracles in chaps. 50-51 show, but he wants his stubborn people to stop *telling* God what he must do, and instead *listen* and heed God's word.

Isaiah had faced the political intrigues and military hopes of Judah over a hundred years before with the same stern warnings to stop and to listen. Again and again he spoke of God's plan that called for obedience and silence, not scheming and building stronger armies or cities. Isa 30:15 puts it into a single saying: "For thus says the Lord God, the Holy One of Israel: By waiting and by calm you shall be saved, in quiet and in trust your strength lies. But this you did not wish." See also Isa 5:12-13, 18-19; 7:9; 9:7-11; 28:26-29; 29:13-14; 30:1-2; 37:26. Now Jeremiah takes up the call. God's plan is one of welfare for Israel, even if it seems otherwise. To go ahead and plot and scheme will not lead to freedom but to greater suffering. God may not work with the speed that our plans call for, but he truly has a plan of his own for *shalom* and not for evil. Seventy years is not tomorrow. God intends the lesson of infidelity and disobedience to sink in for this people. No one who goes into exile will come out from it. Only the next generation shall see his mercy actually bring them back as a nation to their homeland. But when they do return, they will better understand what God wants of them as a people. In vv. 12-14, Jeremiah echoes the cries of earlier prophets, of Amos 5:4-6 and Hos 2:16-20, for the people to turn back to God and rediscover him, to get to really know him in the covenant. But to do this they must first see their sin and resolve to obey God's word. The call to return has been a keystone of Jeremiah's preaching (Jer 3:7, 10; 8:4; 15:7; 18:11; 23:22), but disaster alone did not seem to be enough to change the sinful habits of an entire nation overnight. We still find Ezekiel calling for a true conversion during his ministry from 593 to 572 (Ezek 33:17-20). Only when Israel again "finds" God (v. 14), will he restore their fortunes and let them return to the Promised Land.

The real reason for this long explanation of how the exiles should act finally comes in v. 15 taken together with vv. 20-24. Already among the exiles, at least two prophets, whom Jeremiah names specifically as Ahab and Zedekiah, had arisen claiming that God sent them and had preached the hopeful word that the exile would not last. They undoubtedly also encouraged ideas of armed rebellion to speed the day, for Jeremiah predicts that the Babylonians will execute them for sedition and treason. The capital sentence is well-deserved, in Jeremiah's view, because their real crime is to preach the falsehood, the *lie (sheqer)*, that God will only save and not punish. Jeremiah has repeatedly returned to this theme in chaps. 26-29 (see esp., 27:10, 14, 15, 16; 29:21, 23, 31) and elsewhere (5:2; 7:4, 8, 9; 8:8, 10; 9:3, 4; 10:14; 14:14; 16:19; 23:25,32). He favors this expression because it is rooted in the legal language of the trial. It was the technical word for false testimony (Exod 20:16; Deut 19:18; Ps 27:12; Prov 6:19; 14:4, 25:18) and also for a false oath (Zech 8:17; Lev 5:22 and Jer 5:2). Jeremiah builds the legal case against the prophets Ahab and Zedekiah based on the covenant law which demands obedience and justice, not happiness and prosperity. Only when Israel shows itself faithful can it count on the blessing and the prosperity, the *shalom*, to follow. And if the covenant violations are not enough to convict these two men as false prophets, Jeremiah throws in the charge of immorality as a final proof. They themselves commit the same adultery for which Israel is now paying the price, and yet claim authority to speak healing from Yahweh (v. 23).

If we now return to the small oracle sandwiched into the middle of this letter in vv. 16-19, we find it is directed to the king and people left back in Jerusalem, and clearly does not belong with the rest of the message directed to the exiles. In fact, it has many similarities to the two baskets of figs described in chap. 24, but with the added note that the reason why God has rejected the king and people is that they did not listen to the prophets (v. 19). The editors probably took the substance of chap. 24 and included it here in order to reinforce the point that both the people in the land *and* the exiles must beware of false prophets.

By inserting vv. 16-19 in exactly this spot, the editors have created a small *chiastic* structure that unites all of vv. 1-22 into one whole unit by reversing the direction of the thought in the middle and returning to the starting point. In this way, the parts are balanced like the two legs of the Greek letter *Chi* ("X"). If diagrammed, this passage would look like this:

vv. 4-9   (A) *Babylon's* welfare
vv. 10-14 (B) *Jerusalem's* welfare
vv. 16-19 (B) *Jerusalem's* judgment
vv. 20-23 (A) *Babylon's* judgment

This indicates that the editors were very careful in their choice and arrangement of Jeremiah's words when putting the book together. Since vv. 16-19 are totally lacking in the Greek Septuagint version of the 3rd century, B.C., it may mean that this chapter was put into its final shape only after many years had passed, and an earlier edition had been circulated long enough for a copy to have found its way to Egypt. The Greek translators had only the earlier edition and not our present Hebrew version.

The chapter ends with a third opponent of Jeremiah entering the fray. Shemaiah was among the exiles, and no doubt personally felt the sting of Jeremiah's letter against false prophecy. He wrote back to the overseer Zephaniah insisting that he lock up Jeremiah for claiming to be a prophet, just as the former overseer priest, Pashhur, had done back in chap. 20. Shemaiah even quotes from Jeremiah's letter to prove that Jeremiah was a "madman" (v. 26). For one reason or another, Zephaniah showed this letter to Jeremiah. Perhaps he was a friend of Jeremiah (Zedekiah sends him to Jeremiah again in chap. 37), or maybe he was issuing the prophet a warning to cease. In any case, hearing the message of Shemaiah became the occasion for a new word from God to Jeremiah. It was directed to all the exiles, not just to Shemaiah, and it condemned Shemaiah in language very much like that used against Hananiah in the previous chapter. Again, one prophet stands against another, and the proof must come from a divine sign. As with Hananiah, Jeremiah foresees the death of Shemaiah, or at least the total failure of his family to survive the exile, as the ultimate witness that God's word must be taken seriously. Jeremiah began and ended (vv. 5 and 28) with God's command for the people to settle down in Babylon; all three opponents—Ahab/Zedekiah, the king and people of Jerusalem, and Shemaiah—shall not live to enjoy either that life in Babylon nor return home.

Thus chap. 29 brings to a close the group of reports on the fate of those who opposed the prophetic word of Jeremiah. Despite the strong opposition to other prophets who look only for good, Jeremiah himself ends with a guarded optimism that God will be found when they turn back to him, that he works good, that he will end the exile, and that he has a future plan full of hope (vv. 11-14). With this caution in mind, we turn to Jeremiah at his most hopeful in chaps. 30-33.

II. The "Book of Consolation" Jeremiah 30 - 33

These four chapters contain the greatest concentration of salvation oracles in the Book of Jeremiah. But they are by no means all the same. Many are short bursts of poetic exaltation (30:10-11; 31:7-9), others are a balance between judgment and hope (31:15-22; 33:2-9), and still others are lengthy prose reflections or prayers (32:6-15, 16-25, and 26-44). Because Jeremiah stresses the coming inevitable judgment on Jerusalem and Judah so strongly throughout the rest of the book, many scholars have doubted these words of promise could really come from the same man. After all, they sound more like Hananiah or Shemaiah or the other "false" prophets. Moreover, the style of many of these passages differs from that of Jeremiah elsewhere. 30:10-11, for example, resembles the message of hope in Isa 4:8-10 much more closely than it does Jeremiah's way of speaking. The oracle on the "new covenant" in 31:31-34 clearly foresees an action of God which does *not* demand that Israel return to him in humility, even though *shub*, "return," is a key concept of the prophet elsewhere. On the other hand, few would deny all sense of hope to Jeremiah. The story of his purchase of a field from his relatives in chap. 32 must surely be based on a real incident from the prophet's life. It stands as a sign of hope in the face of the coming Babylonian attack and incorporates a symbolic action with a message for this people to see.

In fact, if we put these chapters aside for a moment, and look back at other passages of judgment in earlier parts of the book, we already can find key elements of Jeremiah's hope in his words to the exiles in chap. 24 that they will be treated as good figs, and in his advice to the exiles in chap. 29 to settle down and wait for God to restore them to their homeland. Jeremiah had hope—but only for those who first endured the punishment of exile and loss. He had little or no sympathy for the people still in Judah who continued the evil ways of their fathers and mothers before them, or based their hopes on the same old ideas of divine support.

When we return to chaps. 30-33, we can see both the limited promise that God will restore those in exile, and a far more sweeping vision of great days ahead. Like so much of the rest of the book, these chapters too have their mix of oracles delivered directly by Jeremiah and those that have been reflected upon, preached, expanded, and edited to highlight Jeremiah as the basis of a new order, both for the exile and for the period of restoration afterwards. At the heart of all the different passages is Jeremiah's keen insight into the plan of God, who upholds his covenant fidelity by demanding good, punishing sin, calling for conversion, and offering healing.

The section can roughly be divided into two parts, chaps. 30-31 and chaps. 32-33. The first is mostly poetic, the second mostly prosaic. The first deals mostly with infidelity of the heart and healing, the second with the future of the land and the institution of kingship. A close examination of these two sections also reveals that they are never an *unconditional* promise of salvation. Judgment is part of the hope for restoration and the effect of all four chapters together is to keep that hope muted and within limits. Quite possibly, many of the most optimistic oracles, such as those in chap. 31, came from the earliest days of Jeremiah's preaching and not from the last days of despair. Many of these were first addressed to the Northern Kingdom which had fallen over a century earlier in 722 (*cf.*, 31:2-6, 7-9, 10-14, 15-22; and 30:18). In the days of Josiah's reform and expansion northwards (627-609 B.C.), Jeremiah had foreseen God's restoration of the two kingdoms into one as in the days of David and Solomon. That hope had been dashed by the rise of the Babylonians and the death of Josiah in 609 B.C. But at a later time, when Judah itself had gone into exile, Jeremiah may have added these oracles to others specifically aimed at the Judah of 586 in its devastation (31:23-26 and 31:27-31). This made up a small collection of hopeful words from Yahweh. Later, the editors of the book added several other oracles of an even more upbeat nature (*e.g.*, 31:31-34, 35-37 and 38-40), either from

Jeremiah himself or from his times, and attached the two incidents in chaps. 32-33 from Jeremiah's period in the guardhouse, as positive illustrations of that hope. The resulting combination has a strong *eschatological* outlook, in that it pictures a coming time of salvation when everything will be restored, northern kingdom with southern kingdom, king, temple, and covenant. In short, all the failures of the past will be erased and Israel will be healed and return to the ideal wholeness that characterized the days at Mount Sinai under Moses or in the time of king David.

Many commentators are particularly skeptical about oracles that use the phrase "Behold, the days are coming," in 30:3; 31:27, 31, 38. They see in it the optimisim of a group that came long after the melancholy days of Jeremiah himself. But even if these oracles were adapted or borrowed from other sources to express a highly positive outlook, this does not mean that they contradict or change Jeremiah's basic meaning. St. Paul borrows hymns in Phil 2:6-11 and in Col 1:15-20 to give color to his message—so, too, here, the editors underline the significance of God's intention to restore Israel in the future by including dynamic illustrations of that hope. But note that they carefully place the entire section of hopeful oracles into the midst of the terrible story of Jerusalem's fall and the prophet's sufferings so that no one will mistakenly accept only the words of salvation and forget the meaning of judgment. The promise of release stems from God's eternal covenant fidelity and is already promised even before the destruction of the nation is reported in chaps. 37-45.

Finally, these chapters provide a series of tableaus about the community of the future. Different oracles describe separate aspects of the restored vision of Israel: 31:31-34, the covenant; 31-35-37, the renewal of creation; 31:38-40, the new Jerusalem; 33:1-12, the new temple; 33:14-26, the role of the Davidic king, etc.

A SPECIAL WORD ON CHAPTERS 30-31

Chapters 30 and 31 are built around a solid core of poetic oracles from Jeremiah's own preaching. Some were delivered to the northern tribes and some to Judah, and so they range in date across the whole ministry of Jeremiah from before 609 down to 587 B.C. Most scholars assume that the "book" mentioned in 30:2 consists of these poetic oracles in 30:5—31:22. Few experts, however, accept that every single passage in this section actually came from Jeremiah himself. For example, many think the exaltant tone of 30:10-11 or 31:10-14 betrays the work of Second Isaiah or his school.

In any case, we may suggest that 30:5 to 31:22 forms a basic collection of salvation oracles, and to it were added, first the prose and poetry of 31:23-34, which treats the renewal of the individual, and secondly the final unit in 31:35-40 which glorifies the new creation.

The two chapters contain 15 separate units in all, mostly short. Briefly, these are: (1) 30:1-3, the introductory label for chaps. 30-31; (2) 30:4-9, a hopeful reflection on the theme of the Day of the Lord; (3) 30:10-11, an oracle of salvation in the style of Second Isaiah; (4) 30:12-17, healing for the incurable wound of Judah (*cf.*, 8:21; 10:19, 14:17; 15:18); (5) 30:18-22, a promise to restore the Northern Kingdom; and (6) 30:23—31:1, a poem on the wrath of the Lord.

Chapter 31 has nine oracles: (1) 31:2-6, a lyric hymn about the covenant; (2) 31:7-9, praise for the return of the North; (3) 31:10-14, a hymn to Zion also reminiscent of Second Isaiah; (4) 31:15-22, Rachel mourns for the northern exiles and is given hope; (5) 31:23-26, a blessing on Judah; (6) 31:27-30, the call to individual responsibility; (7) 31:31-34, promise of the new covenant; (8) 31:35-37, the creator's guarantee of redemption; (9) 31:38-40, the rebuilding and repopulation of Jerusalem.

"FEAR NOT, O JACOB MY SERVANT!"
30:1-31

30 The word that came to Jeremiah from the LORD:
²"Thus says the LORD, the God of Israel: Write in a book
all the words that I have spoken to you. ³For behold,
days are coming, says the LORD, when I will restore the
fortunes of my people, Israel and Judah, says the LORD,
and I will bring them back to the land which I gave to
their fathers, and they shall take possession of it."

⁴These are the words which the LORD spoke concerning Israel and Judah:
⁵"Thus says the LORD:
We have heard a cry of panic,
   of terror, and no peace.
⁶Ask now, and see,
   can a man bear a child?
Why then do I see every man
   with his hands on his loins like a woman in labour?
   Why has every face turned pale?
⁷Alas! that day is so great
   there is none like it;
   it is a time of distress for Jacob;
   yet he shall be saved out of it.

The oracles of salvation open with a very brief summary
of the basic message to come: Jeremiah must write down
these words as a sign and proof that God does intend to
bring the people back from exile. Two phrases in 30:1-3
stand out as important terms to remember. "Behold the
days are coming" first occurs in Amos 4:2; 8:11 and 9:13
as a warning of judgment and then later in Jeremiah
fourteen times, usually with the same sense. But its presence
here signals a shift in meaning—no longer the ferocious
threats of 7:32 that Jerusalem will be a valley of slaughter,
but a promise. The expression recurs three times in the last

verses of chaps. 30-31, in 31:27, 31 and 38; thus it ties the two chapters together by its repetition at beginning and end. The second phrase is "restore the fortunes." The Hebrew words, *shub shebut*, mean to "return what was turned away." While generally translated correctly by saying "restore the fortunes" it probably had the much narrower meaning in Jeremiah's day of literally coming back from exile. It becomes a key expression in the oracles of hope; 30:18; 31:23; 32:44; 33:7, 11, 26; and has already played a role in the letter to the exiles in 29:14. It suggests total restoration of all that Israel enjoyed before the disasters of 598 and 587, above all independence with secure borders and peace in the land. It also suggests that God never fails to "turn back" to his beloved people, even if they so often refuse to turn back to their God.

The first oracle in the series, 30:5-11, sketches the overall message. Men have become like women in labor! That is, the tables are turned; the order of normal reality is reversed; the pain is not only great, it is unnatural. Jeremiah uses this image of childbirth to express the terrible anguish of the Babylonian siege more than once (see 4:31; 6:24; 13:21 and 22:23), but never in such an upside down fashion. Jeremiah becomes like an enemy soldier who shouts out a curse against the opposing force, "May all your soldiers become like women in battle!" (as in 50:37). At the end, Jeremiah returns to the same theme in 31:22, to show the amazing power of Israel's God that he can take even the so-called "weak" woman and use her to establish salvation. Nothing is impossible to our God!

The oracles of hope in vv. 8-9 and 10-11 come as an answer to this description of distress. Where v. 7 speaks of a "day of judgment," vv. 8-9 envision instead a day of release from exile. The RSV, like most modern Bibles, prints these two verses in prose, to indicate that they seem to be an intrusion from somewhere else. Not only do they break the usual meaning of the "Day of the Lord" in Jeremiah (*cf.*, 4:23-28), but they speak of the return of the Davidic king, something Jeremiah gives little or no attention to.

(Note how he carefully avoids calling the restored ruler a king in the oracle at v. 21.) It appears that this comment was made in the margin of the text to explain or emphasize a new "Day of the Lord," the *real* Day when God saves and does not punish. At some point in later recopying of the text, a scribe carefully added it right into the text itself. The practice is fairly common in ancient times, and does not differ much from notes today's students make in the margins of textbooks before an exam.

Certainly the next oracle in vv. 10-11 follows more naturally as the actual response to the agony described in vv. 5-7. The word of Yahweh opens with the call to "fear not!", and follows with the threefold promise of salvation, a return from exile, and punishment for all the enemy nations who have oppressed Israel. But it keeps the careful balance we find everywhere in Jeremiah between chastening and deliverance.

> [10]"Then fear not, O Jacob my servant,
>   says the LORD,
>   nor be dismayed, O Israel;
> for lo, I will save you from afar,
>   and your offspring from the land
>   of their captivity.
> Jacob shall return and have quiet and ease,
>   and none shall make him afraid.
> [11]For I am with you to save you,
>   says the LORD.
> I will make a full end of all the nations
>   among whom I scattered you,
>   but of you I will not make full end.
> I will chasten you in just measure,
>   and I will by no means leave you unpunished.

The confident and highly personal tone of this oracle of hope resembles the typical oracle of salvation found in Second Isaiah (chaps. 40-55). These verses are very close to Isa 41:8-10 in language and spirit. They do not appear in the Septuagint Greek at this point, but can be found in 46:27-28 in both the Hebrew and Greek. This has led many commentators to hold that they too, like vv. 8-9, have been added at a late date, and that we must look ahead still further to vv. 12-17 for the real word of hope called for by vv. 5-7.

Yet there is good reason to assume that this really is a genuine word of Jeremiah. Many of the expressions are typical only of his preaching: "I will make a full end of" or "not make a full end of" (4:27; 5:10; 5:18), and "I am with you to save you" (1:8 and 15:20). Other expressions that occur here are also used by Ezekiel a short time later, but never by Second Isaiah. Thus, "The nations among whom I have scattered you" appears here and in 9:16, but also in Ezek 11:17; 20:34, 41; 28:25; 29:13; 34:12. The expression, "None shall make him afraid," can be found in Jer 7:33; 30:10 and 46:27, as well as in Ezek 34:28 and 39:26. Moreover, the language tenderly addressed to "Jacob my servant" suggests that originally Jeremiah proclaimed these words to the Northern Kingdom, perhaps during Josiah's reform and his resettlement of Samaria and its area after Assyria could no longer hold it. When combined with other oracles aimed mainly at Judah, the same message could be later directed to the South after their disasters. And just as Ezekiel borrowed many of his expressions from the words of Jeremiah, so too did the author or authors of the second part of Isaiah most likely borrow their wording for the salvation oracles in Isa 41:8-13; 43:1-6 and 44:1-6.

From this word of promise, the text moves back into a favorite theme of Jeremiah, the nation's incurable wound. Verses 12-17 summon up a different type of pain from that of childbirth, but one even more frightening. Israel has a gaping wound, delivered by enemy forces, which is surely fatal, yet there are no medics in sight. Verses 14-15 twice repeat the real meaning of this imagery—the people's guilt is so great, that God had to allow them to receive this wound. Even Israel's allies cannot be found to help at this moment. The major ally of Israel during this period of rebellion against Babylon turned out to be Egypt. In fact, the pharaoh sent an army to help king Zedekiah during the final days of Judah's life in 588. But the Babylonians successfully drove the Egyptians back across the border and renewed the siege. Probably this oracle came from that period.

After such an ominous warning, the mood suddenly changes in v. 16, with a "therefore" that really does not follow from what Jeremiah has been hinting at, namely that God himself has punished them. But with a powerful fourfold repetition, the prophet insists that Israel's enemies shall themselves be punished. This reversal of fortune reflects God's promise to restore the covenant. God himself had sent the enemy to "devour" the nation as punishment (2:3; 10:25 and elsewhere), and had caused the gaping wound (8:22 and 10:19), and made them outcasts (24:9). Now what had been judgment on Israel's sins will be delivered equally against her foes for their sins. Covenant Law demanded an eye for an eye, a tooth for a tooth (Exod 21:23-25). The Lord of the covenant will apply the same standard against Babylon and thereby reestablish the covenant law in its full strength. So despite its dramatic change of outlook, the whole of vv. 12-17 fits nicely into the overall perspective of Jeremiah and above all keeps its hope rooted in the fidelity of Yahweh, not in the strength of Israel.

18"Thus says the LORD:
Behold, I will restore the fortunes of
    the tents of Jacob,
    and have compassion on his dwellings;
    the city shall be rebuilt upon its mound,
        and the palace shall stand where it used to be.
19Out of them shall come songs of thanksgiving,
    and the voices of those who make merry.
    I will multiply them, and they shall not be few;
    I will make them honoured, and they shall not be small.

Verses 18-22 contain another oracle directed to the northern tribes. The vision looks forward to rebuilding the old capital city of Samaria which was leveled by the Assyrians in 722 when they put an end to the northern state. As a sign of God's fidelity, it shall be rebuilt even on the same mound, or tell—the heap of earth and ruins that grew larger from the debris of each succeeding town on the site. And it will prosper under the blessing of Yahweh, and the leaders shall not only be one with the people but shall be close to God as well. The entire scene reminds us strongly of the vision of Balaam the prophet at the moment when Israel was on the edge of entering the Promised Land to conquer it. Tradition remembered how Balaam had foreseen the great population explosion of Israel (Num 23:10), and how God would be close to them (Num 23:21), and how fair were Jacob's tents (Num 24:5) and how a ruler would come forth from their midst (Num 24:17). This combination of promised restoration and divine blessing can be found in many Ancient Near Eastern hope oracles; cf., the Hittite example in ANET 206: "(If you, Kurtiwaza, the prince, and the Hurrians, fulfill this treaty) may these gods protect you . . . (and) may the Mitanni country return to the place which it occupied before, may it thrive and expand . . . May the throne of your father persist, may the Mitanni country persist." Ezek 34 and 37, as well as most of Isa 40-49 show similar patterns. But it contains the unique covenant formula that once again emphasizes that Yahweh will do this out of his covenant love, not because of Samaria's just deserts. The deuteronomic authors of 2 Kgs 17:7-18 give a vivid picture of the corruption of Samaria in the days before its fall. Jeremiah would have undoubtedly agreed completely with their analysis, yet he holds out hope for restoration based on relationship of God and people. Verse 22 repeats the words of Jer 7:23 and 11:4, although the same formula occurs also in Leviticus, Deuteronomy and Ezekiel.

The last small fragment in chap. 30 reinforces the message
of this covenant renewal. In fearsome imagery, vv. 23-24
return to the theme of the Day of the Lord as a wrathful
storm from the desert which burns and destroys the wicked.
This poem concludes in v. 31:1 with a version of the covenant formula, but expanded to include all groups of
Israelites. The coming hope will reunite North and South,
former exiles and present ones. Verse 31:1 thus closes out
the promises of restoration in chap. 30, and at the same time
opens up a broad picture of the future and its new potential
which will become the main topic of chap. 31. Quite
probably, Jeremiah's editors placed this particular oracle
here to serve as a transition to chap. 31, since vv. 23-24
are found already in 23:19-20.

"I WILL MAKE A NEW COVENANT"
31:1-40

31 "At that time, says the LORD, I will be the God of
all the families of Israel, and they shall be my people."
²Thus says the LORD:
"The people who survived the sword
found grace in the wilderness;
when Israel sought for rest,
³the LORD appeared to him from afar.
I have loved you with an everlasting love;
therefore I have continued my faithfulness to you.
⁴Again I will build you, and you shall be built,
O virgin Israel!
Again you shall adorn yourself with timbrels,
and shall go forth in the dance of the merrymakers.
⁵Again you shall plant vineyards
upon the mountains of Samaria;
the planters shall plant.
and shall enjoy the fruit.

> ⁶For there shall be a day when watchmen will call
> in the hill country of Ephraim:
> 'Arise, and let us go up to Zion,
>   to the LORD our God.'"

The first oracle, in vv. 2-6, recreates the greatest of Yahweh's saving acts in the past as a model for those who need a new liberation by their God. This description of the exile in the language of the Exodus and Sinai covenant is surely among the most powerful passages in the whole Book of Jeremiah. Although it clearly states the parallel to the escape out of Egypt in v. 2, it directs its main focus to the divine mercy and favor that reached out from afar to the people in the wilderness of Sinai, pledged divine love to them, led them to the Promised Land, and gave them blessing and rest. All the major accounts of the great miracle of the Exodus were celebrated in similar language throughout Israel's history, from the early song of victory in Exod 15 down to the prayer for the Feast of Weeks in Deut 26:5-10. We have good reason to believe that this sequence of slavery—freedom—help in the desert—gift of the Promised Land reflects the temple liturgical service. Not only is Exod 15 a hymn, but three of the most detailed examples of its use can be found in Pss 78, 105 and 136.

What stands out among the Psalms and hymns, however, is the lack of any mention of the covenant-giving on Mount Sinai. Since the covenant plays such an important role in the narratives of the Book of Exodus about the escape from Egypt and journey to the Promised Land, it strikes many readers as surprising to discover this absence. The usual answer distinguishes two separate feast days each of which celebrates only one aspect of the whole story, just as Christian worship distinguishes Easter from Jesus' Ascension or the Coming of the Holy Spirit on Pentecost, and tells only part of the great salvation narrative at each feast. We owe the prophets much of the credit for bringing the two together in their preaching. Jeremiah, Ezekiel and

Second Isaiah, following in the footsteps of Hosea before them, stress that God's liberating power and his covenant love are closely united. Because all three of these prophets faced the great trauma of the Exile, they were able to explain the disaster in terms of failure to obey the covenant, and at the same time to offer hope because the God of the covenant, who remained faithful to his side of the relationship, always showed his mercy and his fidelity by liberation.

This oracle expresses strong emotion. Israel in exile experiences its alienation and distance from God, yet that God comes to it across the great distance, as he did in the days of Moses. He offers them his eternal love, the same love with which he loved their ancestors, and promises them the same mercy that he had given in the terrible desert. The phrases are alive with tenderness, and yet draw together all the major themes of Israel's national past. This is because they speak to the present moment with urgency and exhortation. God did not just do these things in the past, he does them *now*, and he promises to make the future even better. They shall rebuilt, they shall celebrate in joy, they shall plant and cultivate rich fields again. The way that Jeremiah develops his thought here has many similarities with the prologue to the Book of Deuteronomy in Deut 1-11. Reading those chapters will give much of the same flavor that we discover in Jeremiah. Who borrowed from whom? We cannot say. But both Jeremiah and the deuteronomic writers represent a new synthesis of faith and emphasize the love obligations of the covenant *before* and *over* the confidence inspired by the Exodus liberation.

The oracle closes in v. 6 with a vision of both Northern Israel (Mount Ephraim) and Judah joined in worship at the temple in Jerusalem (Zion). Because of the mention of Samaria in v. 5, of virgin Israel rather than virgin Zion in v. 4, and of Mount Ephraim in v. 6, most scholars believe that Jeremiah first spoke this oracle to the people in the North and then later reworked it as a promise to the whole nation when Jerusalem had been destroyed as well. It looks

forward to the solemn oath of God in 31:28, that he will not
only uproot and destroy but will build and plant—the whole
purpose of Jeremiah's mission, according to 1:10.

The next two oracles, in vv. 7-9 and 10-14 share much of
the same spirit of exaltation and joy over the great work
God is about to do. Verse 7 calls on the northern tribes
(Jacob) to shout for joy. This command occurs often in
prophetic books (Isa 12:6; 24:14; Zeph 3:14; Zech 2:14 and
others) in passages where the prophet delivers an oracle
of salvation. Probably the origin of this custom lies in the
liturgy, in which hymns of praise were sung in response to
the proclamation of a salvation oracle over the whole
congregation. The hymn of praise serves also as a profession
of faith, in this case, the confession that God has indeed
saved the remnant of the northern exiles. The reason why
God saved them, and the point of the whole confession,
comes only at the end of the poem, in v. 9, where God
declares "For I am Israel's father, and Ephraim is my first-
born son." This much of the oracle sounds very much like
Hos 11:1-4, but the intermediate lines in vv. 8-9 sound more
like Second Isaiah and his promise of a new Exodus in
which all the exiles shall return in triumph to Judah. Note
the common themes in the following examples: Isa 35:5-6,
in which the blind, lame and mothers shall return; Isa 40:11,
in which he guides them; Isa 41:9; 43:6; 45:22; 48:20, in
which God gathers the exiles from the ends of the earth; and
Isa 40:3-5; 41:18-20; 43:1-7; 44:3-4, in which God will lead
a new exodus on a level road. Because of these similarities,
we can presume that Jeremiah reused an earlier oracle to the
northern tribes after the fall of Jerusalem, and added
liturgical phrases and language to raise the spirits of the
people and to provide continuity with the past sense of hope
once the temple and its liturgy had disappeared.

The oracle in vv. 10-14 also has strong reminiscences of
both Second Isaiah and liturgical usage. Note the reference
to the "nations" and the "farthest shores" (Isa 41:1, 5, 9;
42:4, 10; 49:1; 51:5) in v. 10, and "redeem" in v. 11 (Isa 41:14;
43:1, 14; 44:6, 22, 23; 48:17), and a "well-watered garden"

in v. 12 (Isa 58:11). The whole scene is further pictured as a liturgical procession to Mount Zion with its shouts uttered in response to the prayers and words of the priests. There can be no denying the close connection in imagery and conception between the oracles of Second Isaiah and the language embedded in Jer 30:10-11; 31:2-6 and 10-14. Many commentators simply write off these parts of Jeremiah as late additions by followers of Second Isaiah who wanted to update Jeremiah with more of a sense of optimism about the restoration. They would have done this close to the time that Cyrus, the king of Persia, finally overthrew the Babylonians and released the Israelites to go home, about 539 B.C. However, such simple solutions may not be quite correct. In order to deny Jeremiah's authority in these passages, the skeptical reader must put aside the fact that many of the words are unique to Jeremiah (and sometimes to other prophets) but do not form any part of Second Isaiah's language. For example, in 31:11, the poem says that God will ransom Jacob. The verb for "ransom," *padah*, is known to Jeremiah and Hosea (Hos 7:30 and 13:14) but not to Second Isaiah. Nor should we concede the use of "islands" or "distant coasts" as typically Second Isaiah's. Jeremiah himself uses these terms in oracles which certainly are original to himself: 2:10; 25:22; 47:4. In general, the best policy is to assume that much of this language originated with liturgical prophets before either Jeremiah or Second Isaiah, and both make some use of it in their salvation preaching. It seems strange in Jeremiah because he has so little in the way of salvation proclamation, and it seems to be part of the very being of Second Isaiah because he has almost nothing else than salvation words!

> [15]Thus says the LORD:
> "A voice is heard in Ramah,
>   lamentation and bitter weeping.
> Rachel is weeping for her children;
>   she refuses to be comforted for her children.
>   because they are not."

¹⁶Thus says the LORD:
"Keep your voice from weeping,
    and your eyes from tears;
for your work shall be rewarded,
                    says the LORD,
    and they shall come back from the
        land of the enemy.
¹⁷There is hope for your future,
                    says the LORD,
    and your children shall come back
        to their own country.
¹⁸I have heard Ephraim bemoaning,
'Thou hast chastened me, and I was chastened,
    like an untrained calf;
bring me back that I may be restored,
    for thou art the LORD my God.
¹⁹For after I had turned away I repented;
    and after I was instructed, I smote upon my thigh;
I was ashamed, and I was confounded,
    because I bore the disgrace of my youth.'
²⁰Is Ephraim my dear son?
    Is he my darling child?
For as often as I speak against him,
    I do remember him still.
Therefore my heart yearns for him;
    I will surely have mercy on him,
                    says the LORD.

²¹"Set up waymarks for yourself,
    make yourself guideposts;
consider well the highway,
    the road by which you went.

Return, O virgin Israel,
    return to these your cities.
²²How long will you waver,
    O faithless daughter?

> For the LORD has created a new
>   thing on the earth:
>   a woman protects a man."

Jer 31:15-22 is still another example of an oracle addressed to the Northern Kingdom. It has the form of a dialogue in a very artistic construction:

v. 15   (A)   Rachel weeps her loss

vv. 16-17 (B)   Yahweh comforts her

vv. 18-19 (C)   Ephraim moans his sin and guilt

v. 20   (B)   Yahweh comforts Ephraim

vv. 21-22 (A)   Jeremiah calls to virgin Israel to repent

As noted above in chap. 29, this passage clearly shows the rhetorical device of *chiasmus*, in which the action moves to a center and then returns to its starting point. It opens and closes with reference to a woman in need of comfort; in between these lines, Yahweh speaks twice; and at the center stands the real heart of the oracle, the announcement of the Northern Kingdom's repentance.

Rachel was the favorite wife of Jacob, the father of Israel, and was the mother of Benjamin, the favorite son and nearest territory to Judah. Although one tradition placed her tomb in Bethlehem (Gen 35:19), northern traditions had her buried near Ramah in the territory of Benjamin (1 Sam 10:2). As the symbolic mother of Israel, she performs the mourning rite for her dead children, and no one can give her comfort. Yahweh then speaks to her with the command not to mourn, for the children are not dead but shall return to their homeland. Some of the words in vv. 16-17 are very difficult to understand. What is the work that Rachel does that can bring back the exiles? What is this future hope? "Work" carries the sense of performing a chore or duty by necessity and loses much of the real meaning that Jeremiah intends. It is indeed *action* that will bring about Yahweh's saving "work," but not the mourning—it is rather the following action of Ephraim, *repentance*, that moves God to merciful forgiveness. Rachel, the tender mother who turns to the Lord, is none other than Ephraim, the people, turning back to the Lord. The "future" hope might better be understood from the Hebrew as "hope for your descendants." The future looks bright for those long exiled from their native land.

The centerpiece of this oracle in vv. 18-19 borrows heavily from the thought of Hosea. Hos 4:16 first speaks of Israel as a stubborn calf and the prophet returns to it in 10:11. It is Hosea who first traces Israel's stubbornness to its youth, *i.e.*, in the desert years of the Exodus (Hos 11:1-9). The expression to "smite upon the thigh" recurs in Ezek 21:17. It was an almost universal gesture in the ancient world to indicate shame and sorrow. Homer uses it in the *Iliad* and *Odyssey*, and even Sumerian literature knew of the gesture in the 3rd millennium before Christ!

Yahweh again responds by reaffirming the love that he had for Israel in the covenant at Mount Sinai. This continues the theme of Hos 11:1-4, and alludes to the call of Yahweh for the people to come back to him in Hos 6:1-4. The final word of Yahweh affirms that he will have mercy upon Israel. The word construction for this is very striking: The actual verb comes from the root word meaning a woman's womb, and it is repeated in two forms in the same sentence, so that the sense should be rendered something like: "I will certainly have a mother's compassion on him, says the Lord."

Jeremiah the prophet adds a final comment in vv. 21-22. The call to return has some of the urgency we might expect if in fact the exiles had already been freed and yet were reluctant to return home. Possibly life was better in Assyria or Babylon than in the rocky hills of Palestine; perhaps, if these words were originally addressed to northern

Israelites far away and three generations after their great-grandparents had been forced to move, they no longer felt any obligation to live in the ancestral territory. Certainly, the message *demands* that the time for return is at hand and no delays should hinder it. However, this makes the final words even more difficult to explain. The wonderful new creation involved is that a woman protects a man. The Hebrew suggests that the woman encircles the man, and a much stronger sexual image may be present than the RSV translation reveals. But every commentator has tried a new explanation and none have much certainty. Does the woman play the man's role in order to reverse the soldiers who have become like women in 30:6? Or is God's new work so powerful that he reverses the natural expected roles of all creation? Or does the protective love of Yahweh's womb take over the care of Israel the beloved son because he can no longer do it for himself? Or finally, does Israel the faithless wife now run back to her husband, Yahweh, and cling to him completely?—something she has never done fully before! Of course, it may have been just a popular proverb of the time, "the woman protects the male!" to indicate everything is upside down and makes no sense.

A short oracle follows immediately upon these words to Ephraim and the northern exiles. It addresses the same promise to Judah and its cities in vv. 22-26. God will dwell in their midst and establish his residence as a place of right-eousness and holiness, a source of blessing to them. We can even detect the echo of the priestly blessing on the people from Num 6:24-25, "The Lord bless you and keep you, the Lord let his face shine upon you and be gracious to you, the Lord grant his kindness and give you peace." However, it still remains a mystery what the closing line of this unit really signifies. It seems to end something—perhaps a series of dreams or visions by the prophet; but there was no beginning mentioned earlier. The prophet wakes up and is refreshed by what he has seen, or perhaps by the confidence he has now gained that God will act to save the people from the consequences of their evil ways.

If v. 26 seems to be an ending, v. 27 definitely marks a new beginning. The phrase, "Behold the days are coming" serves as a catchword for three of the four remaining oracles in the chapter. They all formed a series built around future restoration: vv. 27-30 on the restoration of the Promised Land; vv. 31-34 on the reestablishment of the covenant; and 38-40, on the rebuilding of Jerusalem. Only the small poem on creation in vv. 35-37 does not form part of this series.

The first of the oracles stresses the repopulation of the land with both people and animals. One of the immediate effects of the Exile was to leave the land abandoned and severely underpopulated. The writings of the prophets Haggai and Zechariah at the end of the Exile, about 520 B.C., and the descriptions in Ezra and Nehemiah some seventy years after that (458-440 B.C.) leave no doubt of the desperate state of affairs that those who returned from exile found in Palestine. The residents of Jerusalem and Judah were so weak that they could not even defend themselves. Jeremiah bolsters the confidence of the few disheartened individuals left in the land by repeating the words of his commission. It has the ring of truth—just as he predicted the tearing down, the overthrow, and the bringing of evil upon the land, so now he can predict that God will bring about the second side of his mission: to build and to plant (*cf.*, 1:10).

The Israelites had a second complaint, however, which Jeremiah takes up in vv. 29-30. If the evil was done by the generations before them, why should the children and the young be taken into exile for the sins of their parents? Jeremiah quickly answers this with the quotation of a proverb, probably often used by the religious teachers to help explain such hard facts of life. But he rejects the common wisdom of the ages and announces a new order of responsibility. All will not suffer for the sins of a few. Each will bear the responsibility for his or her own conduct. To an ancient ear, this was radical. Unless someone rose to special importance in the society, individuals got little concern. War and revolution, sicknesses, natural disaster, all seemed to kill large numbers of people indiscriminately. Public work projects, all done by hand labor, required whole towns and villages to be mobilized for action. Political and religious practices lumped everyone in the same category. If your city fell, your god fell; if your god fell, you went down with it. This way of looking at life is often called "corporate thinking." The individual generally submerges personal interests in favor of the group or community.

In contrast to this, the 6th century saw a major shift in awareness that placed the burden of religious responsibility on to the shoulders of each person in turn. Ezekiel goes a step beyond Jeremiah in Ezek 18, and spells out the whole gamut of obligations and practices which everyone must learn to do. This movement from group to individual responsibility has been called the "axial crossover" by Karl Jaspers. He proposed that all over the world, in Zoroaster in Persia, Lao-Tzu in China, Buddha in India, Thales and Pythagoras in Greece, as well as in the Exilic prophets, a revolution took place in human consciousness that has affected us ever since. The problem with this approach is that it makes us look for some common cause for all these great religious thinkers' views. It is better to avoid such guesswork and simply be reminded that what Jeremiah says here does not represent a fundamental break with the past, or even with his own earlier preaching. Instead, the call to personal ethical responsibility is part and parcel of the love relationship of the covenant and of the basic Hebrew insight that a covenant with God means imitating the holiness of God and acting as God would act (Lev 19; Gen 1:27, we are the "image" of God!).

Verses 31-34 describe a *new* covenant, and have become the most famous passage in the Book of Jeremiah.

[31]"Behold the days are coming, says the LORD, when I will make a new covenant with the house of Israel and the house of Judah, [32]not like the covenant which I made with their fathers when I took them by the hand to bring them out of the land of Egypt, my covenant which they broke, though I was their husband, says the LORD. [33]But this is the covenant which I will make with the house of Israel after those days, says the LORD: I will put my law within them, and I will write it upon their hearts; and I will be their God, and they shall be my people. [34]And no longer shall each man teach his neighbour and each his brother, saying, "Know the LORD', for they shall all know me, from the least of them to the greatest, says the LORD; for I will forgive their iniquity, and I will remember their sin no more."

Although his younger contemporary, Ezekiel, talks about giving the people a new heart and writing an ever-lasting covenant with them (Ezek 36:26-27; 37:26), nowhere else do we find an Israelite suggesting God would actually enter into an *entirely new* covenant with his people, thus *rejecting* the old covenant. Ezekiel does say Yahweh will put his spirit into the people and make them keep his statutes, which nearly quotes the main point of Jeremiah in v. 33. This suggests that Ezekiel wanted to proclaim the same message but was sensitive enough to tradition not to imply that God would break the original covenant or be un-faithful to it. But Jeremiah was not so shy! This is exactly what he wanted to put across to the exiles. Already in 5:20-25; 14:22; 17:1; 18:13-15; 24:4-7 he has emphasized that the people's evil ways stand directly against God's desire to help them and free them. As 17:1 puts it, their sin was written in stone on their hearts, and they absolutely could not respond to God's covenantal offer. Can a leopard change its spots (13:23)? Yahweh finally told Jeremiah not to even intercede for them any longer (14:11-12). There are two other prose reports about Jeremiah, in 15:1-4 and

25:1-14, which stress that the Lord can no longer respond to Israel, but must punish her infidelity.

Thus to Jeremiah's way of thinking, Israel totally rejected the old covenant, and continued to pursue a way of evil until the final punishment sent by God in the person of the Babylonians finally cancelled the old way of living the covenant. Of course, at no point did Jeremiah believe that God had cut Israel off from his concern and care, and in no place does he give the impression that terminating the older understanding of the covenant means that God just forgets about all he has done in the past and all his special relationship to his people. The end had to come when the priests, prophets, princes, king and people alike pushed and pushed past the breaking point. God takes the opportunity to chastise the people and so soften their hearts and bring them back to fidelity. At the same time, the key to the new relationship between God and people must not start with tablets of stone, but with the heart and will. If the old covenant died because the people failed, a new one must overcome this deficiency! External obedience did not work, so the renewed relationship must center on internal communion and profound change of the will. Only Yahweh can bring this about, and he chooses to do so by offering a deeper and totally personal relationship as the basis.

The background of covenant terminology lies in the unequal status between the parties. One was an *overlord* who dictated the terms, the other was a *vassal* who pledged obedience. In the political order, such treaties usually meant that the vassal threw over the agreement and rebelled as soon as the overlord or his nation proved too weak to force compliance. Israel's own experience proved very similar. When weakened and in dire trouble, they were glad to pray to the Lord of their covenant; when prosperity struck and they felt independent, they turned to other gods and less demanding loyalties.

In the face of this, the profound trust of Jeremiah comes through. He does not give up his people, nor does he lose belief in the lasting promise of Yahweh. God will not only not drop his people altogether, he will fashion an even better relationship with them. The hoped-for change would be so great that the teachers and priests and wise who labored so hard to pass on the traditions and the faith would not even be needed, for Israel would know God so intimately and so well from personal experience that they would not have to be taught who this Yahweh was. And the beginning of that experience is the coming forgiveness and mercy of God in restoring the people Israel to their land.

The covenant on Sinai revealed a God of great compassion and mercy, but it was conditional on the people's ability to obey the Law. In the same way, the covenant with David was conditional, especially on the power and piety of the kings to be faithful. Neither succeeded well. Now Jeremiah foresees a whole new basis for covenant. It is intriguing to think that such a trustful vision of God giving a totally free gift of union was born from Jeremiah's own suffering and uncertainty about God's presence during his ministry. From that doubt and pain, expressed most fully in the Confessions of chaps. 12, 15, 17, 18 and 20, came a deepened understanding of God's action in his life and in that of Israel.

Verses 35-37 break the pattern of "Behold, the Days are Coming" oracles, but play an important role in backing up the almost unbelievable offer of the new covenant in the preceding oracle. The ultimate witness to God's power is his creation in all of its breadth and majesty. Jeremiah calls on two aspects of that creation to give testimony to God's plan. The first aspect recalls the divine decree of Gen 1 that fixes the order of the universe forever. To see the sun rise and set each day without fail gives proof enough that divine order can be trusted completely. But, even if it would fail, he says ironically, God would never fail. And secondly, only if you could play God for a day—which you can't—and measure all of creation's vast borders, and take his place, would it then be conceivable that God would not keep his promise. See similar challenges to human *hubris* in Job 28, 38-41, and Isa 40:1-31. Only God controls and directs the world—this is the absolute barrier between creator and creature which can never be crossed from our side. Indeed, the words of the prophet have a lasting message for us today despite our tremendous scientific and technological advances. We may master the atoms and the energy that form the sinews and muscles of the created world—something our ancient forebears would never even have dreamed possible!—but we will never find the true answer of why it exists and why it works until we discover our own proper role as creature, and our proper source of life and meaning, God.

The final oracle in the collection of chaps. 30-31 describes the rebuilding of Jerusalem. We witness the engineers stretching the measuring rods and lines to lay out the new city (see Zech 2 and Ezek 40-43). The excitement in the prophecy stems from the newness of it. People do not simply erect their old house on top of the rubble. This city will be planned in a new way, it will be enlarged and extended to the North and West. What had previously served as two dumping grounds and profane areas outside the city, the Kidron and Ben-Hinnom valleys, will now be included in the central area. At the same time, since Tophet lay in the Hinnom valley and was the scene of the worst violation of the covenant, the slaughter of children (7:31-33; 19:1-13), this *new* city would *reverse* the evil done there and consecrate the land to the Lord. Verse 40 puts the final word into place by referring yet again (for the third time—see 31:4, 28) to the divine commission to uproot and also to build.

INVESTING IN THE FUTURE
32:1-15

⁶Jeremiah said, "The word of the LORD came to me: ⁷Behold, Hanamel the son of Shallum your uncle will

come to you and say, 'Buy my field which is at Anathoth, for the right of redemption by purchase is yours.' [8]Then Hanamel my cousin came to me in the court of the guard, in accordance with the word of the LORD, and said to me, 'Buy my field which is at Anathoth in the land of Benjamin, for the right of possession and redemption is yours; buy it for yourself.' Then I knew that this was the word of the LORD.

[9]"And I bought the field at Anathoth from Hanamel my cousin, and weighed out the money to him, seventeen shekels of silver. [10]I signed the deed, sealed it, got witnesses, and weighed the money on scales. [11]Then I took the sealed deed of purchase, containing the terms and conditions, and the open copy; [12]and I gave the deed of purchase to Baruch the son of Neriah son of Mahseiah, in the presence of Hanamel my cousin, in the presence of the witnesses who signed the deed of purchase, and in the presence of all the Jews who were sitting in the court of the guard. [13]I charged Baruch in their presence, saying, [14]"Thus says the LORD of hosts, the God of Israel: Take these deeds, both this sealed deed of purchase and this open deed, and put them in an earthenware vessel, that they may last for a long time.[15]For thus says the LORD of hosts, the God of Israel: Houses and fields and vineyards shall again be bought in this land.'

Chapter 32 consists of Jeremiah's purchase of a family estate in his home village of Anathoth (vv. 1-15), a prayer that he utters in light of this experience (vv. 16-25), and a divine response to his prayer (26-44). The entire chapter is written in prose, but not entirely in third person narrative. It contains two accounts in Jeremiah's own words: vv. 6-15 and 16-25. Thus there may be evidence here that Jeremiah did write down, or dictate, some prose reports during his own ministry. Many commentators, however, take the entire 44 verses as a part of the biographical source for the life of Jeremiah which has frequently been credited to the scribe Baruch.

The incident in vv. 1-15 takes place late in the reign of Zedekiah, the final king of Judah. Since v. 1 places the date and correlation to Nebuchadnezzar so precisely, we can identify the time as 588/587 B.C., while the Babylonian army had temporarily withdrawn from surrounding the city of Jerusalem in order to face an Egyptian army sent by pharaoh Hophra to relieve the Israelites. From remarks in Ezek 25-32, we can understand a little more of the international intrigue behind this drama. It seems that Egyptian troops marched north through the Sinai into southern Palestine, while their allies, the Phoenician cities of Tyre and Sidon, aided and supplied them by sea. Thus Judah did not stand alone but formed part of a coalition of western states to oppose Babylonian expansion in their area. The immediate circumstances are given in some detail in Jer 37:11-21, and are summarized here in 32:2-5. Unfortunately the two accounts do not agree completely. In this chapter, the editors say that Jeremiah was already in prison in the court of the palace guard when he received word of the need to buy the land in Anathoth. Verses 3-4 explicitly state that the reason for his imprisonment was his claim that Zedekiah would be taken prisoner by the Babylonians and that Judah would lose the battle. Chapter 37 describes his arrest on the way to buy the field and imprisonment in the vaulted dungeon; *then* a secret meeting with Zedekiah in which he uttered the condemnation of the king; and his *subsequent* removal to the court of the guard. Both cannot be right—they probably represent different sources telling of the same complex of events that all happened about the same time and were remembered together: the purchase of the field that led to his arrest, his condemnation of the king, his time in the guard area prison.

The Law on inheritance in Lev 25:25-28 gives first rights for purchase of property, especially rural property, to the nearest kin in order to keep the property in the family. The thinking behind this regulation sees possession of a piece of land as the sign of the Israelite's membership in the covenant. God gives the land as a gift to Israel as part of the covenant. For the bountiful land which God blesses to be used merely as a means of trade and profit speculation undermines the lasting pledge that each family shall have an inheritance in the Lord. See the arguments along this line proposed by Naboth when King Ahab wants to take his vineyard (1 Kgs 21:3). When his cousin Hanamel comes to Jeremiah in v. 7, we don't know if poverty has forced this move on him or whether he simply seeks to flee the terror of the Babylonian invasion which undoubtedly has devastated the countryside. More than likely the Babylonians have lived off the land, stripping the farmers of their livestock and crops in order to feed the soldiers. Possibly, too, Jeremiah was not the first relative to be asked to buy the land—under the conditions people would not care much about their money if they threw it away on a farm overrun by the enemy. The Book of Ruth offers some good examples of this "redemption" process at work to use as a background to this text (Ruth 2:20, 4:1-12).

The story tells us that Jeremiah had a forewarning of this offer before his cousin arrives. Jeremiah takes this sign as a command from Yahweh to purchase the field regardless of the difficult times. He goes through all of the standard procedures to make the deal legally airtight. Once committed, there will be no going back on his decision. Verses 9-12 stress that not only was payment handed over, but that the deed had proper witnesses and was entrusted to Baruch as a third party to guarantee its safety. The use of two deeds, a sealed copy and an open copy, was part of ancient practice. After being written and witnessed, the owner put his own seal in wax over the deed so that no one could tamper with it. But in order that it could be read or filed without breaking the seal each time, a second copy was prepared and attached for consultation.

All of this solemn activity was not just to perform a favor for his cousin Hanamel. Jeremiah understood it as a divine sign of hope for the future. Therefore he orders Baruch to store it in a jar so that it would last. It would also allow the documents to be hid away in a cave or the ground during the Babylonian attack and so survive intact, just as the Essene community at Qumran in the time of Christ managed to roll up their scrolls, put them into vases with lids, hide them in caves around the Dead Sea, and then escape before the Roman Army of 68 A.D. arrived to wipe out their settlement. Nearly 1900 years later, these scrolls were recovered in generally good condition from the same caves, and have provided remarkable information on the biblical text and the Jewish sects of the first century.

Verse 15 provides the solemn word of Yahweh: houses and fields and vineyards shall again be bought in this land. This short statement provides us with the strongest evidence we have that Jeremiah already intended words of hope before the final fall of Jerusalem a year later. The many positive oracles of chaps. 30-31 raise endless difficulties about their authenticity and the dating of their delivery. But here, in an incident related twice in separate texts, we have a good indication that Jeremiah understood his own role to include both judgment and promise of deliverance at the same time.

JEREMIAH'S PRAYER
32:16-44

> [16]"After I had given the deed of purchase to Baruch the son of Neriah, I prayed to the LORD, saying: [17]'Ah Lord GOD! It is thou who hast made the heavens and the earth by thy great power and by thy outstretched arm! Nothing is too hard for thee, [18]who showest steadfast love to thousands, but dost requite the guilt of fathers to their children after them, O great and mighty God whose name is the LORD of hosts, [19]great in counsel

and mighty in deed; whose eyes are open to all the ways of men, rewarding every man according to his ways and according to the fruit of his doings; [20]who hast shown signs and wonders in the land of Egypt, and to this day in Israel and among all mankind, and hast made thee a name, as at this day.

The prayer in vv. 16-25 is quite lengthy and filled with typical language of the covenant. Like many Psalms (Pss 33; 103) and late prayers (Ezra 9:6-15; Neh 9:6-37; Dan 9:3-19), it recites a litany of the great deeds of God for the people Israel. In particular it hearkens back to the great covenant proclamations of Yahweh at the Exodus:

I the Lord your God am a jealous God, visiting the iniquity of the fathers upon the children to the third and fourth generation of those who hate me, but showing steadfast love to thousands of those who love me and keep my commandments (Exod 20:5-6).

Or:

The Lord, the Lord, a God merciful and gracious, slow to anger and abounding in steadfast love and faithfulness, keeping steadfast love for thousands, forgiving iniquity and transgression and sin (Exod 34:6-7).

Some of Jeremiah's phrases actually seem to borrow from the Exodus narratives. For example, the acclamation of God who "made heaven and earth" comes from Exod 20:11 and 31:17, and the mention of both "great power and an outstretched arm" cites Exod 32:11. A few phrases are typical of the prayers of Nehemiah and Daniel: "rewarding everyone according to his or her ways" in v. 19 resembles Neh 9:36; while the expression "a great and mighty God," parallels Neh 9:32 and Dan 9:4.

Other passages throughout the Scriptures also echo a phrase here and there, but by far the largest single source for thought similar to this prayer comes in the Book of Deuteronomy. Certain unique expressions, such as "Nothing is too hard for thee!" in v. 17, and the combination of "great terror and an outstretched arm" in v. 21, can be found only in Deuteronomy (Deut 17:8; 26:8; *cf.*, Deut 4:34; 34:12). Other phrases are extremely common in Deuteronomy, although sometimes found in other covenantal texts: "to bring the people out with signs and wonders" (Deut 4:34; 6:22; 7:19; 13:2, 3; 26:8; 28:46; 29:2; 34:11), "a land flowing with milk and honey" (Deut 6:3; 11:9; 26:9, 15; 27:3; 31:20; but compare also Exod 3:8, 17; 13:5; 33:3), and "with a strong hand and outstretched arm" (Deut 4:14; 5:15; 7:19; 9:29; 26:8; *cf.*, Exod 6:6).

The final verses of the prayer in 23-24 are almost a summary of the deuteronomic point of view, paralleling the message of Deut 1-11, with its narration of God's great mercy in the Exodus and warning the people to obey the voice of the Lord and walk in his ways. Now that the worst has come to pass, Jeremiah could hardly be expected to do something so foolish and wasteful as buying *that* field unless he expects God to once again deliver and rescue his people as in the days of Egypt.

> 26The word of the LORD came to Jeremiah: 27"Behold, I am the LORD, the God of all flesh; is anything too hard for me? 28Therefore, thus says the LORD: Behold, I am giving this city into the hands of the Chaldeans and into the hand of Nebuchadrezzar king of Babylon, and he shall take it. 29The Chaldeans who are fighting against this city shall come and set this city on fire, and burn it, with the houses on whose roofs incense has been offered to Baal and drink offerings have been poured out to other gods, to provoke me to anger. 30For the sons of Israel and the sons of Judah have done nothing but evil in my sight from their youth; the sons of Israel have done nothing but provoke me to anger by the works of their hands, says the LORD.

God's reply to Jeremiah's prayer can be divided into two parts: vv. 26-35 recite the basic message of judgment which Jeremiah has preached, and vv. 36-44 counter it with the message of hope found in chaps. 30-31. The whole divine response has been put together by the editors as a summary of the two-fold message of the prophet. As must have been the case often in his own ministry, the two sides stand in some tension to one another. The transition from the judgment to promise of release is sudden, and despite its opening "therefore," no reason or cause why God should save the people is to be found in the preceding dreary listing of their complete rejection of the covenant. In this way, it appears as a pure gift of God's favor and mercy to Israel, undeserved and unexpected by all reasonable standards. Scholars often overlook this intentional break that serves to dramatize the gift, and seek to remove the tension by getting rid of the judgment secton as an intrusion. It may well be true that vv. 28-35, or even 28-41, reflect a gathering up of Jeremiah's major thoughts by a third party, and that only vv. 42-44 actually address the situation portrayed in the story of the buying of the field. But even the editors understood clearly that the *meaning* of this purchase of land captured the essence of Jeremiah's mission. From the devastation, promise would be born. For this reason they thought rightly that a summary of Jeremiah's prophesying at this point would highlight the lesson. The deuteronomic editors, if that's who they were, appreciated Jeremiah's unique combination of rejection and re-institution, or re-consecration, to explain the true *conditional* nature of the covenant, rather than the *absolute* promise of divine support preached by the "false" prophets. They themselves were probably heavily influenced by Jeremiah's approach when they put together their history from Joshua through 2 Kings. Key passages, such as 2 Sam 7; 1 Kgs 3 and 9; 2 Kgs 17, all deuteronomic interpretations, reveal an intentional emphasis on the conditional side of the promises to David.

THE PROMISE TO JERUSALEM AND JUDAH
33:1-26

33 The word of the LORD came to Jeremiah a second time, while he was still shut up in the court of the guard: ²'Thus says the LORD who made the earth,' the LORD who formed it to establish it—the LORD is his name: ³Call to me and I will answer you, and will tell you great and hidden things which you have not known. ⁴For thus says the LORD, the God of Israel, concerning the houses of this city and the houses of the kings of Judah which were torn down to make a defence against the siege mounds and before the sword: ⁵The Chaldeans are coming in to fight and to fill them with the dead bodies of men whom I shall smite in my anger and my wrath, for I have hidden my face from this city because of all their wickedness. ⁶Behold, I will bring to it health and healing, and I will heal them and reveal to them abundance of prosperity and security. ⁷I will restore the fortunes of Judah and the fortunes of Israel, and rebuild them as they were at first. ⁸I will cleanse them from all the guilt of their sin against me, and I will forgive all the guilt of their sin and rebellion against me. ⁹And this city shall be to me a name of joy, a praise and a glory before all the nations of the earth who shall hear of all the good that I do for them; they shall fear and tremble because of all the good and all the prosperity I provide for it.

The opening verse of chap. 33 tells us that the following words came to Jeremiah about the same time as did the command to buy his cousin's field. The message that follows can be divided into two major parts: vv. 1-13, a word of promise to restore Jerusalem which is then extended to Judah's other cities and to the rural areas; and vv. 14-26, a series of three oracles on the return of a Davidic king.

The first part, in vv. 1-13, has many similarities with the previous words of hope in chaps. 30-32, especially with

Jeremiah's prayer and God's response in 32:16-44. Note, for example, how both 33:2 and 32:17 begin with praise of God as creator. 33:10-11 and 12-13 end the oracle, as did 32:43, with a vision of the fields and cities being repopulated. The thought is pure Jeremiah—note his characteristic expressions about the voices of the bridegroom and the bride in v. 11 (*cf.*, 7:34; 16:9; 25:10; 31:19), and restoring the fortunes of the land in v. 7 (*cf.*, 29:14; 30:3, 18; 31:23; 32:44), the summons to call upon Yahweh so that he can heal in v. 3 (*cf.*, 29:12), the promise to heal them in v. 6 (*cf.*, 8:22; 31:17), and the return of the flocks to the hillsides (*cf.*, 17:26; 31:24). Apparently, chaps. 32-33 formed a little booklet that was inserted at the present place, and which summarized the main points of Jeremiah's preaching on restoration that he had delivered during the last days of Judah's life just before the final catastrophe. However, it was not edited until late, and this permitted the addition of several very different oracles to be attached to it (vv. 14-26 as well as the prayer and divine response in 32:16-44) before it was included in the official edition of Jeremiah. See the points made below on why vv. 14-26 do not necessarily reflect the thinking of Jeremiah himself.

While vv. 1-13 are made up of a web of Jeremiah's sayings, the whole unfolds a very definite *new* line of argument. It begins with the reminder that God is creator and he alone can establish the order of the world, and therefore he alone can make known the future. This carefully stated opening leads the believer to expect that God will create again as he did in Gen 1. The subsequent mention of God's praise and glory before the nations in v. 9, the fear and awe of the nations of the whole earth, and the joy and gladness of couples about to share God's creative power in marriage, develop the theme further.

This rooting of our human hope for deliverance in the power of God as creator was an aspect of biblical faith developed during the exile. Jeremiah alludes to it in a simple form in 31:35-37; 32:17 and now in 33:2-3; but it is used much more extensively by Ezekiel who ends nearly every oracle with the expression, "in order that you (or they) will know that I am the Lord" (Ezek 6:7, 14; 7:27; 13:16; 28:26; 37:14 and others) or "I the Lord have spoken" (Ezek 12:25, 28; 21:22, 37, etc.), which serve as proofs that God indeed has created and controls the entire universe and all the events of history. Second Isaiah makes the fullest use of the theme of creator and redeemer by joining them together in both oracles of salvation and in divine lawsuits against the claims of false gods (Isa 41:21-24; 42:5-9; 43:5-9; 44:6-8, etc.). The God who *created* was the god who *redeemed* Israel at the Red Sea, and this same God will redeem the exiles from across the Euphrates and the Jordan and restore the creation to its former bounty. A new creation and a new Exodus become the twin bases for understanding a God who wills to save and not to destroy.

The remaining three oracles of hope in 33:14-26 are all tied to the promise of a Davidic king. But they do not all share the same focus. Verses 14-18 relate to the coming king in a purified Jerusalem; vv. 19-22 unite the promise to David with a promise to the levites; and vv. 23-26 foresee the union of northern and southern tribes under a king as in the days of David himself. None of these passages can be found in the Greek Septuagint, which has led most scholars to consider them quite late additions to the present text, perhaps after the final editing of Jeremiah's own materials had long been completed. If indeed this is so, then it would explain why they were inserted at the *end* of the whole section on hope.

Verses 14-18 generally repeat the small oracle in 23:5-6, which contrasts a future king who will be *truly righteous* with the present king Zedekiah, whose name means "My righteousness is Yahweh," but whose conduct does not bear witness to such a claim. Andrew Blackwood suggests that the best explanation for the seeming repetition of these lines in 33:14-17 is that they reflect a rabbi's sermon on 23:5-6, developed perhaps in the late 6th century or even in the 5th century at a moment of despair in order to rekindle faith in Jeremiah's promise. This certainly could be possible, but we must note the slight differences between the two texts as well. In chap. 23, the hoped-for king is both the "righteous branch" and the "Yahweh is our Righteousness," while in chap. 33, the king is a "righteous branch" (*cf.*, Zech 3:8 and Isa 11:1) but *Jerusalem* will be named "Yahweh is our Righteousness." Chapter 33:17 adds the further note about the levitical priests being established with a similar "everlasting covenant" as will be extended to the kings. Both hopes are based on the oracle of Nathan in 2 Sam 7, which apparently became the central support for the Davidic dynasty through the centuries, because it was regularly celebrated in the temple liturgy in honor of the king (*cf.*, Pss 89 and 132). From this use, the priests began to apply the promise to themselves.

The second oracle in vv. 19-22 takes up the motif of the promise to the levitical priests again and associates it with the unbreakable nature of the Davidic covenant. To strengthen this lasting quality further, the oracle refers the hearer to the unchangeable will of God in creation. The question is purely rhetorical since to an Israelite of faith, the notion was patently absurd that humans could interfere in God's plan of creation (*cf.*, 31:35-36). To reinforce the idea even more, v. 22 continues with an allusion to the covenant with Abraham in Gen 15:5 and 22:17, that God would multiply his descendants like the stars or sand of the shore. The same blessing extends both to the kings and the levitical priests.

The final oracle in vv. 23-26 approaches the reunion of the two kingdoms from the same perspective. It summons up the lesson of the covenant in creation in v. 25, and re-affirms the pledge given to the patriarchs in v. 26, in order to strengthen confidence in the promise to David. Just in case all of this fails to be strong enough, the author associates David and Jacob together. For those who know the Old Testament backward and forward, this would recall the plea of Jacob in Gen 32:13 that God indeed lived up to his promise to make him and his offspring as numerous as the sands.

One must acknowledge that these three oracles contain many difficulties if they are to be attributed to Jeremiah himself. First of all, he almost never mentions any real hope for a new king to sit on the throne (at least in clearly authentic oracles). He does not affirm the value of the Davidic covenant as everlasting—in fact he indirectly accuses the false prophets of preaching this as their "lie" (27:10, 14, 15, 16; 29:21, 23, 31). He further shows little or no concern with the special position of the priests, and certainly not with the levitical priests as distinct from others. Finally, the general interest in the "righteous branch" fits well the later focus of the prophets Haggai and Zechariah about 520 B.C. If we add to this the importance of the levites in post-exilic thought in the Books of Ezra and Nehemiah (about 450 B.C.) and the fact that the whole section is lacking in the Septuagint, we can scarcely come to any other conclusion than that vv. 14-26 represent a later period's reflection upon the meaning of Jeremiah's words in chaps. 22-23, with their lack of hope, when mixed with his words of promise in chaps. 30-32. If we had to pick a suitable date for such a reflection, Zechariah 3-4 would provide an ideal occasion, with its hopes for a double messiah from Yahweh—the governor Zerubbabel and the high priest Joshua (see esp. Zech 4:14)—sometime between 520 and 516 B.C.

III. Warnings to Attend to the Warning
Jeremiah 34-36

Chapters 34-36 continue the series of biographical narratives and reports about incidents from the prophet's life that began in chaps. 26-29, and which were interrupted by the oracles of salvation in chaps. 30-33. Just as the first group called the reader's attention to the dangers of a false prophecy that pretended God could not and would not punish Israel, this series adds several new incidents showing foolish neglect of the word of judgment. They come from different periods of Jeremiah's life. The first two, in chap. 34, from late in the reign of Zedekiah; the next two, in chaps. 35-36, from the reign of his predecessor, Jehoiakim.

They are also quite diverse, and little holds them together except the dramatic interest they create. All of them deal with colorful incidents which must have been well-remembered by many at the time. Above all, chap. 36 reaches a kind of climax for this message. Nothing could be more helpful to Jeremiah's point than the scene of the king slowly and deliberately ripping up his prophecies and burning them in 36:22-23. This chapter not only brings to a close the large unit of chaps. 26-36, but it prepares the reader for the next section, 37-45, with its sad, despairing story of the final failure of Judah.

"OBEY THE WORD OF THE LORD, ZEDEKIAH!" 34:1-22

34 The word which came to Jeremiah from the LORD, when Nebuchadnezzar king of Babylon and all his army and all the kingdoms of the earth under his dominion and all the peoples were fighting against Jerusalem and all of its cities: 2"Thus says the LORD, the God of Israel: Go and speak to Zedekiah king of Judah and say to him, 'Thus says the LORD: Behold, I am giving this city into the hand of the king of Babylon, and he shall burn it with fire. 3You shall not escape from his hand, but shall surely be captured and delivered into his hand; you shall see the king of Babylon eye to eye and speak with him face to face; and you shall go to Babylon.' 4Yet hear the word of the LORD, O Zedekiah king of Judah! Thus says the LORD concerning you: 'You shall not die by the sword. 5You shall die in peace. And as spices were burned for your fathers, the former kings who were before you, so men shall burn spices for you and lament for you, saying, "Alas, lord!"'" For I have spoken the word, says the LORD."

Chapters 34-35 stress the need for obedience to Yahweh. The first incident, in vv. 1-7, must have made a strong impression on people around Jeremiah—the date for this one word is given twice with elaborate detail in both vv. 1 and 7. The full siege of Jerusalem in 588-587 is under way and the rest of the nation has already fallen except for the large fortified towns of Lachish and Azekah. Jeremiah makes what amounts to a final offer to Zedekiah: change now, and God will deliver you from this disaster. The promise of a sign accompanies the prophet's words. But whereas he predicted the death of Hananiah in chap. 28 and of Shemaiah in chap. 29, he now offers Zedekiah the assurance of life if he will change. In v. 5, he calls it *shalom*, that peace and prosperity every Israelite wished for (*cf.*, Pss 29:11; 35:27; 85:11; 125:5; 128:6 Isa 48:18; 54:13; 60:17; 66:12). It will be a highly charged moment when Zedekiah humbly meets the Babylonian king, "eye to eye and mouth and mouth," as v. 3 calls it, and is spared. But if he refuses to reform, the city shall be burned and the king handed over to die by the sword.

The saying was particularly memorable because in fact Zedekiah did not escape in mercy. Instead, 2 Kgs 25:5-7 and Jer 52:8-11 tell us that when he was finally captured trying to flee (see Ezek 12:13), the Babylonian king had him brought to his camp to meet him face to face; then he executed his sons before his eyes, blinded Zedekiah and took him away as a prisoner to Babylon. We have heard already Jeremiah's warnings to the king in chaps. 21 and 32; we will hear them repeated again in chaps. 37 and 38. Apparently, Zedekiah represented for Jeremiah, and the followers of Jeremiah who saved these stories, the epitome of one who could have turned back to the Lord and did not. He thus becomes the exemplar of Israel as a whole. In this one king, all the possibilities of fidelity or infidelity are at war, tugging him in two different directions. His particularly gruesome fate only accents the tragedy of the nation as a whole.

The custom of burning spices for the king is recorded of Asa, one of Zedekiah's predecessors, in 2 Chron 16:14. It was considered a great shame to be denied burial rites (*cf.*, 22:19 and 1 Kgs 13:22), especially for a ruler. Note the serious manner in which Amos levels the charge of defiling royal bones against the Moabites in Amos 2:1.

The statement of v. 5, "You shall die in peace," cannot be right. The whole idea clearly indicates that Jeremiah makes this promise conditional upon obedience. Indeed, the mistake lies in the very first word of v. 4, where the RSV takes Hebrew *'ak*, a small particle, to mean "yet," when its much more basic sense is restrictive: "only," or "if only" fits better. "If only you hear the word of the Lord, . . . you shall die in peace."

Finally, a small fragment of a letter was found in the ruins of Lachish that dates from the very siege mentioned in v. 7. The commander of a local garrison nearby reports back to the regional headquarters in Lachish that he has posted the notice sent out to his men, presumably from the commander. He then added that no one was left in the outpost of Beth-haraphid, probably because it has been overrun by the Babylonian army. His final paragraph is the most ominous: "And let my lord know that we are watching for the signals of Lachish, according to all the indications which my lord has given, for we cannot see Azekah" (ANET 322). It must date to a very short time after the incident of 34:1-7.

8The word which came to Jeremiah from the LORD, after King Zedekiah had made a covenant with all the people in Jerusalem to make a proclamation of liberty to them, 9that every one should set free his Hebrew slaves, male and female, so that no one should enslave a Jew, his brother. [10]And they obeyed, all the princes and all the people who had entered into the covenant that everyone would set free his slave, male or female, so that they would not be enslaved again; they obeyed and set them free. [11]But afterward they turned around and took back the male and female slaves they had set free, and brought them into subjection as slaves.

The second incident in chap. 34 fills the remainder of the chapter. When the siege was at its most terrifying stage, the king and all the slave-owners entered into a solemn covenant to free their slaves, perhaps to win over the favor of God and show an act of piety that would move him to have mercy upon them. But when Hophra brought his army to aid Judah, Nebuchadnezzar had to lift the siege and go down to meet the Egyptians. This gave Judah a breathing spell and buoyed their hopes that victory might come to them. In that moment, the landowners, nobles and slave-holders reversed their solemn vow and reenslaved the Israelites who had been freed. A more blatant act of disregard for the covenant could hardly be imagined. Jeremiah's reaction is to announce that Yahweh will call the Babylonians back to finish the job of destroying the city (vv. 21-22).

Slavery was permitted in Israel, apparently from very early days, since the law is included in the Covenant Law Code found in Exod 20-23. Exod 21:2-6 allows Hebrews to enter slavery for economic reasons, but they must have the choice of freedom in the 7th year. The law seemed to be well-accepted. It was still included in Deuteronomy's vision of the community in Deut 15:12-18, although updated in terms of a more prosperous and more urban economy. It specifies now that the master must give the freed slave something to start out with to make it on his or her own. However, permanent slavery had a place, too, if the Hebrew man wanted to marry another slave; or if married, they bore children while in slavery. Males could not take a wife or children to freedom with them; so to maintain their families, they could declare themselves slaves in perpetuity.

The incident has particular significance for Jeremiah because the king and the people chose to make a covenant (v. 8) and a public proclamation. Their later decision to break this solemn form of agreement only revealed their true attitude toward the Sinai covenant and God. Loyalty and obedience were fine when trouble made it necessary to turn to God, but in good times or when local interests would be hurt, they felt free to break the commandments and foresake the way of Yahweh.

Verses 12-22 comprise the divine judgment upon this act of betrayal. It recalls the mercy of Yahweh in making his covenant with them when they had been slaves (Exod 20:2), cites the law of Exod 21 on slavery, and then praises their act of mercy to their slaves as true to the Sinai covenant. But because they revoked it and proved unfaithful, God will now do a new act of liberation—he will free them from his covenant protection to become victims of the Babylonians! The phrase, "sword, famine and plague (or pestilence)" is common throughout Jeremiah (21:9; 24:10; 27:13; 29:17; 32:24; 38:2) to describe the disaster of war. The fate of those who violated their word can be fittingly compared to the calf used in the ceremony of ratifying the covenant. Literally, the Hebrews "cut a covenant," i.e., they symbolized the solemnity of the agreement by cutting an animal in two. Verse 8 actually uses the verb "cut" where RSV says they "made" an agreement. Gen 15:9-19 pictures Abraham cutting up animals, with God's divine fire passing between the parts as a sign of his acceptance of the agreement. However, other Ancient Near Eastern treaties suggest that the cut-up animal graphically illustrated the curse expected to fall on whichever party broke the treaty. Thus, one treaty reads: "(he) cut the neck of a sheep, saying: Let me so die if I take back that which I so gave thee," and another treaty, from Sefire, describes in detail the fate

of the offender in terms of the slaughter of a spring lamb
(ANET 532).

Jeremiah brings the threat to a climax in v. 20 by repeating his earlier dire warnings of non-burial and disgrace
for the corpses of the offenders (see 7:33; 16:4; 19:7; Ezek
39:4, 17; and Deut 28:26). Although he had granted the
people a respite, Yahweh will now give the command to
his instrument, the Babylonians, to resume the siege and to
finally destroy the city. They will leave Judah nothing
more than a deserted wasteland. This particular curse was
standard fare in the ancient world—note how biblical
oracles use it against Babylon itself in Isa 13:20-21 and Jer
51:37, but it especially echoes the threats that Jeremiah
had used for so long against Israel (4:27; 6:8; 9:10; 10:22;
12:10; 32:43). Interestingly enough, the phrase, "to make the
cities (or the land) a devastation," occurs regularly in Isaiah
and Zephaniah, still more in Jeremiah, but above all in
Ezekiel, who makes it an even greater part of his prophesying than Jeremiah did (21 times in all).

THE RIGORISM OF THE RECHABITES
35:1-19

⁵Then I set before the Rechabites pitchers full of
wine, and cups; and I said to them, "Drink wine," ⁶But
they answered, "We will drink no wine, for Jonadab the
son of Rechab, our father, commanded us, 'You shall
not drink wine, neither you nor your sons for ever; ⁷you
shall not build a house; you shall not sow seed; you
shall not plant or have a vineyard; but you shall live in
tents all your days, that you may live many days in the
land where you sojourn.' ⁸We have obeyed the voice
of Jonadab the son of Rechab, our father, in all that he
commanded us, to drink no wine all our days, ourselves,
our wives, our sons, or our daughters, ⁹and not to build
houses to dwell in. We have no vineyard or field or seed;

¹⁰but we have lived in tents, and have obeyed and done all that Jonadab our father commanded us. ¹¹But when Nebuchadrezzar king of Babylon came up against the land, we said, 'Come, and let us go to Jerusalem for fear of the army of the Chaldeans and the army of the Syrians.' So we are living in Jerusalem."

The next story from the life of Jeremiah comes from a much earlier period, sometime late in the reign of Jehoiakim. It involves members of what must have been considered a very small sect within Israel since the whole "household" (which may mean a clan, or more likely, a group) had moved en masse to Jerusalem for safety during the Babylonian invasion of 598 (v. 11). Their unusual presence in the city provides Jeremiah with an opportunity to perform another symbolic action. From vv. 6-9, we learn that this group drank no wine, did no agricultural farming or cultivating of vineyards, and lived in tents rather than houses. If they had brought their tents and pitched them in a corner of Jerusalem, everybody would have been talking. No doubt these Rechabites were already well known as a very strict and quite conservative sect within Israel, much as we might look upon the Mennonite or Amish way of life today.

Jonadab, their founder, first appears during the revolt of the general Jehu in Northern Israel at the time of Elijah and Elisha. Under prophetic command, Jehu launched a military coup against the House of Ahab in 842 B.C., and wiped out the royal family. According to 2 Kgs 9:22-26, one cause of the revolt was the injustice rampant in royal circles; according to 2 Kgs 10:18-27, the real cause was royal support for the cult of the Phoenician god Baal by Ahab and his son Joram to please Jezebel, Ahab's Phoenician wife. Both reasons may have worked hand in hand. Jehu suddenly meets Jonadab on the highway in the midst of his revolt and invites him to ride in his chariot so that Jonadab can see for himself how faithfully Jehu carries out the task of eliminating all members of the family of Ahab. Jonadab thus was remembered as a zealot for Yahweh against the pagan cults that flourished under Jezebel. Jehu recognized him and seemed to seek his approval, so that the Rechabites may already have been a known force of opposition to the spread of Baal worship in the North.

We hear little more about them except for a short mention that they are related to the Kenites and lived with the Tribe of Judah in 1 Chron 2:55. Our only real source of information is Jer 35 and its testimony about their practices some two hundred years after Jonadab. The refusal to drink wine has some parallels in Israelite religious practice as a mark of special consecration. The Nazirites, for example, took vows of special rigor in their religious practice, including refraining from wine and not cutting their hair, for either a period of time (Num 6:2-4); or perhaps under special conditions, for life (Samson in Jgs 13:4-7, and Samuel in 1 Sam 1:11). Ezek 44:21 specifies that a priest while in service at the Temple must refrain from wine. Generally, however, such practices were temporary. A more likely source for understanding their rejection of most marks of a settled and civilized culture lies in the Kenite origins. The Kenites were a nomadic clan that lived throughout the Sinai and Southern Judah's Negev desert. They are closely connected to the Exodus events and the early days in the wilderness through Hobab, the father-in-law of Moses according to Jgs 4:11. He is the same as the Midianite Ruel, listed as father-in-law in Exod 18. As part of the tribes of Judah, they were instrumental in establishing David as the king in Hebron (2 Sam 2:4). They may represent a strong reaction to the later developments in monarchy and the assimilation of Canaanite culture with its urban centers and landowning emphases. Nomadic or semi-nomadic tribes have always been part of the landscape around the towns of Syria-Palestine. They are still there today. However, we have no way of knowing if the Rechabites actually come from a group that had always lived in tents, or if their founder

Jonadab (or his father Rechab) made a dramatic return to a simpler and long-treasured way of life. The latter seems more probably given the respect the later members pay to Jonadab and his regulations.

Elijah himself, with his coat of hair and leather belt (2 Kgs 1:8) had represented such a return to a vision of Israel in the desert, without wine or farm produce, living from day to day without established homes, and zealous for the cause of Yahweh. It hearkened back to a time before Israel came into contact with the Canaanites in the land and had been slowly but surely corrupted by their ways. This can be a powerful ideal to live by. Diodorus Siculus (XIX, 94) in his description of Palestine in the 1st century, describes some Nabateans as doing without wine, refusing to plant fields, and living in tents rather than homes. Since he places them in the southern Negev desert, it is attractive to believe that this Roman historian had heard about the remnants of the Rechabites still faithful to their vows some 800 years later!

All of this leads us to the conclusion that the Rechabites were indeed Israelites who pledged themselves to a total rejection of anything that would interfere with the worship of Yahweh. Their denial of most of the ordinary cultural practices of a mixed agricultural and urban economy provided a striking witness of opposition to any traces of Baal worship and its fertility cults. It also provided Jeremiah with a remarkable example of fidelity to the difficult demands of their founder, Jonadab. The prophet now proceeded in elaborate fashion to set up a demonstration of that fidelity, and to use the occasion to announce God's judgment on Israel's infidelity.

Verses 1-11 describe how Jeremiah was able to invite the Rechabites to the temple for a religious meeting in one of the side chambers reserved to the priests and levites (see Ezek 42:1-14; 46:19-24). There he offers them wine to drink as a test. Of all the possible ways to tempt them, this was perhaps the most serious affront possible since the misuse of wine in religious orgies and sacrificial banquets typified the worst of Canaanite practices. Thus, the chief god El is described in one Ugaritic document at a drinking feast for the dead:

> El drank wine until sated,
> The dregs until drunk.
> El left for his house,
> Went down to his courtyard.
> TKMN and SHNM carried him.
> A HBY attacked him,
> With two horns and a tail.
> He cursed amid his excrement and urine,
> El fell; El, like someone entering the underworld.

As the last line makes clear, El was *dead* drunk!

However, the scene does not suggest that Jeremiah offended them by this gesture. In fact, the use of the temple chambers and the willingness of the whole clan to come with him there suggests the prophet enjoyed a certain prestige and even favor with the temple authorities. Perhaps as a priest himself, he had the right to use the rooms, although in this case, it seems that an important friend among the sons of Hanan made it possible.

Their expected refusal leads to the oracle of judgment in vv. 12-17. In it, the text repeats many of the standard charges from Jeremiah about the disobedience and infidelity of the people towards Yahweh, and insists that if the followers of Jonadab can be so faithful to their human master's teachings, how much the more should Israel have been faithful to their God. The judicial sentence is passed in very solemn terms in v. 17. God is listed with all his titles to emphasize that this is no mere human teacher whose words have fallen on deaf ears.

The chapter ends with a word of support to the Rechabites. It takes the form of a covenant; not a national covenant as on Sinai but more of a royal grant of favor. David had received the personal promise of his dynasty in this manner, and Israelite tradition remembered how God had granted the same to Noah in Gen 9 and Abraham in Gen 15. Each of these heroes had been faithful in an age of infidelity and so merited the gift of eternal survival (*cf.*, Ps 132:12). To "stand before the Lord" means no more than to survive the disasters ahead so that the individual can continue to worship Yahewh (*cf.*, Jer 7:10 and 15:19). In the midst of a judgment of death, to be promised life is gift enough.

JEHOIAKIM REJECTS JEREMIAH'S WORDS
36:1-32

[4]Then Jeremiah called Baruch the son of Neriah, and Baruch wrote upon a scroll at the dictation of Jeremiah all the words of the LORD which he had spoken to him. [5]And Jeremiah ordered Baruch, saying, "I am debarred from going to the house of the LORD: [6]so you are to go, and on a fast day in the hearing of all the people in the LORD'S house you shall read the words of the LORD from the scroll which you have written at my dictation. You shall read them also in the hearing of all the men of Judah who come out of their cities. [7]It may be that their supplication will come before the LORD, and that every one will turn from his evil way, for great is the anger and wrath that the LORD has pronounced against this people." [8]And Baruch the son of Neriah did all that Jeremiah the prophet ordered him about reading from the scroll the words of the LORD in the LORD'S house.

Chapter 36 brings to a close the section on the fate of Gods word that has run from chap. 26 on. In chaps. 26-29, the divine judgment was challenged by false prophets; in chaps. 30-33, the question whether the word would survive the disaster arose; in chaps. 34-35, official indifference attempted to undermine its effect; finally in chap. 36, the king himself defiantly tries to wipe out the work of Jeremiah in one blow. The story unfolded in these 32 verses has such a wealth of personal detail and such a carefully noted sequence of events, that almost everybody recognizes some eyewitness has first put his account into writing. By tradition it was the scribe Baruch himself, and there is really no good reason to deny this, even if we maintain that it was probably re-edited to sharpen its point as a conclusion to chaps. 26-36. For it does have all the features of a climax. The drama of the scene unfolds in four stages. The word is delivered to the people, then to the princes, and then to the king. After the king has done what neither people nor princes would do, burn the scroll in contempt, Jeremiah directs judgment against the king, and recreates the scroll so that the word would not only live but grow.

In this, the entire chapter stands in direct contrast to the narrative of 2 Kgs 22-23 in which Jehoiakim's father, Josiah, hears the word of the "Book of the Law," found in the temple in his 18th year as king (622 B.C.). While Josiah had listened in obedience and submitted himself to the words of the Law (2 Kgs 22:11), did penance (2 Kgs 23:1-2) and renewed the covenant pledge to Yahweh (2 Kgs 23:3), Jehoiakim was not afraid and did not even rend his garments as Josiah had done (2 Kgs 22:11). The parallel becomes even more telling when we note that Jeremiah's prediction in vv. 27-31 declares that God will bring the "evil" written in the scroll upon the people and that the king's corpse will be thrown out without proper burial. In contrast, Huldah the prophetess tells Josiah that God will indeed bring the "evil" written in the Book of the Law upon the nation, but that Josiah would be given a burial in peace because of his repentance (2 Kgs 22:14-20). The editors have certainly organized the eyewitness account of Jer 36 to highlight the drastic difference between Josiah's obedience and Jehoiakim's disobedience to the divine word. Even though this incident occurred rather early in the career of Jeremiah (v. 1), it was important enough to stand as the summarizing word of explanation why the nation came to its end. The next two major divisions, chaps.

37-45 and 46-51, direct their attention to the story of the end and to the role of judgment over other nations. But they add no further words of substance to what has now been said.

Chapter 36 is a goldmine of information about the prophetic process. We get an interesting view of the use of the temple grounds for prophecy, we learn of the methods of delivery of oracles, as well as something about the means of writing and preserving them. Above all, we get a fascinating picture of the workings of the officials in Judah's government under the last kings. This chapter has occasioned many articles on the nature of oral versus written tradition in prophecy, and much speculation about what parts of the present Book of Jeremiah can be located in the first scroll that he dictated (v. 2), and what parts in the additions to the second scroll (v. 32). No common agreement has been reached on either of these issues, and they remain hot topics even today.

The chapter opens with a note about the date of these happenings. Jeremiah receives God's command in the fourth year of the king's rule, but Baruch does not deliver the word until the ninth month of the king's fifth year. If Jeremiah received his oracle late in the fourth year, the time can be calculated as February or March of 604; Baruch then appeared in the temple some nine or ten months later, in late November or early December of 604. In any case, a significant period of time elapsed between the two dates. Perhaps it took Jeremiah a long while to complete the dictation; or perhaps the desire to wait for a fast day made him delay the delivery. These were difficult days. Nebuchadnezzar had beaten the Egyptian army badly at the Battle of Carchemesh in the Spring of 605, and pharaoh Necho had retreated back to his own territory. This left his vassal Jehoiakim caught in a dilemma. If he stuck by Egypt, the Babylonians could simply overrun and annex his territory. If he changed sides, he might still have to pay heavy penalties and possibly lose his throne. To make matters worse, the Babylonians attacked the neighboring state of Ashkelon, a Philistine city on Israel's very coast, about the same time that Baruch reads out Jeremiah's words of judgment. No wonder the king did not want to hear any more doom than he had to deal with already!

Jeremiah appears to be barred from the temple because of the words he uttered against it in chaps. 7 and 26. This leads him to extraordinary measures to get his word spoken on the temple grounds. We might well wonder why he could not have spoken at a popular streetcorner instead. Certainly we have no certitude that Jeremiah did not speak in public squares, but this passage and several others (chaps. 7, 20, 28, and 35) suggest that he regularly delivered his more important oracles in the temple courtyards. One reason may have been to attract crowds, another may have been to gain proper authority for the word he spoke. For this reason, he carefully waits for a fast day, even if it falls months after he receives the original command to preach. Could it be that prophetic oracles were regularly delivered on such occasions and the people actually came to the temple expecting such prophecies? The Book of Joel, uttered apparently at the time of a locust plague, might be a good example of just such a fast day oracle. Even the Book of Nahum, with its prediction of Assyria's fall, could be situated reasonably well on a day of fasting and prayer for deliverance. In view of the setting described in Jeremiah 36, it would be most foolish to portray the prophet as a lonely figure of fierce independence who stood against the temple and its priests and prophets, and had no connection whatsoever with them. Part of the effectiveness of a Jeremiah or an Isaiah must have come from their acceptance as genuine members of the Israelite community in good standing, and not as some kind of quack or strangely-possessed madmen. The fast day may well have been to pray for guidance in the crisis of the Babylonian victories at

Carchemesh and Ashkelon; or, in a less dramatic fashion, a part of the prayer and fasting specified in later Jewish Law for drought when rain has not fallen by December.

Another reason for waiting for a fast day was to underscore the repentance theme. Twice the text notes that Baruch was to read these words to both Jerusalem and to everyone of the house of Judah (vv. 6, 9). Jeremiah obviously considered it important that the message be delivered to the whole nation as far as it was possible. Moreover, since v. 2 states that this scroll was to include all words addressed to Israel *and* to Judah *and* to foreign nations, its public reading would draw attention to God's plans on the international scene. Thus it effectively becomes a political message to the Israelites to avoid constant intrigue and plans for revolt, and to accept the de facto situation of Babylonian domination of Palestine. Instead, the people's attention should be focused on internal reform and loyalty to their own covenant. Verse 3 clearly makes the threat of destruction *conditional* upon Israel's refusal to convert their hearts. Yet by v. 31, the situation has changed. There is no hope left for repentance, and the judgment becomes absolutely predicted.

There are many elaborate structures present in this chapter to give it artistic merit of a high grade. Note, for example, how the command to Jeremiah in vv. 1-4 parallels exactly Jeremiah's command to Baruch in vv. 5-8, and that both parallel Yahweh's final word to Jeremiah in vv. 27-32. We can also detect a threefold structure of meaning: Jeremiah arranges for the proclamation of the word (vv. 1-10); the princes and king respond (vv. 11-26); Jeremiah counter-responds with a new oracle and scroll. This brings out the themes of possible repentance, the offer refused by the king despite the caution of the leading men, and the final word of judgment.

Baruch goes to the temple on the fast day and reads from the room of Gemariah, whom we have already noted in chap. 26 as a special friend of Jeremiah. His father had read the Book of the Law to Josiah years before, and no doubt he was among the influential princes of the land. His chambers were located above the courtyard so that Baruch could stand at a window or on a balcony and be seen and heard by many below. Baruch himself is called a "scribe," but this would have meant much more in the ancient world than it does today to speak of a secretary who takes dictation. The role of scribes, educated not just in writing but in literature, included teaching and being among the wise of the land. Scribes were often attached to the temple library as custodians of the records of the royal court, economic contracts, and judicial decisions, as well as the religious texts used in worship and education. Archaeological work at both Thebes in Egypt and Ugarit in Syria have uncovered large libraries and schools attached to the great temples of those important cities. Often, too, scribal schools were the training grounds for government administrators and officials.

Baruch was probably among the princes of the land. Not only do they give him a respectful hearing in vv. 11-19, but they preserve the document in the official records room, the chambers of Elishama, the secretary (v. 20). Later, a small oracle preserved in chap. 45 warns Baruch against high ambition and promises that he will be spared when other officials are executed by the Babylonians. This gives further support to the idea that he held a position of rank. Nevertheless, we find that he is devoted to Jeremiah and eventually even shares his exile in Egypt (43:6). The text, however, carefully distinguishes Baruch's authority as scribe and proclaimer from that of the message he delivers. The reason for Jeremiah's writing of the word, and later for the prince's careful verification of this fact (vv. 17-18), was to insure that all recognize it as God's word through Jeremiah, and not the thought of Baruch, son of Neriah.

¹⁴Then all the princes sent Jehudi the son of Nethaniah, son of Shelemiah, son of Cushi, to say to Baruch, "Take in your hand the scroll that you read in the hearing of the people, and come." So Baruch the son of Neriah took the scroll in his hand and came to them. ¹⁵And they said to him, "Sit down and read it." So Baruch read it to them. ¹⁶When they heard all the words, they turned one to another in fear; and they said to Baruch, "We must report all these words to the king." ¹⁷Then they asked Baruch, "Tell us, how did you write all these words? Was it at his dictation?" ¹⁸Baruch answered them, "He dictated all these words to me, while I wrote them with ink on the scroll." ¹⁹Then the princes said to Baruch, "Go and hide, you and Jeremiah, and let no one know where you are."

Verses 11-19 record the reactions of the major officials in Jehoiakim's government. Generally, they are favorable to Baruch and Jeremiah, and seem to be genuinely concerned to take the message seriously. They go to great lengths to hear it read in its entirety, have it stored for safe keeping, and get Jeremiah and Baruch into hiding before reporting to the king. Some of these men have appeared already in past narratives. Elnathan brought the prophet Uriah back for execution (26:20-23); Elishama seems to be the grandfather of the leader Ishmael who assassinates Gedaliah in chap. 41. They knew that the king would be angry at these words, and do everything in their power to prevent harm either to the scroll or to the authors.

Verses 20-26 give a colorful picture of the king's response. He slices the scroll in pieces as every few columns are read aloud by the prince Jehudi. Not satisfied with destroying the written word, he sends his aides to arrest both Jeremiah and Baruch. At that moment, Jeremiah probably faced the same fate as Uriah, his colleague: death for treason. Luckily the princes had thought ahead to hide the prophet and his friend, for their appeals to the king not to destroy the scroll nor act rashly had fallen on a deaf ear.

The chapter ends with an oracle of judgment in vv. 27-31, and the writing of a new scroll with *even more* words of judgment on it. This passage has been carefully edited to stress the differences between Jehoiakim and his father Josiah, and to make final the threat of condemnation which had still left room for conversion and reprieve in vv. 2-3. The figure of king Jehoiakim again symbolizes the whole people. Just as he has hurled the scroll into the fire, so enemies would hurl his body out on the road in disgrace.

> [32]Then Jeremiah took another scroll and gave it to Baruch the scribe, the son of Neriah, who wrote on it at the dictation of Jeremiah all the words of the scroll which Jehoiakim king of Judah had burned in the fire; and many similar words were added to them.

The mention of a second scroll in v. 32 has led to many suggestions about its contents. Most solutions seek an answer within the present body of oracles in Jeremiah 1-25. Some scholars pick out all the poetic oracles and divide them up between the first scroll and the additions to the second scroll. More recently, William Holladay has proposed a most appealing solution. He notes that chap. 36 clearly states that the first scroll read aloud by Baruch still allows for repentance, while the oracle in vv. 26-31, associated with the production of the second scroll, closes the door on such hope. He further observes that chaps. 1-10, plus chap. 11, contain a mixture of oracles, some holding out hope and some emphasizing the finality of God's judgment. He would look for the first scroll among the oracles in 1-11 that offer a call for repentance, and for the enlargements in the second scroll among the oracles in those same chapters that bar any chance of repentance.

Thus his list would look like the following:

First Scroll	Second Scroll
1:4-10	1:11-19
2:1-37	
3:1-5, 12-13, 19-15	
4:1-4	4:9-12
4:5-8	
4:13-18	4:19-28
4:29-31	5:10-17
5:1-9	6:9-15
5:20-29	6:27-30
6:1-8	7:16-20
6:16-26	7:21-29, 30-34
7:1-15	8:4-10a, 13
	8:14—9:8
	9:9-10
	9:16-21
	10:17-25
	11:1-17

Other commentators believe that the original scroll had to contain some of the oracles in chaps. 13, 14, 18, and 19 as well. Holladay's inclusion of chap. 11 certainly would not win large support. But it does have the great advantage of offering (1) a reasonable way to divide the materials of the two scrolls based on indications in the text of chap. 36, and (2) a first scroll short enough to be read three times in one day.

BOOK II
JEREMIAH 37 – 45
JEREMIAH'S LIFE DURING THE
FINAL DAYS OF JUDAH

THESE NINE CHAPTERS can be treated as a single unity. Some authors have termed it "Jeremiah's passion," to emphasize the suffering that the prophet endured for fidelity to his mission. No clear subdivisions can be isolated from this long narrative account that stretches from the time that the Babylonians began the attack on Jerusalem in 588 down to Jeremiah's final words in Egypt some four to five years later. This does not mean, however, that it was written as a biography by a single inspired author. We have good reason to believe that many incidents have been combined, and that sometimes they overlap. Much of chap. 38 can be understood as a variant account of chap. 37. Also, the events of chaps. 32 and 34 really belong with this period, and may have originally been part of the same prose collection. For convenience sake, our discussion will distinguish chaps. 37-38, the events leading up to the fall in 587, from chaps. 39-45, the events after the fall.

These narrative chapters include a number of oracles, particularly in chaps. 42-44 from Jeremiah's period of exile

in Egypt. They tend to duplicate much of his earlier preaching, and serve as confirmation of the deserved fate of Judah.
They also treat the Jews who took up residence in Egypt
rather harshly, probably because of the irregularities in
their religious practice. In the end, if we had to characterize
the subject of this whole section, it is best to stay away from
a too-personal approach which brings out the terrible
anguish endured by Jeremiah. The purpose here, as with
the whole book of the prophet, centers on the accomplish-
ment of the divine word through Jeremiah. God remains
the main factor in the drama of Israel right to the end.

I. Fainthearted Zedekiah Confronts Jeremiah
Jeremiah 37 - 38

Chapters 37-38 give us a glimpse into the political
power struggle between the weak king Zedekiah and his
princes and chief officials. We have already seen the
tensions among the different factions in Judah, some
supporting Jeremiah's view of peace, such as the family of
Shaphan or the priest Zephaniah (chap. 29); others seeking
a war for independence and resistance to the bitter end.
The king wants to hear Jeremiah's message, but does not
have the courage to openly challenge the war-mongers.
Through the ups and downs of this conflict, Jeremiah
received generally shabby treatment, but remained firm
in his convictions despite his personal humiliation and even
mortal danger. This picture provides us with an important
counterbalance to the impression given in the "Confessions"
of chaps. 11-12, 15, 17, 18 and 20, that Jeremiah himself
was a vacillating and unsure messenger of God's judgment.

JEREMIAH IN PRISON
37:1-21

> ³King Zedekiah sent Jehucal the son of Shelemiah,
> and Zephaniah the priest the son of Maaseiah, to Jere-
> miah the prophet, saying, "Pray for us to the LORD our

God." ⁴Now Jeremiah was still going in and out among the people for he had not yet been put in prison. ⁵The army of Pharaoh had come out of Egypt; and when the Chaldeans who were besieging Jerusalem heard news of them, they withdrew from Jerusalem.

⁶Then the word of the LORD came to Jeremiah the prophet: ⁷"Thus says the LORD, God of Israel: Thus shall you say to the king of Judah who sent you to me to inquire of me, 'Behold, Pharaoh's army which came to help you is about to return to Egypt, to its own land. ⁸And the Chaldeans shall come back and fight against this city; they shall take it and burn it with fire. ⁹Thus says the LORD, Do not deceive yourselves, saying. "The Chaldeans will surely stay away from us," for they will not stay away. ¹⁰For even if you should defeat the whole army of Chaldeans who are fighting against you, and there remained of them only wounded men, every man in his tent, they would rise up and burn this city with fire.'"

The first verses of this section serve as an introduction to all of chaps. 37-45. They make a new beginning after the bloc of oracles and stories from the time of Jehoiakim in chaps. 35-36. What would have been in such a Jehoiakim – collection cannot now be totally identified, although we should probably include many of the narratives in chaps. 11-20, as well as chaps. 25, 26 and 36. In any case, this new "Zedekiah–collection" does not include his whole reign. We jump immediately from a coronation notice in vv. 1-2 down to his tenth or eleventh year, that is from 598 to 588.

Chapter 37 has three units. Verses 1-10 are set in the early summer of 588, when the Babylonians had to lift their total encirclement of Jerusalem to meet the Egyptian army coming from the South (see the comments on 34:8-11). Jeremiah was still operating freely in the city when Zedekiah sought to obtain an oracle for himself and the leaders of the city. He sends two officials to seek the word through Jeremiah. Interestingly, of these two, Zephaniah seems disposed favorably toward Jeremiah (see 29:29) while Jehucal subsequently asks for Jeremiah's death as a traitor (38:1).

Jeremiah's oracle, in vv. 6-10, repeats his message of 34:21 and of 21:3-5. Except for the name of Jehucal here, it could be simply another version of the same visit reported in chap. 21. The language reveals some of the colorful exaggeration and sense of irony that Jeremiah loved. He predicts that even the enemy wounded would be enough to defeat Judah. Left unsaid, of course, is the real reason—because Yahweh stood against Israel. The RSV's "Do not deceive your-selves," literally means "Don't get your hopes up!" Zedekiah and his leaders were banking on the Egyptian support to save them. One of the Lachish letters found in the ruins of that city at the time of the Babylonian conquest, men-tions hopefully the rumor to that effect:

> It hath been reported to thy servant, saying, "The com-mander of the host, Coniah, son of Elnathan, hath come down in order to go into Egypt . . ." (ANET 322).

The arrest of Jeremiah as he leaves for Anathoth in vv. 11-16 seems to conflict with the previous report in 32:1-12. If both are correct, then Jeremiah must have been on his way to a meeting of the family in 37:11-16 to discuss what should be done with the estate. Since Jeremiah never arrived, only later did his cousin come to offer him the right of purchase (32:1-12). Thus the matter may have been on Jeremiah's mind for some time before he understood the meaning of this act as a pledge of hope. The details of his arrest stand out vividly. The guard at the Benjamin gate, which leads north toward Anathoth, probably knew all about *this* Jeremiah who preached surrender and advised giving in to the Babylonians (21:9 and 38:2). He was under-standably disturbed in this hour of mortal danger at how many people had actually deserted already (38:19, 39:9, 52:15). Nothing would convince him that Jeremiah was not joining them while he still had time to escape. The princes, described as enraged, more likely welcomed the opportunity to silence Jeremiah once and for all.

Verses 16-21 describe Jeremiah's terrible conditions in the vaults under Jonathon's house. RSV does not translate the whole phrase for this dungeon. The Hebrew says that they took Jeremiah to the "house of the cistern, to the vaults . . ." It must have been much like the house shown to pilgrims and tourists today in Jerusalem as the House of Annas and Caiaphas with a number of large, airless and lightless rooms carved out of the rock as cellars. From there the king secretly sent for Jeremiah. The true character of Zedekiah as a weak leader afraid of his own officials comes through clearly here (and again in 38:5). Perhaps he felt helpless to suggest a plan contrary to theirs. At least he seemed to respect Jeremiah's word as authentic and has enough self-respect to grant the prophet's request for better treatment; even if, for political reasons, he cannot give him freedom in the middle of the war.

A SECOND STORY OF JEREMIAH'S ARREST
38:1-28

> 4Then the princes said to the king, "Let this man be put to death, for he is weakening the hands of the soldiers who are left in this city, and the hands of all the people, by speaking such words to them. For this man is not seeking the welfare of this people, but their harm." 5King Zedekiah said, "Behold, he is in your hands; for the king can do nothing against you." 6So they took Jeremiah and cast him into the cistern of Malchiah, the king's son, which was in the court of the guard, letting Jeremiah down by ropes. And there was no water in the cistern, but only mire, and Jeremiah sank in the mire.

Chapter 38 seems to duplicate the scene just narrated in 37:11-21. Although the names differ, and the mention of a cistern in the court of the guard is new, the general sequence of events parallel each other. The prophet is arrested and condemned to a cistern or dungeon by the officials. Zedekiah meets with him secretly, received a negative oracle, and allows him to be kept in the court of the guard instead of the pit. Even 37:20, Jeremiah's fear that he might die in the dungeon, fits the cistern of Malciah and its mud better than a house prison. The major difference involves the role of Ebed-melech, who rescues Jeremiah. It seems that at least vv. 1-13 are a separate and more graphic account of the arrest and imprisonment found in 37:11-16. The opening lines in 38:2 match the oracle in 21:5-6, so that we may even have *three* accounts of this one event.

The climate of Palestine leaves the country with little or no rain between May and October. For this reason, the ancients built cisterns out of the rock, plastered them with lime, and collected rainwater to store for the dry summer season. Every city had large cisterns built in any available space, especially in the public courts. Generally these were large underground cavities with narrow openings to prevent excess evaporation from the sun. This would explain the need for the ropes and special cloth to help Jeremiah out. Near the end of the summer and in early fall, many of these cisterns would be nearly empty—in this case down to just damp mud. Apparently the officials wanted Jeremiah to die from neglect—exposure, lack of food, maybe even suffocation. That way they do not directly risk shedding the *blood* of the innocent (Gen 37:21-22).

Ebed-melech, a foreigner from southern Egypt, held some important post in the government. RSV's "eunuch" misunderstands the term. Known from Egyptian and Babylonian documents, the *saris* (in the Akkadian language, "one who is the king's head") held a personal supervisory role for the king. Jeremiah refers to many of them— 29:2; 34:19; 41:16; 52:25. Only in later times, mostly Arabic usage, did the word come to have the specialized sense of a eunuch. In Ebed-melech's case, he had direct access to the king even when he was conducting public hearings in the gates (cf., Ruth 4:1-2; 2 Sam 15). The king gives him 3 men (or, according to the Hebrew text, 30 men) and the responsibility to save Jeremiah. Verse 13 ends exactly as did 37:31, with Jeremiah receiving better quarters.

38:14-28 records the (next) secret meeting with the king. It is most noteworthy for the promise of Yahweh would even now turn back his wrath and spare the city if the king would repent and get up backbone to support a peace-treaty. The king proves even more spineless in this episode than before. At the end of the interview he begs Jeremiah not to let his officials know that they even talked about possible surrender. Verse 22 gives us a wonderful insight into the Jeremianic sense of irony. The lines are poetry, a taunt song in which the trusted friends (literally, "friends of your welfare," cf., 20:10) deceive him so that the king ends up in the mud stuck worse than Jeremiah was. Instead of promising welfare or peace, they urge him onto destruction and war.

II. Jeremiah After The Fall Of Jerusalem
Jeremiah 39 - 45

The series of narratives that make up this section focus on the remnant left from the Babylonian victory. It includes men of character like Gedaliah, the new governor, wandering soldiers, ambitious freebooters such as Ishmael, and the prophet Jeremiah. In many ways, it relates how Jeremiah was pushed and shoved and respected even less than before. It also traces the gradual loss of any hope to be expected from this remnant. First the governor and pious pilgrims are murdered, then the few worthwhile supporters drag Jeremiah and Baruch to Egypt, until all that are left are a few landless peasants. These have no future, and the story of God's saving plan must now move to Babylon and the Exile. When the Book of Jeremiah ends, Ezekiel, Second

Isaiah and the postexilic prophets become the bearers of a new message fought for and forged in the experience of captivity far from the homeland.

JEREMIAH'S RELEASE AND FREEDOM
39:1-18

39 In the ninth year of Zedekiah king of Judah, in the tenth month, Nebuchadrezzar king of Babylon, and all his army came against Jerusalem and besieged it; ²in the eleventh year of Zedekiah, in the fourth month, on the ninth day of the month, a breach was made in the city. ³When Jerusalem was taken, all the princes of the king of Babylon came and sat in the middle gate: Nergal-sharezer, Samgarnebo, Sarsechim the Rabsaris, Nergal-sharezer the Rabmag, with all the rest of the officers of the king of Babylon. ⁴When Zedekiah king of Judah and all the soldiers saw them, they fled, going out of the city at night by way of the king's garden through the gate between the two walls; and they went toward the Arabah. ⁵But the army of the Chaldeans pursued them, and overtook Zedekiah in the plains of Jericho; and when they had taken him, they brought him up to Nebuchadrezzar king of Babylon, at Riblah, in the land of Hamath; and he passed sentence upon him. ⁶The king of Babylon slew the sons of Zedekiah at Riblah before his eyes; and the king of Babylon slew all the nobles of Judah. ⁷He put out the eyes of Zedekiah, and bound him in fetters to take him to Babylon. ⁸The Chaldeans burned the king's house and the house of the people, and broke down the walls of Jerusalem. ⁹Then Nebuzaradan, the captain of the guard, carried into exile to Babylon the rest of the people who were left in the city, those who had deserted to him, and the people who remained. ¹⁰Nebuzaradan, the captain of the guard, left in the land of Judah some of the poor people who owned nothing, and gave them vineyards and fields at the same time.

Chapter 39 has the looks of a mixture of various odd notes thrown together. Verses 1-10 tell of the fall of the city and the fate of Zedekiah. It generally parallels the accounts in 2 Kgs 25:1-12 and Jer 52:4-16. Verses 11-14 tell of the release of Jeremiah from the court of the guard in Jerusalem. This creates a conflict with a second report about his release from a group of prisoners at Ramah, five miles away in 40:1-6. Finally, the chapter closes with a note on Jeremiah's word of promise to Ebed-melech for his kindness in saving his life from the pit. This rightly should follow 38:13. However, who are we to claim to understand the mind of the ancient editors. They have fooled us more than once with their sense of how to order material differently from our modern chronological compulsion.

The first unit in vv. 1-10 has many textual difficulties. It begins with a verse repetition of the last line in chap. 38: "And it was when Jerusalem was taken . . ." RSV transfers this to the beginning of v. 3, but it may well be the leftover of a label heading a new section. Ancient scribes often repeated the bottom line of a previous tablet or scroll at the top of the next one so readers would know what order the documents were in. The second problem is the list of names in v. 3. It differs from the list in v. 13, and has generated many solutions. The RSV has copied v. 13 into that spot. The original list in v. 3 seems to have been: (1) Nergal Sharezer, of Samgar, Nebo-Sarsechim the *rab saris*, and Nergal Sharezer, the *rab mag*. All are high officials. The first becomes king of Babylon in 560, and the other two bear the title of military generals, *rab*. In fact, Nebo-Sarsechem might be a spelling variation on Nebushazban, who appears in v. 13.

The scene is rushed. The Babylonian leaders are already holding court in the breached gateways before Zedekiah escapes. When he does flee, he takes the obvious road out of the Kidron Valley eastward down to Jericho attempting to make it across the Jordan River to Ammonite country with his whole army. He was desperately hoping to escape detection before dawn broke. But it was no use. He was caught and sent all the way to Syria to the town of Riblah where the Babylonian king had made his headquarters, leaving the actual campaign to his generals. Verse 9 adds Nebuzaradan to the list of Babylonian generals. He functions as the military commander over the conquered territory from this time on, although 2 Kgs 25:8 tells us that he did not arrive until a month after the city was taken.

Zedekiah's fate seems especially cruel, even though it was not exactly what Jeremiah had predicted. Since at a later date Babylonian records still mention supplies for the exiled Jehoiachin in Babylon but nothing about Zedekiah, we can presume the blinded and heartbroken king did not survive long in exile. Not only were the royal princes executed to prevent any uprising centered upon a royal pretender to the throne, but many of the nobles lost their lives also. These may have been the counsellors who supported the war, or they may have been royal cousins around whom hopes of revolt might swirl. The Babylonians undoubtedly had good lists of whom to capture and whom to execute both from their own intelligence sources (such as ambassadors) and from interrogation of the deserters from Jerusalem. Thus Jeremiah had surely come to their attention beforehand; it would explain their interest in sparing his life. The account of his rescue in vv. 11-14 involves the commander of the military occupation, Nebuzaradan, who did not arrive in the city until a month after the actual capture (52:12). Thus a problem arises whether these military chiefs actually released Jeremiah from the court of the guard or not. More likely, the second account in 40:1-6 which relates that they found him chained among prisoners waiting to be exiled, is the more accurate. The text further specifies, along with both 2 Kgs 25:11-12 and Jer 52:15-16, that the Babylonians left no one but a few poor people in the land. This must be read as a theological reflection stressing that no one of worth was spared, or at least no one in whom the further divine plan would operate. The continuing stories in chaps. 40-44 reveal that many people stayed behind; and according to an anonymous list giving the number of exiles which Babylon deported (Jer 52:28-30) only 832 persons went into exile in 587.

The final small story in chap. 39 reports Jeremiah's blessing of Ebed-melech and his promise that the Ethiopian official who had saved his life would survive the destruction of the city (vv. 15-18). It seems out of place here after the prisoners have already been freed from the prison courtyard, and should follow 38:13, or at least 38:28. It is a kind of legal repayment. For just as Ebed-melech had given Jeremiah his life, so now Jeremiah returns the favor. This new gift of life for life reverses the old legal principle of *vengeance* found in the covenant law of Exod 21:23-24: a life for a life, an eye for an eye, a tooth for a tooth. Jeremiah later offers the same gift to Baruch (45:5).

AN UPRIGHT GOVERNOR, GEDELIAH
40:1-16

40 The word that came to Jeremiah from the LORD after Nebuzaradan the captain of the guard had let him go from Ramah, when he took him bound in chains along with all the captives of Jerusalem and Judah who were being exiled to Babylon. ²The captain of the guard took Jeremiah and said to him, "The LORD your God pronounced this evil against this place; ³the LORD has brought it about, and has done as he said. Because you sinned against the LORD, and did not obey his voice, this thing has come upon you. ⁴Now, behold, I release you today from the chains on your hands. If it seems good to you to come with me to Babylon, come, and I will look after you well; but if it seems wrong to you to come with me to Babylon, do not come. See, the whole land is before you; go wherever you think it good and right to

go. ⁵If you remain, then return to Gedaliah the son of
Ahikam, son of Shaphan, whom the king of Babylon
appointed governor of the cities of Judah, and dwell
with him among the people; or go wherever you think
it right to go." So the captain of the guard gave him an
allowance of food and a present, and let him go. ⁶Then
Jeremiah went to Gedaliah the son of Ahikam, at
Mizpah, and dwelt with him among the people who
were left in the land.

40:1-6 gives a second version of Jeremiah's release from
captivity, and places the event some time after the fall of
the capital city when Jeremiah is found among those being
deported to Babylon and freed by the commanding general
himself. Ramah is a town in Benjamin, some five miles
north of Jerusalem, and famous as the home town of the
prophet Samuel (1 Sam 7:17; 8:4). It apparently served as a
convenient local headquarters for the Babylonian forces of
occupation now that Jerusalem was in ruins, and a holding
place for Judeans being gathered for the long trip to
exile in Babylon.

The account differs from the statements in 39:11-14,
according to which Nebuchadnezzar himself ordered the
release of Jeremiah from the court of the guard. We cannot
make the two stories match, unless we suppose that in the
confusion of the times, Jeremiah had been released, but
was swept up in some later round-up of citizens. There he
was noticed and released a second time. How it actually
happened does not make much difference to the tradition.
The repetition of his release at the command of the highest
authority serves rather to stress that Jeremiah was perfectly
free to go into exile or to stay in the land, and he chose the
latter. To highlight the freedom of his choice, the oracle
we would ordinarily expect from the prophet is spoken by
the captain of the guard in vv. 2-5!

In choosing to stay, Jeremiah joins Gedaliah, a grandson
of Shaphan, whose family had played such an influential

supporting role in the years under Jehoiakim and Zedekiah. The new governor had set up his government at Mizpah, about eight miles north of Jerusalem and not far from the Babylonian commanders at Ramah. It, too, was one of the cities connected with the work of Samuel (1 Sam 7:5-11). No evidence has been found in the excavations at the site (Tell en Nasbeh) of any destruction levels during the 6th century—a very unusual occurrence since almost all Israelite ruins from that period show extensive destruction through siege and burning. It seemed to have remained an important government center through the early post-exilic period (Neh 3:15, 19).

Gedaliah had a formidable task of restoring normal life. Chapter 40 draws a portrait of him as a very humane and prudent person. He takes over the care of the poorest of the land and encourages them to return to farming and harvesting to prepare for the first harsh winter. He wins over the trust of the military leaders of the Jews who had escaped with various ragtag battalions and now lived off the land as guerillas. He also stood up as a mediator and liaison with the Babylonians to prevent reprisals against the remaining Jews.

Among the former military leaders that he wins over, two stand out: Ishmael, who comes from royal blood and may have already been a high official in the past, and Johanan, the son of Kareah. The former turns traitor to the new governor, while the other remains fiercely loyal to the end. Verses 13-18 relate how Johanan and the other leaders from rural areas discovered the plot of Ishmael to assassinate Gedaliah, and tried to warn the governor. But Gedaliah would not believe them. He obviously trusted that nobles would be honorable and true to their word. Even when Johanan pressed the case dramatically by offering to kill Ishmael outright, Gedaliah would not change his mind. The stage was set for tragedy, as Johanan realized all too well and Gedaliah seemed to miss. Nobody would be able to hold the struggling survivors together if Gedaliah died.

We might wonder why a man of such character as Johanan would not rise to assume the office after the murder takes place. But he clearly believed that if he did make claims to leadership, the Babylonians would act against him. The reason may lie in his origins. If he was a commoner who gained power, the Babylonians would not tolerate his taking title to an office. On the other hand, Ishmael was from the royal family, even if only a distant cousin, and may have been outraged that Gedaliah, who lacked royal blood, had been named governor in the first place. Ishmael's grandfather was Elishama, the secretary, or highest official, under king Jehoiakim (Jer 41:1); while Gedaliah's family were among the faction that opposed the king on many issues, including the case of Jeremiah! Possibly, then, Ishmael had only the highest patriotic motives. He may have been zealous for the Davidic covenant and opposed any usurper who claimed to succeed to the Davidic throne. We do not have enough information about his motives, but his brutal violation of the ancient world's law of hospitality by murdering his host, his bizarre and cruel treatment of the pilgrims shortly after, and his alliance with the Ammonite king, a bitter enemy of Israel, show that the author or authors of this narrative did not think they were very noble.

THE ABOMINATION OF ISHMAEL
41:1-18

41 In the seventh month, Ishmael the son of Nethaniah, son of Elishama, of the royal family, one of the chief officers of the king, came with ten men to Gedaliah the son of Ahikam, at Mizpah. As they ate bread together there at Mizpah, ²Ishmael the son of Nethaniah and the ten men with him rose up and struck down Gedaliah the son of Ahikam, son of Shaphan, with the sword, and killed him, whom the king of Babylon had appointed governor in the land. ³Ishmael also slew all the Jews who were with Gedaliah at Mizpah, and the Chaldean soldiers who happened to be there.

⁴On the day after the murder of Gedaliah, before any one knew of it, ⁵eighty men arrived from Shechem and Shiloh and Samaria, with their beards shaved and their clothes torn, and their bodies gashed, bringing cereal offerings and incense to present at the temple of the LORD. ⁶And Ishmael the son of Nethaniah came out from Mizpah to meet them, weeping as he came. As he met them, he said to them, "Come in to Gedaliah the son of Ahikam." ⁷When they came into the city, Ishmael the son of Nethaniah and the men with him slew them, and cast them into a cistern. ⁸But there were ten men among them who said to Ishmael, "Do not kill us, for we have stores of wheat, barley, oil, and honey hidden in the fields." So he refrained and did not kill them with their companions.

Ishmael ruthlessly slays the trusting Gedaliah, and kills all the witnesses at the scene, thus giving him valuable time to escape undetected. However, he does not take the opportunity, for two days later he was still present to kill 80 pilgrims on their way to Jerusalem in mourning for the temple. They were imitating the funeral rites for the dead, and probably intended to hold a mourning feast at the site of the ruined temple. The lamentation for the temple was popular during the Exile. Note the language of Ps 74:2-3 and Lam 1:4 and 2:6. The customs of gashing the body and shaving the hair were forbidden by Deut 14:1, but popular nevertheless (see Jer 16:6; 48:37). For the torn clothes, see 2 Sam 1:2; 3:31. The incident made a strong impact on the people—even the cistern in which the corpses were thrown was remembered (v. 9; *cf.*, 1 Kgs 15:22).

Johanan catches the fleeing Ishmael at Gibeon, which was west of Mizpah, in the opposite direction from Ammon, to which Ishmael was supposedly headed. Apparently,

The major sites mentioned in Jeremiah 40-41 involving Gedaliah's assassination and the pursuit of Ishmael.

Mizpah: seat of Gedaliah's administration
Ramah: where Jeremiah was taken
Gibeon: Johanan overtakes Ishmael
Anathoth: Jeremiah's hometown
Jerusalem: destroyed by Babylon
Bethlehem: Johanan flees here
Hebron: major town of southern Judah

the murderers tried to elude capture by taking a roundabout means. Although the villain escaped, the prisoners, including Jeremiah, were freed. At this point, Johanan faces a dilemma. Since the Babylonian governor had been assassinated, and he had failed to take the culprit, he himself may bear the penalty. Not knowing what to do, he retreats south to Bethlehem to provide an escape route to Egypt if needed. Thus chap. 41 ends.

Though colorful, the story does not actually tell us enough even to calculate how long Gedaliah was governor. Since the pilgrims were on their way to Jerusalem at the time of the Fall festival of weeks in September or October, the whole governorship may have lasted only five months in 587. But on the other hand, if the 3rd deportation of prisoners mentioned in 52:30 occurred as a result of this assassination, then Gedaliah ruled five years until 582. In order to achieve the program of pacification, this seems the more realistic likelihood. Outside the Bible, one tempting discovery may link us to these events. In the ruins of Lachish, a signet ring with a seal on it was unearthed with the words: "Of Gedaliah, who is over the house." This title belongs to a high official (*cf.*, Isa 22:15), and may well be our Gedaliah. But for more specific details and motives, the reader can search out Flavius Josephus, *The Antiquities*, Books IX and X, who describes these events at length. But his sources remain unknown, and most scholars suspect that he builds his descriptions largely from other biblical texts. One independent note, however, is his remark in Book X, ix, 7, that Nebuchadnezzar brought the Ammonite kingdom to an end in his campaign to the West in 582.

JEREMIAH'S WARNING AGAINST GOING TO EGYPT 42:1-22

[7]At the end of ten days the word of the LORD came to Jeremiah. [8]Then he summoned Johanan the son of Kareah and all the commanders of the forces who were with him, and all the people from the least to the greatest,

⁹and said to them, "Thus says the LORD, the God of
Israel, to whom you sent me to present your supplication
before him: ¹⁰If you will remain in this land, then I will
build you up and not pull you down; I will plant you,
and not pluck you up; for I repent of the evil which I did
to you. ¹¹Do not fear the king of Babylon, of whom you
are afraid; do not fear him, says the LORD, for I am with
you, to save you and to deliver you from his hand. ¹²I will
grant you mercy, that he may have mercy on you and let
you remain in your own land.

Johanan was uncertain over what course of action to
follow, and perhaps had to deal with strong disagreements
among his followers. Should they stay and hope for the best,
or flee to Egypt and have to face exile and difficulty there.
They turned to Yahweh through the prophet Jeremiah for
an answer. All approved this means of making a decision,
but the ten day delay between the request and the coming
of the divine word may reflect a period of unsettled decision
until all fell into line. When the word does come, it comes
definitively. Yahweh answers, "No," and repeats his call
to trust that had been the heart of Jeremiah's message from
the beginning. The promise, however, is full of new hope.
God has *turned* from his anger (v. 10); he will *be with* the
people just as he promised to the exiles in Babylon (29:13-
14); he will *build up* and not tear down (1:10). The text
stresses the mercy of Yahweh to those who have endured
so much. It sets the stage for the later message of Second
Isaiah, that Israel has suffered double for its sins, and so
God wishes to show only graciousness and mercy (Isa
40:1-11).

On the other side, if the people, despite their solemn
pledge in v. 6, refuse to stay in the land and trust, but flee
out of fear to Egypt; then they will receive much of what
Jeremiah has long threatened and they have now seen come
about. The wrath of Yahweh will be a fire against his people
even in Egypt (v. 18; *cf.*, 4:4; 5:14; 9:3; 11:16; 17:27; etc.);

they will perish by the sword, famine and plague (v. 17; *cf.*, 14:12; 21:7, 9; 24:10; 27:8; etc.); and they will be a horror and reproach to all (v. 18; *cf.*, 42:18; 44:12). The entire oracle makes the point with extreme force. In case the reader does not get the message quickly, the oracle develops and redevelops the threat, first in vv. 13-18 and then again in vv. 19-22. God does not wish to start again with his people in Egypt! He intends to work salvation through the exiles in Babylon and among those who will center themselves about his prophet while remaining in the land. The oracle almost seemed to presuppose that the refugees would not accept the command to settle down and trust.

JEREMIAH TAKEN INTO EGYPT
43:1-13

43 When Jeremiah finished speaking to all the people all these words of the LORD their God, with which the LORD their God had sent him to them, ²Azariah the son of Hoshaiah and Johanan the son of Kareah and all the insolent men said to Jeremiah, "You are telling a lie. The LORD our God did not send you to say, 'Do not go to Egypt to live there'; ³but Baruch the son of Neriah has set you against us, to deliver us into the hand of the Chaldeans, that they may kill us or take us into exile in Babylon." ⁴So Johanan the son of Kareah and all the commanders of the forces and all the people did not obey the voice of the LORD, to remain in the land of Judah. ⁵But Johanan the son of Kareah and all the commanders of the forces took all the remnant of Judah who had returned to live in the land of Judah from all the nations to which they had been driven—⁶the men, the women, the children, the princesses, and every person whom Nebuzaradan the captain of the guard had left with Gedaliah the son of Ahikam, son of Shaphan; also Jeremiah the prophet and Baruch the son of Neriah. ⁷And they came into the land of Egypt, for they did not obey the voice of the LORD. And they arrived at Tahpanhes.

Chapter 43 opens with an intriguing incident in vv. 1-7 explaining how the group which had just pledged to obey the oracle of God now found a way to denounce not only the word, but the man who spoke it. Did the ten day delay make many suspicious? Did Jeremiah actually speak as his opponents claim in chap. 42, in terms that sounded like his earlier political positions? Did Baruch really have influence on the prophet? We shall never know. The text itself makes the rejection a very serious matter. It speaks of the leaders as insolent, who turn the very charge levelled against Judah's sins over all the years back on Jeremiah: he preaches the *lie*. The strong terms of Jeremiah's warning in the previous chapter show he must have foreseen this outcome. It gives all readers of the words of Jeremiah the chance to reflect on the power of *fear*—fear of the Babylonians, of reforming oneself, of the unknown—to block religious decisions about life.

The leader Johanan brought many people to Egypt—all the people around Gedaliah, their families, and any other stragglers and individuals who sought safety. Whether Johanan forced Jeremiah to go along (the Hebrew verb in v. 5, means "take" but does not necessarily imply force), or persuaded him out of a sense of duty to the group, we do not know. But Jeremiah went knowing that this would not have God's blessing.

The second part of chap. 43 relates a word of Jeremiah combined with a symbolic action. Was it soon after arrival, or a long time after? Again no answer can be reached. The action typifies Jeremiah's style—the stones will be signs of judgment, and even though hidden in the ground, they will endure until the prophecy comes to fulfillment. Tahpanhes is a town on the Northeastern edge of Egypt facing Asia. It probably served as a regional administrative headquarters, possibly even the forward military base for Egyptian army expeditions to Palestine. Ezek 30:18 includes it in the list of important Egyptian strongholds to be devastated by Yahweh. Jeremiah foresees the day when

Nebuchadnezzar will set up his own military encampment on the spot in order to conquer, or at least defeat, the Egyptian forces. The terms of the threat are familiar from Jeremiah's oracles against his own people: sword, captivity, fire and pestilence. To these he adds the specific prediction that the famed obelisks which stood before most major temples, and above all before the sun temple at Heliopolis (literally "the house of the sun"), would be destroyed; and the innumerable temples that filled every city would suffer the most. The most striking statement is the metaphor of a shepherd cleaning his cloak of lice and other insects—in the same way Nebuchadnezzar will rid Egypt of its vermin.

From the partial records of the Babylonian Chronicles and from a report in Josephus, the Jewish historian, scholars believe that Nebuchadnezzar did invade Egypt about 568 and managed to win limited victories in the Delta region without conquering the whole country or unseating the pharaoh, Amasis. Whether Jeremiah lived to see it or not, we will never know.

JEREMIAH'S FINAL WARNING
44:1—45:5

[15]Then all the men who knew that their wives had offered incense to other gods, and all the women who stood by, a great assembly, all the people who dwelt in Pathros in the land of Egypt, answered Jeremiah: [16]"As for the word which you have spoken to us in the name of the LORD, we will not listen to you. [17]But we will do everything that we have vowed, burn incense to the queen of heaven and pour out libations to her, as we did, both we and our fathers, our kings and our princes, in the cities of Judah and in the streets of Jerusalem; for then we had plenty of food, and prospered, and saw no evil. [18]But since we left off burning incense to the queen of heaven and pouring out libations to her, we have lacked everything and have been consumed by the sword

and by famine." ¹⁹And the women said, "When we
burned incense to the queen of heaven and poured out
libations to her, was it without our husbands' approval
that we made cakes for her bearing her image and poured
out libations to her?"

Chapter 44 includes the last major oracle of Jeremiah,
delivered to the Judean refugees in Egypt. The construction
of this chapter makes it clear that this stands as a summary
of *all* Jeremiah's preaching during the years of their independence from 627 down to 587. Everything that he had
spoken about the kings and people of Judah apply just as
much to the remnant that now lives in Egypt. Moreover,
the language of this very lengthy section bears many marks
of re-interpretation, *i.e.*, phrases added to bring out the
long-range historical significance of what Jeremiah had
preached. Note, for example, the people's answer to
Jeremiah (vv. 15-19) spoken in a great assembly of all the
people in Egypt; it cites all the major actors of the drama
before the fall of Jerusalem: princes and king, people of
the land, and citizens of the capital; and stresses that these
will no more listen to Jeremiah's word than had the people
before the judgment came upon them. We can also see in the
choice of accusation—that they burned incense to the queen
of heaven—a clear reference back to the major single
summary passage of Jeremiah's earlier preaching, the
Temple Sermon of chap. 7 (and 26). Many commentators
have also pointed to the pervasive deuteronomic language
in this chapter as evidence of extensive editorial additions.
Chapter 44 can be divided into three parts. Jeremiah gives
an oracle, the people respond, and Jeremiah strengthens
his message. The first section, vv. 1-14, breaks the natural
continuity between the threat he utters at the end of chap. 43
and what should have been the people's answer in 44:15-19.
We can thus reasonably assume that the editors of Jeremiah
especially added this particular narrative to reinforce the
threat of doom and the symbolic action reported in 43:8-13.

44:1 lists a number of towns in Egypt which had become residences for exiled Jews. Most of these are also known from Ezek 29:8-16; 30:13-19, and from the fascinating collection of Aramaic texts found in the Jewish colony at Elephantiné in the far south of Egypt. It flourished under the Persians as a military outpost manned by Jewish mercenaries and their families, but the evidence suggests that these settlers may have been at Elephantiné since the 7th century. In any case, the number of Jews in Egypt certainly was much higher than the few who straggled out with Johanan and Jeremiah.

Most of the expressions used in vv. 2-14 are typical of Jeremiah and have been noted in earlier passages. The heart of his accusation here, however, specifically reflects the message of 7:16-20. Burning incense may also symbolize any kind of sacrifice. The Hebrew word occurs in Lev 1:9 and 3:16 for the burning of fat offerings, for example. Note too, the use of the phrases "persistently sent my servants the prophets" from 7:35, and the combination of "wrath and anger" from 7:20. The emphasis on the wives in v. 9 reflects the practice of this particular type of idolatry which was mainly performed by the women, although Jeremiah emphatically includes the whole family in the guilt, as he does in 7:18.

What they should have done is stated in v. 10: humbled their hearts before God. A comparison with Ps 51:17 will show that this summarizes the covenantal obedience that prefers doing God's will above any sacrifices whatsoever, even the legally required ones.

The final lines of this section give the sentence of judgment—no remnant shall survive from among those in Egypt. RSV captures the imagery of vv. 11-12 better than any other English translation, but even it weakens the force of Jeremiah's message. The text reads: "I have set my face to do evil" against those who "set their faces" to go to Egypt. Their insolent disobedience stands out. Phrases such as "my servants the prophets" and "to walk in my laws and statutes" have strong deuteronomic overtones, but other expressions such as a "single escapee or survivor" (which lies behind the RSV translation of v. 14) are not typical of Deuteronomy (*cf.*, Jer 42:17; Lam 2:22).

The people deny in vv. 15-19 that the worship of other gods and goddesses was a crime; after all, "we had plenty of food and prospered" at that time. The goddess may be Ishtar, the Babylonian fertility deity; or the goddess worshipped in the West under the name of Astarte, who played a similar role for Canaanite religion. These goddesses were often interchangeable in function, but all of them combined the ideals of love, fertility, jealousy and often warlike behavior. A similar goddess, known primarily in Ugarit, Anat, was both sister and wife to the great Canaanite god Baal, and not only made love profusely but fought his battles bloodily. Shrines to her have been found in northern Egypt where Semites settled in some numbers, and surprisingly, the Elephantine documents revealed that the Jewish settlers there not only worshipped Yahweh, but a companion goddess, Anat-Yahu, who may have been understood as Yahweh's wife. That text dates from the late 400's, over a century after Jeremiah, but provides a good background for understanding the vehemence of the anti-idolatry stance in this chapter.

> 20Then Jeremiah said to all the people, men and women, all the people who had given him this answer: 21"As for the incense that you burned in the cities of Judah and in the streets of Jerusalem, you and your fathers, your kings and your princes, and the people of the land, did not the LORD remember it? Did it not come into his mind? 22The LORD could no longer bear your evil doings and the abominations which you committed; therefore your land has become a desolation and a waste and a curse, without inhabitant, as it is this day. 23It is because you burned incense, and because you sinned against the LORD and did not obey the voice of the LORD or walk in his law and in his statutes and in his testimonies, that this evil has befallen you, as at this day."

The final section in vv. 20-30 repeats the judgment again. We might recognize the sandwich pattern created by placing the judgment first in vv. 1-14, a defense in 15-19, and re-judgment in 20-30. Such repetition delighted ancient ears, even though it now strikes the modern readers as verbose and often boring. But these verses use a second structure as well. The prophet quotes the women (and all the people!) in v. 25 so that their *word* of defiance becomes almost an oath. After reciting the expected list of terrible evils that will come upon them for this, the passage ends with the choice between their word and God's word. The decision will be made known by a sign. Jeremiah twice has given signs, once to Hananiah in chap. 28, and once to Shemaiah in chap. 29. Both were the death of the false prophet. Now, using a third example, the defeat and humiliation of Zedekiah, he pronounces the same sign on the Judean exiles in Egypt.

> **45** The word that Jeremiah the prophet spoke to Baruch the son of Neriah, when he wrote these words in a book at the dictation of Jeremiah, in the fourth year of Jehoiakim the son of Josiah, king of Judah. ²"Thus says the LORD, the God of Israel, to you, O Baruch: ³You said, 'Woe is me! for the LORD has added sorrow to my pain; I am weary with my groaning, and I find no rest.' ⁴Thus shall you say to him, Thus says the LORD: Behold, what I have built I am breaking down, and what I have planted I am plucking up—that is, the whole land. ⁵And do you seek great things for yourself? Seek them not; for behold I am bringing evil upon all flesh, says the LORD; but I will give you your life as a prize of war in all places to which you may go."

45:1-5 belongs with the story of the scroll in chap. 36. The editors have separated these words and placed them at the end to serve as a closing, both for chaps. 37-45, but also for the words of Jeremiah to his own people. It is dated to the same time as 36:1. Jeremiah rewards Baruch's willing service with a promise of life that parallels the oracle he

made over Ebed-melech in 39:15-18. The context draws
out the parallel between Jeremiah and his helper even
more fully, however. The text quotes Baruch giving a
lament much like that of Jeremiah's own confessions in
15:10-15 and 20:7-11. The prophet must rebuke Baruch as
Yahweh did Jeremiah himself for wanting too much, for
expecting a reward for the mission that God imposes on
him. The divine answer promises little if any respite, but
concedes that Baruch can escape from the coming disasters
with his life. A look at the passages where Jeremiah has
used this phrase before (21:9; 38:2; 39:18) indicates that
survival was to be considered gift enough. We must remember that biblical thought had almost no positive concept of
the Afterlife. Hope in divine mercy and the longed-for goal
of fidelity were usually expressed in terms of long life
(Isa 38:17-19; Deut 5:15-16; 30:19; Pss 34:12; 35:28; 91:16).

All in all, chap. 44 (and 45) shows much reworking and
highlighting of the prophet's message. Jeremiah probably
never had a chance to deliver such an oracle to all the
Judean settlers in Egypt and thus have the divine word
penetrate to every corner of the land. But the ancient faith
in the power of God's word did not require that an audience
always hear it spoken. It was enough that God had solemnly
put it into existence through a prophet for it to begin its
work. This insight should help us deal with the last section
of the book, the *Oracles against Foreign Nations*, mostly
against peoples whom Jeremiah never met.

BOOK III
JEREMIAH 46 – 51
ORACLES AGAINST
FOREIGN NATIONS

THE FINAL MAJOR DIVISION in the Book of Jeremiah consists of a considerable collection of oracles delivered against traditional enemies of Israel. Many of these come almost untouched from the hand of the master himself. Their power and dramatic imagery stand near the top of the list in any evaluation of Jeremiah as poet. Others may be much older than the prophet but cherished in the circle of his followers for their expressive power. Some, no doubt, come from anonymous members of his circle who carried on the work of the master sometime longer into the exile. The reason editors include such additional oracles to supplement Jeremiah's own words involves their sense of completeness. Oracles against Nations were part of the deepest-rooted traditions in prophecy. Prophets were associated with national decisions to enter wars from early times (see the stories of Balaam in Num 22-24, and the career of Samuel in 1 Sam 1-12, as well as the narrative about the Aramean wars in 1 Kgs 22). They were expected to seek God's word of support and victory.

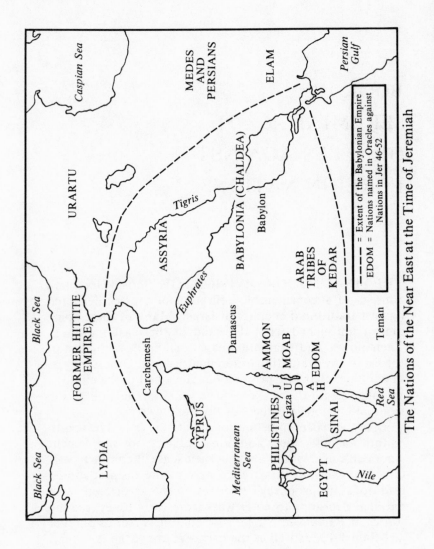

The Nations of the Near East at the Time of Jeremiah

A very instructive example comes from the ancient city of Mari on the Euphrates River in Syria. It can be dated to the reign of king Zimri Lim (c. 1730-1700 B.C.) and is a report to the king in letter-form. It opens with mention of taking omens: "For a report on the campaign my lord is waging, I inquired of a man and a woman . . . for the signs, and the (oracular) word was very favorable to my lord." It goes on to report a favorable oracle:

> "No battle will be fought. Right after arriving his (Ishme-Dagan, the enemy king) auxiliary troops will be scattered, and they will cut off the he(ad of Ishme-Dagan) and then put it under the foot of my lord" (ANET 629-630).

The Assyrians have also left us a number of prophetic texts which encourage the king in battle. One from the reign of Esarhaddon (680-668) reads:

> "'O king of Assyria, fear not! The enemy of the king of Assyria I will deliver to slaughter' (This oracle is) from the woman Sin-qisha-amur of Arbela" (ANET 605).

In Israelite tradition, Amos had included a full range of such oracles as a preface to his radical proclamation against his own people. The Book of Isaiah contained a broad collection in chaps. 13-23. So, too, Jeremiah, the prophet to nations (1:5), should have a complete collection. Thus a few here and there would be added to fill in missing oracles, or to expand existing ones to match types from his predecessors.

In their present position, these oracles are tacked on to the end of the book. The Septuagint places them after 25:13 and before 25:14 and that may be their original position. If we look to the model of Isaiah or Ezekiel, we must conclude that the Septuagint placement has the better case. However, the actual order of the individual oracles appears better in the Hebrew text; here Jeremiah moves consistently from far west to east, an order that far excels the mixed-up one

within the Septuagint. Because the language of this genre
of prophecy is stereotyped and controlled by traditional
usage, it often is impossible to distinguish unique styles
from one prophet to another. However, one sign of authentic Jeremiah material can be located in allusions to historical
events of his day. Both chaps. 46 and 47, for example, are
not only dated by their labels, but actually fit the situations
that the labels announce. Others, such as the oracles
against Moab and Edom in chaps. 48-49, are so general that
they could have been spoken by Amos or by Ezekiel just as
easily as by Jeremiah.

ORACLES AGAINST EGYPT
46:1-28

46 The word of the LORD which came to Jeremiah
the prophet concerning the nations.

²About Egypt. Concerning the army of Pharaoh Neco,
king of Egypt, which was by the river Euphrates at
Carchemish and which Nebuchadrezzar king of Babylon
defeated in the fourth year of Jehoiakim the son of
Josiah, king of Judah:

³"Prepare buckler and shield,
   and advance for battle!
⁴Harness the horses;
   mount, O horsemen!
Take your stations with your helmets,
   polish your spears,
   put on your coats of mail!
⁵Why have I seen it?
They are dismayed
   and have turned backward.
Their warriors are beaten down,
   and have fled in haste;
they look not back—
   terror on every wide!
                    says the LORD.

Chapter 46 contains three separate oracles, vv. 2-12, 13-24 and 25-28. The first two certainly come from Jeremiah; the last may have been added to extend the prophecy down to the end of the exilic period, since vv. 25-26 sound like Ezekiel, 27-28 like Second Isaiah!

46:2-12 comes from the year that the Babylonians defeated the Egyptian army at the battle of Carchemesh, *i.e.*, 605 B.C. When Assyria had fallen in 609, Babylon took over her old territories in the East, but left the Egyptian army, which had come to help defend Assyria, in control of Syria and Palestine. Some three years later, the Babylonians were ready to drive Egypt out of Asia altogether. The two armies met in northern Syria at the great city of Carchemesh, and Nebuchadnezzar won an important victory. This poem dates to that battle, perhaps as Jeremiah's interpretation that it was not Babylon but the God of Israel who gave victory.

The poem progresses in two stages. The Egyptian army is described arrayed fearsomely for battle in vv. 3-4 and then in total rout in vv. 5-6. The second stage opens with the army redescribed in almost mythical terms as the primeval waters of chaos surging over the earth, helped by allies from the farthest corners of the earth (vv. 7-9). But just as suddenly, Yahweh crushes their evil force in a slaughter feast.

In vv. 3-6, the picture is highly realistic. One can almost feel the shouted commands and the troops falling into line. The Egyptian battle array must have been an impressive sight, with their gleaming shields in two sizes (RSV's "buckler" is a small shield), their spears and chariots. Middle Kingdom Egypt (2000-1800 B.C.) filled the tombs of the nobles with small wooden models of the marching battle line of troops—they were exceptionally proud of their military strength! But suddenly, like the click of a camera shutter, we see the next scene with panic everywhere as defeat overwhelms them. "Terror on Every Side," one of Jeremiah's special phrases for characterizing an enemy (6:25; 20:3 and 10) catches the mood perfectly. The phrase probably originated as a curse long before Jeremiah, but now the curse is on Egypt.

Seeing the Nile as a flood covering the land captures both the factual situation of the annual Nile flooding of the Egyptian farmland and the ancient myth of the Sea (Yamm) as the symbol of chaos and evil in Ugaritic literature (ANET 130-31, a part of Canaanite religion), as well as the similar role of Tiamat in the Babylonian Creation Epic (ANET 60-72). Just as Tiamat had her monstrous helpers, so Egypt brings its mercenaries from the hinterlands of Africa: Ethiopia, Somalialand and Libya. But Yahweh's power more than equals these forces of evil. His "Day of the Lord" will be a smashing victory, pictured as a feast in which the butchers are covered with blood trying to meet the demands of the celebrators. This mythical imagery appears fairly often in the exilic period and after (*cf.*, Ezek 39:17-20; Isa 34:5-7). The sword drunk with blood reminds us of Deut 32:42. The poem ends with the mocking challenge to go to Gilead and obtain some of its famous healing ointment. But Egypt cannot any longer reach Gilead, for Babylon had taken it away from her control, and of course her wound is too great to be healed at all (*cf.*, 8:22).

> ¹³The word which the LORD spoke to Jeremiah the prophet about the coming of Nebuchadrezzar king of Babylon to smite the land of Egypt:
> ¹⁴"Declare in Egypt, and proclaim in Migdol;
>   proclaim in Memphis and Tahpanhes;
> Say, 'Stand ready and be prepared,
>   for the sword shall devour round about you.'
> ¹⁵Why has Apis fled?
>   Why did not your bull stand?
>   Because the LORD thrust him down.
> ¹⁶Your multitude stumbled and fell,
>   and they said one to another,

'Arise and let us go back to our own people
   and to the land of our birth,
   because of the sword of the oppressor.'
17Call the name of Pharaoh, king of Egypt,
   'Noisy one who lets the hour go by.'

18"As I live, say the King,
   whose name is the LORD of hosts,
like Tabor among the mountains,
   and like Carmel by the sea, shall one come.
19Prepare yourselves baggage for exile,
   O inhabitants of Egypt!
For Memphis shall become a waste,
   a ruin, without inhabitant.

The second poem in vv. 13-24 can be dated not too long
after the first. Nebuchadnezzar brought his army down to
wipe out the Philistine city of Ashkelon, an Egyptian ally
in 604 (see 47:2-9), and drove Egyptian forces back across
their border. It describes the defeat of the Egyptian army
under the image of its patron god Apis, who was worshipped in the form of a black bull. The Hebrew word for
"bull," *'abbir*, frequently occurs as a metaphor for warriors
(see Isa 10:13; 34:7; Pss 22:13 and 68:30), and even as an
ancient name for Yahweh (Gen 49:24; Ps 132:5; Isa 49:26;
60:16). Verse 15 draws the sharp contrasts between the
two bulls, Apis and Yahweh; and vv. 17-18 between the two
kings: Yahweh, Lord of Hosts, and Hophra (whose mysti-
fying name in v. 17 makes a pun between *h-ib-r* for Hophra,
and the Hebrew verb, "to let go by," *he-ebir*). There is no
contest! Yahweh stands out like the two great mountain
peaks of Palestine, Carmel and Tabor (v. 18). And if
Yahweh has the might of a mountain, pharaoh's army can
be compared to pampered calves that bolt in terror at the
bite of a horsefly (vv. 20-21).

Verses 23-24 draw the most varied interpretation from modern commentaries. A recent favorite portrays hunters chasing a snake and cutting down the whole forest to finally get it. More probably, the image sees Nebuchadnezzar's army decimating the population of Egypt (by far the greatest in the ancient world!) as woodsmen would chop down a whole forest stand for lumber. Egypt's hordes are more numerous than locusts, but no more courageous than the small snakes that slither away from a person's approach.

The final four verses in chap. 46 are much more problematic. Verses 25-26 resemble Ezek 29:13-16 with its modified word of hope for Egypt, and Ezek 29:19 in which Yahweh makes a gift of Egypt to Nebuchadnezzar. For the great similarity of vv. 27-28 to the prophecies of Second Isaiah, see the comments on Jer 30:10-11. An oracle to Israel would seem out of place in this collection, and it may serve to indicate the purpose of these oracles against foreign powers—to give Israel hope in her restoration and confidence that the God who controls the destinies of nations will not forget his special care for the people who have covenanted with him.

THE ORACLE AGAINST THE PHILISTINES
47:1-7

> [5]Baldness has come upon Gaza,
>   Ashkelon has perished.
> O remnant of the Anakim,
>   how long will you gash yourselves?
> [6]Ah, sword of the LORD!
>   How long till you are quiet?
> Put yourself into your scabbard,
>   rest and be still!
> [7]How can it be quiet,
>   when the LORD has given it a charge?
> Against Ashkelon and against the seashore
>   he has appointed it."

The label in 47:1 specifies a particular occasion for this oracle against the Philistine cities on the southern coast of Palestine. But like so many other biblical dates, we can no longer discover exactly when it happened. Egypt attacks the southernmost city of the Philistine league, probably to keep it as a buffer against the Babylonians. Since we do know that Nebuchadnezzar attacked and took Ashkelon, another Philistine city, about 604, we can guess that Egypt responded to this threat by driving the Babylonians out of the area as soon as possible. This, in turn, led to a new Babylonian attack on Egypt somewhere near Gaza about 601. At that time, the Egyptian army held the Babylonians in check at least, and may even have administered a stunning defeat to them. Nebuchadnezzar brought his army back to Babylon and waited three years before he could again muster an army strong enough to try another invasion of the West. It was this same defeat of Babylon in 601 that gave king Jehoiakim the courage to rebel and seek to gain his freedom from Nebuchadnezzar—an attempt that ended in disaster when the Babylonians finally did return in 598. This Philistine oracle would thus fit well into one of the moments of drama between 604 and 601.

The Philistines were from the Mediterranean islands of Crete and Greece. They had settled the coastline at the same time the Hebrews had moved into the Promised Land from the East. In the beginning, the Philistines were clearly superior (*cf.*, 1 Sam 4-5), but after the time of David, Judah either controlled them or could hold its own against them.

The imagery of this oracle resembles that of the oracles against Egypt. The foe from the north is portrayed as the chaotic flood, the battle is sketched in sharp and breathless images, the victory of Babylon becomes a "Day of the Lord." Verse 4 associates the Philistines with the maritime republics of Tyre and Sidon in Phoenicia, probably because of their common interest in the sea trade. Caphtor, in v. 4, refers to Amos 9:7 which traces Philistine origins to there. Possibly it is Crete. Verse 5 lists Gaza and Ashkelon, two of the five cities making up the Philistine alliance, while Ashdod, Gath and Ekron are missing. Since the end of v. 5 has textual difficulties in Hebrew, each translation seeks to unlock more names in its wording. The RSV's "anakim," which follows the Septuagint, were a race of giants who lived in Palestine before the Hebrew conquest (Num 13:22-23). The New American Bible puts in "Ashdod" for "Anakim" to recover one more city of the alliance. Both guesses have about equal value. Some years ago, an Aramaic letter was found at Saqqara in Egypt, asking for the pharaoh's help, and sent by one of the Philistine city-states at this time. Scholars have usually identified the city, whose name was unclear except that it ended in-*on*, with Ashkelon. But recently some believe it should be Ekron. That would add one more Philistine city to the list!

Chapter 47 ends with a poignant plea that the sword of the Lord end its slaughter. The words are those of the Philistines, but the reply comes back as an oracle of the Lord: it cannot stop once his word has commanded it!

ORACLES AGAINST MOAB
48:1-47

48 Concerning Moab.
Thus says the LORD of hosts, the God of Israel:
"Woe to Nebo, for it is laid waste!
　Kiriathaim is put to shame, it is taken;
the fortress is put to shame and broken down;
²the renown of Moab is no more.
In Heshbon they planned evil against her:
　'Come, let us cut her off from being a nation!'
You also, O Madmen, shall be brought to silence;
　the sword shall pursue you.
³"Hark! a cry from Horonaim,
　'Desolation and great destruction!'
⁴Moab is destroyed;
　a cry is heard as far as Zoar.

⁵For at the ascent of Luhith
    they go up weeping;
for at the descent of Horonaim
    they have heard the cry of destruction.
⁶Flee! Save yourselves!
    Be like a wild ass in the desert!
⁷For, because you trusted in your
    strongholds and your treasures,
    you also shall be taken;
and Chemosh shall go forth into exile,
    with his priests and his princes.
⁸The destroyer shall come upon every city,
    and no city shall escape;
the valley shall perish,
    and the plain shall be destroyed,
    as the LORD has spoken.

Chapter 48 consists of several oracles, some in poetry and some in prose. No common agreement has been reached about the exact divisions among them, and the editors may well have considered the entire chapter a single poem, no matter how many pieces had been joined together to fashion it. One possible criterion, not used by the RSV, is to start a second major section at v. 29. Much of the material in vv. 29-39 duplicates the oracles against Moab in Isa 15-16 and may be largely traditional phrases added to the poetic sections in vv. 1-28. For purposes of discussion, we shall treat the text in four sections: 1-10, 11-20 with 21-28, 29-39, and 40-47.

Moab was long an archrival of Israel. It played a role in the stories of the conquest (Num 21-24) and is the subject of many prophetic condemnations (Amos 2:1-3; Isa 15-16; Ezek 25:8-11; Micah 6:5; Zeph 2:8-9; and Dan 11:41). When Israel had power under David and the early kings of northern Israel, it subjected Moab as a vassal state; when Israel grew weak fighting the Aramaeans in the 800's.

Moab won its independence. Ever after, it took oppor-
tunities to seize territory from the Israelites or to support
their enemies. 2 Kgs 24:2 tells how Nebuchadnezzar used
Moabites to harass Judah during his invasion.

The history of the Moabites is not completely known.
Besides the note from Josephus in his *Antiquities* that the
Babylonians ended the kingdom in 582, we have one other
major piece of information outside the Bible: the Mesha
Stone. Mesha was king of Moab between 840 and 820 B.C.,
and overthrew the control of Israel about 830 in the time
of Jehu. To commemorate his victory and the new independence of Moab, he erected a memorial account of it,
which was uncovered by accident in 1868. It was a goldmine
of information on Moab's relations with Israel, the practice
of ritual slaughter of captured villages, attributes of the
God Chemosh, and identification of geographical sites.
Many of the names that dot Jeremiah 48 are found on that
stone and help confirm the accuracy of place and people
references in his Oracles against Nations.

Moab lies east of the Dead Sea and party north of it in the
old tribal area of Reuben (*e.g.*, Nebo and Kiriathim in v. 1;
cf., Num 32:3 and Josh 13:19). Mesha took over many of
these areas when he made his break for freedom.

The first poem in vv. 1-10 has many authentic touches of
Jeremiah. Verse 2 has a double pun: In Heshbon, they
"planned evil" (*hash-bu*), and Madmen is "brought to
silence" (*tiddomi*) Madmen itself literally means a "dung-
hill" and makes a play on the real city name: Dimon (Isa
15:9). The irony, too, is typical of Jeremiah. Chemosh
their great god will be led into exile like everyone else.
Solomon had built a temple to Chemosh for his foreign
wives (1 Kgs 11:7), which Josiah destroyed (2 Kgs 23:13),
and 2 Kgs 3:21-27 relates the horrifying tale how the king
of Moab sacrificed his eldest son to Chemosh to prevent an
Israelite victory. On the Mesha Stone, the king brags that he
had "fought against (Ashtaroth) and took it and slew all of
the people of the town as a satiation for Chemosh," and later
that he took Nebo and slew all "seven thousand men, boys,

women, girls and maidservants, for I devoted them to destruction for Ashtar-Chemosh" (ANET 320-21). This terrible god now meekly goes to captivity and shame!

Verse 5, on the other hand, almost literally repeats Isa 15:5, suggesting it was a well-known saying. RSV's "ass" in v. 6 does not make much sense, but other suggestions for the mysterious Hebrew word *aroer* (Tamarisk tree, sandgrouse, a city) don't clear up the meaning much better. Whatever the image involved, it captures their idea of a creature or object perfectly suited to living in the desert and surviving. Finally, v. 10 adds a curse line to specify that the fate of Moab is Yahweh's work.

The second poem and prose combination follows in vv. 11-28. It combines several small units. The first is a metaphor of Moab settling in like fine wine, and suddenly being spilled and shattered on the ground. Apparently Moab had escaped the trial of losing her population to exile up to this time. Verse 13 has an interesting reference to Israel's worship of Bethel. This does not mean the city Bethel as city, but a *divine being* or manifestation at the city. The Elephantiné documents from Egypt (mentioned in chap. 46) list a shrine to *Bethel* there; so that this cult, otherwise unstated in the Bible, may have had more of a following than we know. Verses 14-15 change the image to the destruction of all the choice warriors, and vv. 15-16 to the breaking of its independent rule (the sceptre of its king). Verses 18-20 imitate a dirge sung at a funeral—this time the corpse is Moab herself.

The prose additions in vv. 21-27 list a number of cities found also on the Mesha Stone and end with the images of a broken arm and horn, both ancient symbols for strength (*cf.*, Ezek 29:17-21 for comparable images applied to Egypt). The imagery of drunkenness in vv. 26-27 is traditional, as in 25:17-29. Moab who always derided Israel will herself be the object of derision as it flutters about seeking safety like the doves (v. 28).

Jeremiah follows the wording of Isa 16:6-10 almost exactly in vv. 28-33. He simply takes over the traditional

taunt song as valid. The same can be said of the prose
passage in vv. 34-39. Nearly all of the expressions can be
found somewhere in Isa 15 or 16. The account may be a free
rendering of the older materials. As it stands now, the effect
of the whole section is to begin a funeral lament. Moab's
desolation is greeted by the reed pipe by which the wailing
for the dead would be chanted. The shaving of the head,
gashing the body, and the sackcloth are all common
mourning customs. When these are combined with the
poetic lamentation over her fall because of pride and
insolence, the prophet or his editors have created an
extended image of the collapse before the wrath of Yahweh
of all human pretensions to divine power. It bears a faint
resemblance to the great poems on human *hubris* found
in Isa 14 and Ezek 31 and 32.

The final poem against Moab also appears to be a patch-
work quilt. Verses 43-44 resemble Isa 24:17-18 and vv. 45-
46 are very close to the "Song of Heshbon" in Num 21:28-29.
Verses 40-41 are reused in a similar manner for the oracles
against Edom in 49:22. The point of the image of an eagle
(or vulture) is to stress the swiftness of the attacker and his
ability to move in the mountainous country of Moab
without trouble. Ezekiel 17 chooses a similar metaphor.
And the purpose of repeating so many well-worn phrases
and old poems is to bring their power and effectiveness to
bear once again. They have become embedded in the traditions of the people and express the terrible fate of enemy
attack and the common experience of devastation and
hopelessness known to all Near Eastern peoples. There
can be no better way of saying how awful Moab's fate will
be than by repeating these favorite gems.

ORACLES AGAINST AMMON AND EDOM
49:1-22

49   Concerning the Ammonites.
Thus says the LORD:
"Has Israel no sons?
Has he no heir?

Why then has Milcom dispossessed Gad,
and his people settled in its cities?
²Therefore, behold, the days are coming,
says the LORD,
when I will cause the battle cry to be heard
against Rabbah of the Ammonites;
it shall bcome a desolate mound,
and its villages shall be burned with fire;
then Israel shall dispossess those who dispossessed him,
says the LORD.

Chapter 49 contains a series of shorter oracles against foreign powers, of which the condemnation of Edom is the longest. The shorter passages are generally single poems, but the Edomite section mixes prose and poetry together.

49:1-6 are directed against the Ammonites, whom we have already met in the person of their king Baalis, the sponsor of Ishmael's revolt against Gedaliah (40:14). Ammon covered the area inland from the Jordan River just above and to the east of the Dead Sea. Its capital, Rabbath-Ammon, still flourishes as Amman, the modern capital of Jordan. Because of its location away from the Jordan River, Ammon was bound to come into conflict with the Israelite tribe of Gad that also lived on the East bank of the river. Fights and border struggles were common (Jgs 11 and 1 Sam 11) until David subdued the land harshly (2 Sam 10). Border battles still continued, however, for Amos mentions them in Amos 1:13-15. The Assyrian king, Tiglath-Pileser III, deported the people of Gad when he put down an Israelite revolt in 734-733, and Ammon took over their territory for itself. We hear little of them again until the rebellions in Judah against Nebuchadnezzar in both 598 (2 Kgs 24:2) and 587 (Ezek 21). They worshiped the god Milcom, and Israel had a special loathing for their practices of child sacrifice (see Lev 18:21; 20:2-5; 1 Kgs 11:7). The name "Moloch" in these passages makes a pun on both Milcom, "the king," and on *molk*, the word for a sacrifice.

The oracle of Jeremiah begins with a reminder of how Ammon took over the land belonging to Gad, then launches into the threatening prediction that "the days are coming" (but compare its positive use in 31:27, 31, 38!) when this shall be reversed in a terrible battle and the people of Ammon shall go into exile the same as Israel's people had. References to the people of Ammon in the personification of its major cities, Rabbah and Heshbon, the deportation of its god and priests, the description of the funeral laments, all share the imagery used against the Philistines and Moab in the preceding chapters (see 48:2, 7, 8). The mention of Heshbon in v. 3 is probably the same city that belongs to the Moabites in 48:2. A border town, it changed hands often. Ai, on the other hand, is not the same Ai that Joshua conquered in Josh 7. They stand on opposite banks of the Jordan River. The translation "valleys" in v. 4 of the RSV has been shown to mean "strength" in texts found at Ugarit, and this would make much more sense here. The oracle ends with a promise to restore Ammon's fortunes. Note the same wording for Moab in 48:47 and for Elam in 49:39. This expression, *shub shebut*, "to restore the fortunes of," occurs in several oracles of hope for Israel (30:3, 18; 33:7, 11), and indicates the close connection between God's plan of punishment-plus-salvation for the Israelites, and a parallel providential care for all nations.

[7]Concerning Edom.

Thus says the LORD of hosts:
"Is wisdom no more in Teman?
    Has counsel perished from the prudent?
    Has their wisdom vanished?
[8]Flee, turn back, dwell in the depths,
    O inhabitants of Dedan!
For I will bring the calamity of Esau upon him,
    the time when I punish him.
[9]If grape-gatherers came to you,
    would they not leave gleanings?

If thieves came by night,
   would they not destroy only enough for themselves?
¹⁰But I have stripped Esau bare,
   I have uncovered his hiding places,
   and he is not able to conceal himself.
His children are destroyed, and his brothers,
   and his neighbours; and his is no more.

The oracles against Edom in vv. 7-22 are printed partly in poetry and partly in prose in the RSV, but perhaps more of vv. 17-22 really belong to the poetry than the translation shows. Yet even the poetry itself shows very strong connections to other passages in the prophets or to other parts of Jeremiah, so that hardly an original line can be found in these verses.

Edom's territory covered the land below the Dead Sea and to the east of the great valley that ran down from the Dead Sea to the Red Sea. The story of Jacob and his brother Esau personifies the age-old hatred between the two nations and yet at the same time showed Israel understood that they were related. Like Moab and Ammon, it began life about the same time as Israel in the 13th century, was subjected to David's empire, was controlled on and off by the kings of Judah down through the 8th century, and finally won its real independence in the 7th. Judean oppression for so long a time led to undying hatred on the part of the Edomites, and when Judah was helpless in exile, it moved in with a vengeance. Some of the poems of pure hate against Edom from the exilic period suggest that the Edomites took an active role in the Babylonian destruction of Jerusalem (Lam 4:21-22; Obad 1-14; Ezek 35:1-15). Later, they themselves suffered defeat by Arab invaders from the desert and moved west into the Negev area of Judah. Oracles against Edom are frequent in the Old Testament, and because of their intense spirit of vengeance, most critics see many, if not all, of them coming from this period when Edom took part in the attack on Jerusalem and then occupied southern Judah (Ezek 25:12-14; Mal 1:2-5; Amos 1:11-12; Ps 137; Isa 34:5-14; 63:1-6).

Jeremiah 49:7-16 seems to be a variation of Obad 1-9. The language is nearly identical. Compare Obad 1-4 with 49:14-16, and Obad 5-6 with 49:9-10 to get the flavor. Both probably use a common cursing poem much older than either prophet. The second part of the oracle in 49:17-22 quotes other sections of Jeremiah, *e.g.*, v. 18 = 50:40, vv. 19-21 = 50:44-46, v. 22 = 48:40-41.

The first poem opens with a reference to the Edomites' fabled expertise in wisdom (Job comes from the Edomite area!), and how useless it has now become. God will trick them out of their land more than Jacob did Esau of his birthright, and strip them cleaner than a harvester does the field. To bolster this fearsome threat, the editors have added a note in vv. 11-13 referring back to the general threat against all nations that God will make them drunk on the cup of wrath (25:15-29); and tenderly noting how God will take care of the survivors (v. 11). This comment is not part of the poem itself, which continues in vv. 14-16 as a specific prediction that Edom's enemies will attack and conquer her mountainous land that seems so impregnable. Esau will be reduced to a humiliated and insignificant nation (*cf.* Ezek 29:13-14).

The second oracle in 49:17-22 repeats many of Jeremiah's typical threats. The imagery of the shepherd who must confront the lion that mauls his flock was an Old Testament favorite, but operates in both directions. Here God is like the lion, as in Amos 1:2; 3:8 and 3:21. But in Ezek 34, God is the shepherd who protects the flock. From the extended references to the eagle in this chapter (vv. 16 and 22), the rocky territory of Edom must have been frequently called an eagle's nest by the people. Its fate will be complete, destroyed like Sodom and Gomorrah. Biblical passages don't tell us the precise location of these symbolic capitals of evil, but the evidence seems to point to an area near the bottom of the Dead Sea on the borders of Edom. Jeremiah was

particularly pointed, therefore, in naming Edom's fate in
v. 18. This prophecy came true to a large extent when the
Arab tribes moved into Edom and set up their own kingdom
of Nabatea there, with its capital at Petra. The Edomites
who survived crossed the Jordan and intermixed with what
Jews were there, forming the later region of Idumea, homeland of king Herod the Great in the Christian era.

ORACLES AGAINST DAMASCUS,
KEDAR AND ELAM
49:23-29

28Concerning Kedar and the kingdoms of Hazor which
Nebuchadrezzar king of Babylon smote.

Thus says the LORD:
"Rise up, advance against Kedar!
Destroy the people of the east!
29Their tents and their flocks shall be taken,
their curtains and all their goods;
their camels shall be borne away from them,
and men shall cry to them:
'Terror on every side!'
30Flee, wander far away, dwell in the depths,
O inhabitants of Hazor!
says the LORD.
For Nebuchadrezzar king of Babylon
has made a plan against you,
and formed a purpose against you.

Damascus was the capital of an Aramaean kingdom and
the chief city of a league of small states in Syria which
included Hamath and Arpad. Most of them flourished in
the 9th century, but fell to the terrible assaults of the
Assyrian Tiglath Pileser III in the 730's (see Isa 10:9;
36:19). When powerful, they had caused a great deal of
trouble to northern Israel at the time of Elijah and Elisha
(1 Kgs 20; 22 and 2 Kgs 1-9). This oracle uses old traditions

much like those found elsewhere in Jer 46-51, and which often stem from treaty curses common to the Ancient Near East. See Amos 1:27 to understand the curse of the last verse of the oracle against Damascus (vv. 23-27).

The oracle against Kedar and Hazor in vv. 28-33 should be changed from the RSV to read "Kedar and Hazer." The language of this poem conjures up the picture of desert life: living in tents, herding rather than farming, camel travel, refuges in caves and cutting the corners of their hair (see 9:26, 25:23). Kedar was such an Arab nomadic or semi-nomadic group (*cf.*, Gen 25:13; Isa 21:16-17; Ezek 27:21). It is closely identified with Edom and with unwalled villages (*hazerim*) in Isa 42:11 and 60:7. Because of this link between Kedar and *hazer*, almost no one believes that the text should refer to the great citadel city of Hazor, known as one of the largest Canaanite cities of the 13th century, B.C., and fought against by Joshua (Josh 11).

The oracle generally describes an attack by the Babylonians which drives the Arabs from their settlements and forces them to flee into waste areas on camels or on foot, leaving most of their meagre possessions behind as booty. The final line in v. 33 throws the best curses in Jeremiah's collection at them (see 46:19; 49:2; 50:13; 51:29, 37). The scene described here regularly fills the records of Assyrian kings from Tiglath Pileser (745-728) down to Ashurbanipal (668-632). Tiglath Pileser, for example, writes in his annals, "As for Samsi, queen of Arabia . . . 1,100 inhabitants, 30,000 camels, 20,000 cattle, 5,000 containers (of her possessions), I took away from her and she herself fled to save her life" (ANET 284). Even the Babylonians expended large efforts to subdue the Arab tribes which made constant raids against the settled farmlands. Nabonidus, the last king of Babylon, actually spent a good part of his reign in Tema, one of the Arab cities (see ANET 305-306). In fact, the citizens of Babylon resented this so much that they welcomed the Persian conqueror Cyrus the Great into their land in 539, thus ending the Babylonian empire (ANET 315-216). Several excellent Assyrian reliefs showing king Ashurbanipal's wars against the Arabs can be seen in the British Museum.

> [35]Thus says the LORD of hosts: "Behold, I will break the bow of Elam, the mainstay of their might; [36]and I will bring upon Elam the four winds from the four quarters of heaven; and I will scatter them to all those winds, and there shall be no nation to which those driven out of Elam shall not come.

The final oracle about Elam stands against a country far away and hardly an enemy or threat to Judah. We know little about Elam from biblical records except that it was famed for its archers (Isa 22:6; Jer 49:35). It lay east of the lower ends of the Tigris and Euphrates Rivers, in what is now Southwestern Iran. Its history always had more in common with the Sumerians and Babylonians because it shared the flat river valley with them than it did with the fierce mountainous people of Persia and Media (North of Persia). We do not know what led Jeremiah in 597 to give such an oracle—perhaps some battle of the moment between Babylon and Elam that is now forgotten. In any case, the language does not have much original material. Imagery of God setting his throne in Elam has been used before for Egypt in 43:8-13 and for all nations in 1:15, while the promise to restore its fortunes echoes 48:47 and 49:6.

The major value of including such an oracle in the collection is to re-emphasize the rule of God over the destinies of all nations, and to extend the range of his judgment from the West clear over to the major powers in the East. It prepares the reader for the climax of the book, the series of words against Babylon itself.

WARNING AND CURSE OF BABYLON
50:1-32

50 The word which the LORD spoke concerning Babylon, concerning the land of the Chaldeans, by Jeremiah the prophet:
²"Declare among the nations and proclaim,
set up a banner and proclaim,
conceal it not, and say:
'Babylon is taken,
Bel is put to shame,
Merodach is dismayed.
Her images are put to shame,
her idols are dismayed.'
³"For out of the north a nation has come up against her, which shall make her land a desolation, and none shall dwell in it; both man and beast shall flee away.

⁴"In those days and in that time, says the LORD, the people of Israel and the people of Judah shall come together, weeping as they come; and they shall seek the LORD their God. ⁵They shall ask the way to Zion, with faces turned toward it, saying, 'Come, let us join ourselves to the LORD in an everlasting covenant which will never be forgotten.'

Chapters 50-51 are extremely lengthy (110 verses) and thoroughly mixed up in content and imagery so that it helps to read them impressionistically rather than logically. If order does underlie the thinking of the editors who put them together, it is climactic, with the most fearsome descriptions of terror held until the end. The complex concludes with a short story of Seraiah added to confirm the *authority* of the oracles. Perhaps the editors themselves thought that they had to underline Jeremiah's authorship since these oracles seem to contradict his earlier oracles and letter in chap. 29, which counselled acceptance of Babylon and surrender before its power. Yet this does not have to be an impossibly difficult problem from any point of view. The very ferocity of the threat in chaps. 50-51 indicates that Babylon had a fearsome reputation in battle and in conquest. Prophets often told the people to prevent their own suicide by surrendering. Isaiah had done so before the Assyrians in 734-732, and probably again in 705-701 (see Isa 7-8 and 30:12-17). Jeremiah can call Nebuchadnezzar God's servant in 27:7, as Isaiah had called Assyria the rod of God's anger in Isa 10:5-15, but they also foresee the destruction and end of the oppressor nation (Isa 10:15-17; 14:24-27; Jer 27:7; 29:10).

The collection has many prose passages and even whole poems borrowed from other parts of Jeremiah (*e.g.*, 51:15-19 = 10:12-16). Yet much of it consists of fine war songs of a very high caliber. Interspersed are references to the conquest by the Medes (51:11, 28) that would have been unlikely on the lips of Jeremiah since they did not rise to powerful status until about 560 or so. Yet, the whole body of oracles certainly does not date to long after 560 or 550 since it enthusiastically expects the total destruction of Babylon which never happened. Cyrus the Persian entered the city almost as a welcome visitor in 539, and spared the city from destruction. Probably words of Jeremiah make up the bulk of the material, with other poems and comments included to apply and update his message about the time of Nebuchadnezzar's death in 562. The loss of this great leader and the rise of less competent and more troubled rulers may have raised the hopes of Jewish exiles that deliverance was near. But we must remember that these, like all the Oracles against Nations, use very traditional vocabulary. Many scholars have pointed out how closely Jer 50-51 resembles the wording of Isa 13-14 against Babylon. Surely Jeremiah and his book depend to a large extent on the earlier poetry!

50:1-32 can be broken down into a number of smaller sections, but their exact relations to one another are uncertain. The first verse serves as a label for both chapters and solemnly declares that now God's word which has spoken judgment for so many nations, touches also the great power of Babylon. Verses 2-3 then set the theme: Babylon's god Marduk (slightly distorted in Hebrew as Merodach), the lord (Bel) of the world is defeated and shown to be helpless and shamed before all the world. Here the word for idols really means "excrement" and makes the shame more vivid. Then the unthinkable happens: the feared "foe from the north" will itself become victim of a new "foe from the north." Compare this verse to 4:6 or 6:1. As 51:11 and 28 probably intend, that foe will be Persia under the great conqueror Cyrus. Technically, Persia stands east of Babylon, but the invasion will sweep down from the North through the great valley of the Tigris and Euphrates.

Verses 4-7 make the first application to Israel. The language of return reminds us of Second and Third Isaiah (Isa 49:14-18; 59:20-21; 60:14) and the Psalms of the exilic period (Ps 126:4-6). Jeremiah has already promised an everlasting covenant in 32:40. The hope of a flock without their shepherds rests in God's coming as shepherd (Ezek 34).

Verses 8-10 continue with a call to Israel's exiles to get out of Babylon before the foe from the North destroys them along with the city. The he-goat is the most aggressive member of the sheep and goat flocks and bounds out of the pens first each morning. So, too, must Israel make haste.

The following poetic unit in vv. 11-16 recites the theme of God's wrath. Babylon personified as a mother will be the victim of war, ravished, exposed and humiliated by the battle to come. Jeremiah has threatened Judah in earlier days with becoming a desolate waste and a place for people to hiss at (v. 13; *cf.*, 6:8; 9:10; 12:10; 18:16; 19:8), but now the tables will be turned and God's vengeance will return upon Babylon itself, because instead of being simply instruments to punish. Babylon in its greed went on to plunder God's inheritance (vv. 11 and 15). God's vengeance (*naqam*) had been called up against Israel's covenant violations in 5:9, 29 and 9:9. Now it requites justice against the other side equally. This harsh word appears frequently in biblical literature to express God's righteous anger against nations (Jgs 11:36; 2 Sam 4:8; Isa 34:8; 35:4; Deut 32:41).

Verses 17-20 stand side by side with this threatening message to interpret its meaning for Israel. God will indeed punish Babylon and thus restore the land of Israel to its former abundance and security. Like *naqam*, the word for "punish," *paqad*, stands rooted in the covenant obligations. Exod 34:6-7 not only calls God "slow to anger and rich in mercy," but ready to *punish* violaters to the third and fourth generation! See similar uses in Amos 3:2; Hos 1:4; 2:13; 4:9; 8:13; 9:7; 12:3; Jer 5:9 and 9:9. Verse 20 brings forth the theology of the remnant. In Amos and Isaiah it meant little more than those God spared from outright death in his punishment. But in Jeremiah, these survivors receive blessing as well. Verse 20 resonates with the promise of the new covenant in 31:31-34, that they will have new hearts, free from disobedience.

Verses 21-28 offer a stirring little poem on the day of battle in all its color and terror. Note how it opens with the two territorial names. They are puns on small sections of Babylon. *Merathaim* sounds like the Hebrew word, "double rebelliousness," while *Peqod* makes a homonym with *paqad*, "punishment." Twice, in vv. 21 and 26, God hands them over to utter destruction. The word used, *herem*, comes from the ancient practice of dedicating one's enemies to God as a burnt holocaust sacrifice if the God will give victory. When he does, all the enemy, men, women and children must be killed. A fearsome and primitive corollary of identifying God too strongly as a warrior and God of battle! The language of vv. 21-26 contrasts the power of Babylon as a hammer with its fate, trapped like a bird, reduced to nothing, etc. Its bulls (*i.e.,* its soldiers) become the animals for sacrifice. God's vengeance will completely repay their wickedness (v. 28), especially their contempt of the temple in Jerusalem.

Verses 29-32 return to the theme of Babylon's pride as her basic fault. It is this human ambition to act as gods that ultimately sets the nations against God and leads to the judgment made by the prophets against the pagan peoples. The particular thought in these four verses really comes from the tradition of Isaiah. See the characterization of Babylon's pride in Isa 14, and the constant use of the divine title "Holy One of Israel" throughout the Book of Isaiah. It comes in Jeremiah only in this section (51:5 and 50:30).

THE REDEEMER COMES IN POWER
50:33-46

35"A sword upon the Chaldeans, says the LORD,
    and upon the inhabitants of Babylon,
    and upon her princes and her wise men!
36A sword upon the diviners,
    that they may become fools!
A sword upon her warriors,
    that they may be destroyed!
37A sword upon her horses and upon her chariots,
    and upon all the foreign troops in her midst,
    that they may become women!
A sword upon all her treasures,
    that they may be plundered!
38A drought upon her waters,
    that they may be dried up!
For it is a land of images,
    and they are mad over idols.

God is a redeemer, the one who releases a relative from prison, pays the debts, buys the property to keep it in the family if a member has to sell. It captures the essence of the God of the Exodus in Exod 6:6; 15:13. Many of the laws regarding human "redeemers" (*go'el*) can be found in Lev 25:47-55. This proclamation of the saving Lord is followed by the powerful little poem often simply called "the song of the sword" in vv. 35-38. This in turn has appended another threat to make Babylon totally depopulated (see earlier 46:19; 48:9; 49:13; 49:33; 50:3; 50:12). For the significance of the reference to Sodom and Gomorrah, see the remarks on 49:18. The chapter closes with a re-application of 6:22-24, which had been said of Israel, but is now directed in v. 40 against Babylon. It fits the general pattern of threats in the Oracles against Nations (*cf.*, v. 30 with 48:41; 49:22; 51:30). Finally, vv. 44-46 reuse the same comment made against Edom in 49:17-22.

Throughout chap. 50, a theme of God's work or plan is hinted at repeatedly (vv. 15, 25, 45). Isaiah had used this point in his preaching (Isa 5:19; 28:21; 29:14; 30:1) to call Israel to obedience to the covenant and away from political alliances with pagan nations. It implies a trust that God controls the destinies of nations and that he will protect the good as well as punish the wicked. Spoken here against Babylon, it implies God's vengeance will be inexorable. Nothing shall reverse it until it is completed.

GOD'S PUNISHMENT OF BABYLON
51:1-33

51 Thus says the LORD:
"Behold, I will stir up the spirit of a destroyer
   against Babylon,
   against the inhabitants of Chaldea;
²and I will send to Babylon winnowers,
   and they shall winnow her,
and they shall empty her land,
   when they come against her from every side
   on the day of trouble.
³Let not the archer bend his bow,
   and let him not stand up in his coat of mail.
Spare not her young men;
   utterly destroy all her host.

⁴They shall fall down slain in the land of the Chaldeans,
    and wounded in her streets.
⁵For Israel and Judah have not been forsaken
    by their God, the LORD of hosts;
but the land of the Chaldeans is full of guilt
    against the Holy One of Israel.

Verses 1-14 describe an ancient battle in graphic pictures. The spirit of the destroyer is one sent from God with God's own power to act. Note how this theme becomes central to Ezekiel later on. God's spirit makes it possible for Ezekiel to receive God's word (Ezek 2:2), and it is the spirit that makes the nation live again (Ezek 37). For Jeremiah, it has the power of God's justice to punish. The excitement of battle continues from vv. 1-4 to 6-7, and from 11a to 12-14 mixed with poetry lauding God's power to bring it about. Note how often familiar images reappear here: the locusts as in 46:23, the use of an *atbash*, reversing the names of letters of a name to hide it (see the comments on Jer 25:26 in the previous volume; here RSV's "Chaldea" is actually spelled out as "a heart risen against me," *leb qamai*), the use of the Lord's vengeance in v. 6, the balm of Gilead in v. 8 (*cf.*, 8:22), the cup of wrath in v. 7 (*cf.*, 13:12-13; 25:15-29; 49:12-13), and the work of the Lord in v. 10.

The refrain that weaves through these passages calls for the Israelites to praise God's divine vengeance and his work in Zion. This suggests that the viewpoint of the singers was from the temple in Jerusalem and may mean that a few of the verses have been added after the restoration in 539 when the people had more chance to return home. Certainly the note on the Medes in v. 11 reflects a time after the death of Jeremiah, although before the end of the exile. The writer still looks forward to Babylon's total destruction. The most impressive part of the refrain praising God comes in vv. 15-19 and is lifted straight from 10:12-16. The motifs were favorites in Israelite polemics against foreign gods (see their reuse in Second Isaiah, esp. Isa 44:9-20; 40:12-23), and if it was good enough to express this in chap. 10, they are all the better used against Babylon here.

Verses 20-23 could be called "the hammer song" to match the "song of the sword" in 50:35-38. Its theological message stresses that God uses human instruments to achieve his purposes (see Isa 10:5-19; Jer 27:4-11). In this case, the unknown nation will be used against Babylon. But since no such nation was a match for Babylon in Jeremiah's lifetime, possibly he had originally said it about Babylon against Israel! Now the editors found its perfect use against Babylon itself. It suggests that the chosen people will become the instrument against Babylon. Note how the next few verses in 24-26 draw a contrast between Mount Zion, the Lord's mighty strength, and the destroying mountain of Babylon. We are reminded of the great mountain of Babylon, the temple tower of Marduk. Its technical name is a ziggurat, an artificial platform several stories high to serve as a stepping place for the god when he descends from the heavens to visit Babylon. It is featured as the "tower of Babel" in Gen 11, where the mighty ziggurat was so small by divine standards that God had to leave heaven to come down and get a closer look!

Finally, the poem in vv. 27-33 gives us still another war song. The nations of the far North are *called against* Babylon (Ararat, Minni and Askenaz can all be found in Eastern Turkey and Northern Iran), and *sanctified* (translated as "prepare" in RSV) as Jeremiah was sanctified for his task (Jer 1:5). It is a picture of total weakness and collapse for Babylon trembling before the coming of the divine warrior. It is so rapid that the messengers cannot keep from stumbling over each other as one after another brings more bad news. Babylon will be left like a threshing floor ready for the harvest season—it is cleared of all living growth and trampled down to hard dirt.

BABYLON'S FATE
51:34-58

> [34]"Nebuchadrezzar the king of
>   Babylon has devoured me,
>   he has crushed me;
> he has made me an empty vessel,
>   he has swallowed me like a monster;
> he has filled his belly with my delicacies,
>   he has rinsed me out.
> [35]The violence done to me and to my
>   kinsmen be upon Babylon,"
>   let the inhabitant of Zion say.
> "My blood be upon the inhabitants of Chaldea,"
>   let Jerusalem say.
> [36]Therefore thus says the LORD:
> "Behold, I will plead your cause
>   and take vengeance for you.
> I will dry up her sea
>   and make her fountain dry;
> [37]and Babylon shall become a heap of ruins,
>   the haunt of jackals,
> a horror and a hissing,
>   without inhabitant.

The first section in vv. 34-44 contains a dialogue between Jerusalem and Yahweh. Jerusalem lodges a legal complaint by calling for a curse. God accepts the lawsuit and promises to prosecute it because he is the city's *go'el*, "redeemer," bound by blood ties to avenge her wrong. The imagery of lions, lambs, drunkenness and sleep are colorful enough, but the primary weapon will be God's power over the forces of chaos. He will dry up the primeval sea that gives Babylon water and provides the Euphrates River as a protection and travel route. When the life-giving water goes, the place will become uninhabitable. But God promises to restore what the chaos monster has swallowed. We are reminded of Amos 3:12 where the shepherd tries to rescue from the lion a piece of an ear or a tail of his lamb. Death, like Sea, is a symbol of the powers of chaos that oppose God. Death is that great swallower who gulps down human lives into Sheol (see the comments on Jer 23:9-22). Some older commentators have even taken the reference to the great sea monster in v. 44 to be the basis of the Book of Jonah. Jonah would be a *midrash*, or commentary, on the meaning of this passage. Part of the sense of a mythical judgment against Babylon is enhanced by the repeat of the atbash *sh-sh-k* for *ba-be-l* in v. 41, to hide the name of Babylon from ordinary eyes.

Verses 45-53 make up still another powerful poem of destruction. God announces Babylon's death as punishment for the death of Israel which it caused. All of nature shall witness to the justice of God's sentence. As in Deut 32:1, the heavens and earth are the chief witnesses in the divine lawsuit. The constant assassinations and weakness of the rulers after Nebuchadnezzar's death are a sign of God's impending judgment. The rightness of such vengeful language comes from referral to (a) what Judah and Jerusalem have suffered, and (b) to Babylon's pride. She has mounted to the heavens like a god (*cf.*, Isa 14:13-15) by defiling Yahweh's temple and trampling in its precincts. But even her own impregnable walls and moats, seemingly a heavenly fortress in themselves, will not save her now.

Verses 54-58 bring the section on Babylon's destruction to a close by creating an eyewitness account of Babylon's fall. From a distant vantage point this observer can hear the shattering and demolition of the city walls, and watch the warriors captured, the leadership confused and helpless as though drunk, death spreading everywhere, and the flames consuming all the might and glory of the greatest city in the world. But the observer also sees the hand of God behind this unthinkable event. What no human agency could have brought about on its own, the Lord of justice and recompense has. The prophet ends by quoting an old proverb which appears also in Hab 2:13, "The people labor for nought, and the nations weary themselves only for fire." They build only for human masters and world powers. God established the order of creation to bring glory to his name and for nations to know him, but the peoples opted instead for hopes of immortal fame in empire and army. These will not last, but go up in flame as do the walls of Babylon.

THUS SHALL BABYLON SINK, TO RISE NO MORE
51:59-64

[59]The word which Jeremiah the prophet commanded Seraiah the son of Neriah, son of Mahseiah, when he went with Zedekiah king of Judah to Babylon, in the fourth year of his reign. Seraiah was the quartermaster. [60]Jeremiah wrote in a book all the evil that should come upon Babylon, all these words that are written concerning Babylon. [61]And Jeremiah said to Seraiah: "When you come to Babylon, see that you read all these words, [62]and say, 'O LORD, thou hast said concerning this place that thou wilt cut it off, so that nothing shall dwell in it, neither man nor beast, and it shall be desolate for ever.' [63]When you finish reading this book, bind a stone to it, and cast it into the midst of the Euphrates, [64]and say, 'Thus shall Babylon sink, to rise no more, because of the evil that I am bringing upon her.'

Thus far are the words of Jeremiah.

The editors have appended a symbolic act that Jeremiah arranged long before the second fall of Jerusalem. The fourth year of Zedekiah places this at the same time the ambassadors were filling Jerusalem and plotting revolt against Babylon (chap. 27). Jeremiah sent a note (one scroll!) to Babylon with words of judgment on it, had Seraiah throw it into the Euphrates River and pronounce an oracle over it. Seraiah was probably Baruch's brother, for they have the same father (*cf.*, 32:12), and he held a high post. (RSV's "quartermaster" tries to capture the Hebrew words, "prince of the resting places," the one in charge of provisions and royal journeys.) The scroll must have been read to the exiles to reassure them at the very time that Jeremiah was counseling the leaders back at home to accept Babylonian rule and stop planning armed revolt (27:12-16). It gives us a concrete example of a prophet preaching both judgment warnings and salvation hopes at the same time but for two different purposes.

Because the scroll was short, it probably contained some of the oracles now found in chaps. 50-51, but certainly not all of them. The combination of a written word from Yahweh, the symbolic gesture, and a spoken oracle, greatly reinforced the effective power of the divine word. 51:64, "thus far are the words of Jeremiah," looks like the note put at the end of the book when it was first completed. The addition of chap. 52 must have come at a later time.

BOOK IV

JEREMIAH 52

APPENDIX FROM 2 KGS 24:18—25:30

JER 52:28-34

²⁸This is the number of the people whom Nebuchadrezzar carried away captive: in the seventh year, three thousand and twenty-three Jews; ²⁹in the eighteenth year of Nebuchadrezzar he carried away captive from Jerusalem eight hundred and thirty-two persons; ³⁰in the twenty-third year of Nebuchadrezzar, Nebuzaradan the captain of the guard carried away captive of the Jews seven hundred and forty-five persons; all the persons were four thousand and six hundred.

³¹And in the thirty-seventh year of the captivity of Jehoiachin king of Judah, the twelfth month, on the twenty-fifth day of the month, Evilmerodach king of Babylon, in the year that he became king, lifted up the head of Jehoiachin king of Judah and brought him out of prison; ³²and he spoke kindly to him, and gave him a seat above the seats of the kings who were with him in Babylon. ³³So Jehoiachin put off his prison garments. And every day of his life he dined regularly at the king's table; ³⁴as for his allowance, a regular allowance was given him by the king according to his daily need, until the day of his death as long as he lived.

Chapter 52 is taken directly from 2 Kgs 24:18 to 25:30 to establish the details of the last days so that the narrative in chaps. 37-44 can be better understood by the readers. The differences between the account in Kings and in Jer 52 are minor, but we do learn a few details from one that seem to be lacking in the other. In Jer 52:10 we learn that many of the princes were executed along with the sons of Zedekiah. 2 Kgs 24:7 leaves this out. Also, 2 Kgs 25:22-26 tells the story of Gedaliah's assassination, but Jer 52 has removed it since the whole event fills chaps. 40-41 already. The list of treasures taken from the temple is expanded quite a bit in Jer 52:17-23. The list of captives deported to Babylon, given in Jer 52:28-30, cannot be found in 2 Kgs 25, but there is at least some parallel in the listing of captives from the first conquest of Jerusalem in 598 provided by 2 Kgs 24:14, 16.

The entire chapter has four sections: vv. 1-16 relate the events surrounding the fall of the city in 587; vv. 17-23 list the treasures taken from the temple and brought to Babylon; vv. 24-30 name those executed and deported, and vv. 31-34 report the release of king Jehoiachin from prison to a place of honor among the courtiers in Babylon in his last days. It may be intended as a final note of hopefulness.

The narrative about the siege and fall generally parallels the more detailed account we have seen in Jer 39-41. The siege lasted from January, 588, down to July or August of 587, a good year and a half. Verse 8 tells us a new fact lacking in 39:5; namely that the royal troops were scattered when the Babylonians captured the fleeing Zedekiah. These same troops may have been the guerrilla bands whom Gedaliah managed to win over to his side in 40:7-9. It also confirms the fact that the general Nebuzaradan did come only a month after the battle was over; he carried specific orders to burn the city and tear down its walls so that it could not serve as a center again, and to bring back the treasures of the temple and palace to Babylon.

The listing of the booty sent back to Babylon concentrates on those of valuable metals, gold, silver or bronze. The audit taken after the Exile when the Persians gave back the stolen vessels found in Babylon listed thousands, even though no indication of such quantities is found in Jer 52; see Ezra 1:7-11 for the details. The Jeremiah text lists the basins, small bowls, pots, lampstands, incense dishes and libation vessels in vv. 18-19 that are passed over in 2 Kgs 25:13-17. Jeremiah also mentions the twelve bronze bulls (v. 20), and describes the two pillars in colorful detail, including the number of pomegranates decorating the sides (v. 23). A good description of all these temple furnishings can be found in 1 Kgs 6-7 which reports Solomon's construction of the temple. One problem of historical interest arises from the note that the Babylonians broke up the twelve bronze bulls that stood under the great basin of water. According to 2 Kgs 16:17, Ahaz had to cut off the bulls from the basin at the time of the Assyrian tribute in 734-732. Perhaps the later kings had replaced them.

The list of officials in vv. 24-30 represents most of the top leaders who would have prosecuted the war. The high priest was grandson of Josiah's high priest Hilkiah (according to the later remembrance in 1 Chron 6:13-15); Zephaniah, his assistant, may be the same man who dealt with Jeremiah over the letter of Shemaiah in 29:24-32. Besides the king's advisors, the army commanders and directors of personnel, sixty "people of the land" also were executed for their parts in the rebellion of Zedekiah. There has always been some confusion over whom these "people of the land" represented. In many cases in the Bible, they seem to be the landowners of large estates in the rural areas of Judah, but in Jeremiah the term often represents the ordinary people (see 37:2, 44:21) and may hint at a decimation of the army ranks by taking every 60th or 100th soldier for execution.

Verses 28-30 list three separate deportations of citizens. Since the total number reaches only 4,600 persons, we can assume that the repeated claim that only the poor were left in the land (39:10; 52:16) has been slightly exaggerated in order to stress that future hope lay only with those who went into exile. The detailed accounts of the assassination of Gedaliah and the Judean survivors' flight to Egypt also emphasize this point. Moreover, the 3000 deported in 598 make up the largest group of exiles, but is still far smaller than the number quoted in 2 Kgs 24:14, which lists 10,000. The more modest numbers in Jeremiah 52 should be preferred.

Jehoiachin went into exile in 598 after only three months' reign. Ezek 1:2 gives reason to believe that he was recognized as the rightful king even while his uncle Zedekiah had power (see remarks above on Jer 28:1-17). The 37th year of his captivity fell in 561, the year that Evil merodach (from the Babylonian *awil-marduk*, "man of Marduk," made into a pun in Hebrew, "Stupid man of Marduk") became king. The Weidner tablets listed Jehoiachin supplied comfortably by the Babylonian treasury in 592, so why he had ended up in prison in 562, isn't known. Possibly the rebellion in 588 had been seen by the Babylonian authorities as due to hopes aroused by his freedom to move around. In any case, Evil merodach granted amnesty to prisoners upon his accession to the throne as was customary in the East. Clearly, the Babylonians no longer saw any danger in an aging king of the Judeans some forty years after he had last lived in his native land.

For the editors of Jeremiah and for the author of the Book of Kings responsible for this last remark on the pre-exilic history of Israel, the freedom of Jehoiachin had great significance. It represented the continuation of the monarchy through long years of exile and captivity; and it rekindled hope that the promises of Jeremiah for restoration would soon be fulfilled. In fact, it gives a very positive twist to the turn of events, so that the prophecy of Jeremiah will not be taken as totally condemnatory or judgmental, but as a promise of rebuilding and hopefulness.

The Book of Habakkuk

INTRODUCTION TO THE
BOOK OF HABUKKUK

1. The New Testament and Habakkuk

In Christian churches, the small Book of the prophet Habakkuk has been more well-known for its use in the New Testament than it has been known for itself. In fact, its fame rests on the quotation of a single thought from Hab 2:4-5, "The just shall live by faith" (King James rendering of Rom 1:17 and Gal 3:11) which appears in St. Paul twice and in the Letter to the Hebrews once (Heb 10:37-38). Paul found in this passage from Habakkuk an answer to the difficult problem of why his gentile pagan converts could become Christians without first accepting the Jewish Law of Moses and its regulations. The first disciples had all been Jews who practiced their Judaism faithfully while also expressing faith in Jesus the Risen Lord (see Acts 2:46-47 for an idealized description of the first Christian groups in Jerusalem, and Acts 15 and Gal 2:1-14 for the conflicts that arose when non-Jews were first admitted to the community). Paul appealed beyond the necessity of the Law as a way of life to other parts of the Old Testament that showed examples of faith in God without the mention of the Law. His favorite was Abraham, who believed in the promises of God long before Moses ever lived or received the Law. In both Rom 4 and Gal 3, he argues that Abraham received God's blessing because of his faith alone. But Paul also liked Habukkuk as an authority for why the Churches should admit gentiles with nothing more than faith in Jesus as the Risen Savior. Hab 2:3-4 was a prophetic word from God which seemed to go beyond observance of the commandments of Moses to a new level of trust that God would act anew in a coming age. Paul naturally interpreted the prophet to be speaking of Christ's coming.

About the same time, the unknown author of the Letter to the Hebrews wrote to his community or communities, who knew Jewish Law well, and quoted the same verses of Habakkuk in urging them to hold onto their new faith in Jesus despite ups and downs and the seemingly endless delay in his Second Coming. This author found in Habakkuk an excellent example of advice to those who become discouraged at the apparent victory of evil over good, or who insist that God act according to the rules and written explanations of the Law as they think he should. True faith must wait patiently and trustingly for God to take the initiative.

We have spent time on these New Testament quotations of Habakkuk because so many readers of the Bible never get beyond the mention by St. Paul to really look at the original prophet and discover why Paul or the author of Hebrews found it such a rich source of reflection. By the time we have gone through this brief commentary, we will certainly understand better how faithful Paul and Hebrews were to the spirit of Habakkuk, and we will discover that there was much more to Habakkuk than only one message. Habakkuk never knew of a coming figure of Jesus Christ, and if the early Christians did see in his words the hand of God revealing a new dimension beyond the vision of the prophet, this did not destroy or render useless the lessons that he tried to make for his own day and age. An Old Testament commentary has the duty to bring alive the urgency and the relevance of the prophets in their own setting and in their own frame of thought so that modern readers can understand and learn from the Israelites their experience of faith and their divine encounter. Because Habakkuk became so important to Christian interpretation, it provides us with one of the best examples of how an Old Testament word of faith was able to speak in a new way to later generations without losing the power of its original message.

2. Date and Origin of the Book

Mention of Babylon in the first chapter as the instrument of God against Judah helps us to identify the general time frame of the book's events as the late 7th and early 6th centuries. But very little is known of the prophet behind the text. Verse 1 gives only his name and affirms that he was indeed a prophet. All other information must be gleaned from internal hints within the prophecies themselves. A late story in Greek called *Bel and the Dragon* is included among Catholic Bibles as chap. 14 of the Book of Daniel. From it comes the famous story of Daniel in the lion's den in which an angel picks up the prophet Habakkuk by the hair in Judah and transports him and his bowl of porridge to Babylon to feed the imprisoned Daniel and then returns him back home again (Dan 14:32-38). While we cannot trust this fanciful story as a source of reliable information, still it probably developed in circles that read the preaching of Habakkuk against Babylon, and so it largely depends on our present biblical book. The Septuagint has also added a heading that calls Habakkuk the "son of Jesus of the tribe of Levi," but this too cannot be verified and may well result from the psalm format in chap. 3 which could suggest that the author was a levite singer according to the directions of 1 Chron 23 and 25. In Christian times, Pseudo-Epiphanius wrote a *Lives of the Prophets* in which he identified the home of Habakkuk in southern Judah and noted that his tomb was still pointed out in a town called

Keilah. Even if these details cannot be historically ascertained, at least they agree with the general information supplied by the book itself.

In Jewish tradition, the book can be divided into two chapters of narrative and one of prayer. Certainly the third chapter, which has its own heading, forms an independent psalm within the whole. Most scholars also agree that the first two chapters should be divided into two parts with the dividing line somewhere around 2:5. The first section contains a dialogue between that prophet and God which alternates the prophet's lament with a response from God in the form of an oracle. The second part beginning with 2:6 (or a half verse earlier as we shall see) offers a series of five woes against a foreign enemy that runs to the end of chap. 2. Each of these three major sections can be further analyzed into smaller units for the purpose of fuller understanding, but the whole book gives an impression of harmony and cohesiveness rather than of disparate chunks thrown together in a rockpile. The outline followed in this commentary can be diagrammed so:

1:1   Label for the whole book
1:2—2:5a   Dialogue of the prophet with God
2:5b-20   Series of woe oracles
3:1-19   Psalm of the prophet

Nevertheless, despite the apparent unity of the book, commentators have carried on lively argument over both the authenticity of its parts and even the date of its setting. To a trained eye, many inconsistencies stand out in Habakkuk. These include the mixture of references to foreign enemies with condemnation of Judah. Most prophets keep the two separate. Another is exact identification of the enemy nation. Despite the reference in 1:6 to the "Chaldeans," a term gradually used of the Babylonians (see Jer 50:1), critics have sought to name the Assyrians, Egyptians, Greeks, Scythians, and Seleucid Syrians as the real enemy. Another question arises from the rapid changes in style and literary form from section to section. To many scholars, these shifts look suspiciously like additions or later comments that have been edited into the text of an original prophet. The most serious difficulty of this type involves the last chapter with its own heading and musical notation. Was this attached to the *real* prophecy of Habakkuk in chaps. 1-2, or did the prophet make use of a psalm to round off his message? Or, even more unorthodox to some experts, could he have been both prophet and psalmist? Finally, a great number of commentators have claimed that the thought patterns are lacking in logic and with a careful re-arranging of some verses, a clearer and more "correct" text will emerge.

No one can deny the great wealth of literary genres and forms used in this one short book. They give it much of its drama and power. But this fact alone does not tell us much about the composition of the book. Eighty years ago, a critic would credit each different genre to a different author, but we have come to understand so much more about poetic and prophetic literary style in recent decades that we now appreciate the Hebrew genius for mixing and interlocking varied styles and forms together. Even changes from direct address to third person narrative don't bother a modern student of the Psalms since the line between poetry and sermon, story and message was much less rigid than in modern literature. When we examine the total Book of Habakkuk, instead of focusing on individual parts, we find that the interesting little literary units do build toward a single climax in which the oracles and poetry, the dialogues and woes, all reinforce the same message of trust in the God who will act on behalf of Israel.

The only reasonable setting for such a unified book will be the same crucial historical period of the Babylonian rise to power and final conquest of Judah and its capital Jerusalem that gives us the books of Jeremiah, Ezekiel, Zephaniah and Nahum, as well as the Deuteronomistic history of Joshua, Judges, Samuel and Kings. These represent

Israelite response to the shocking and absolutely devastating end of all its hopes in the kingship, the temple, and the Promised Land of Palestine as signs of God's unbroken care. Given the rapid nature of the changes in the world power balance—with Assyria collapsing, Egypt striving to regain its old power base in Palestine, and Babylon slowly rising over them all—Israel's own fortunes went up and down from year to year in the forty years from 626 to 586 B.C. Habakkuk's preaching may have extended over a large part of this time, just as did Jeremiah's. The most convincing dates to give for the various parts of our book might be listed as follows:

1:2-4 which speaks of injustice in Israel can be best understood in the reign of king Jehoiakim from 609 to 598.

1:5-11 which speaks of the Chaldean foe should be located after the great victory of Nebuchadrezzar over the Egyptians at Carchemesh in 605 B.C.

1:12-17 turns on the enemy as evil and probably dates to after the first siege of Jerusalem in 598 B.C.

2:1-4 most likely belongs to the same period as 1:12-17.

2:6-20 may well have been uttered first against the falling Assyrian empire between 626 and 612, when Nineveh went up in flames, but has been placed so that now it stands reused against Babylon itself—a power that seeks to become the new tyrant like the Assyria of old.

3:1-19 has some very archaic parts, making its core by far the oldest piece in the book, predating Habakkuk possibly by centuries. But it is updated to the time of the prophet and used as a conclusion.

3. History of Interpretation

Here we briefly sketch the position taken by this commentary. But although it wins wide acceptance today, in years past other commentaries have held greatly differing positions on the date of the material. The earliest rabbinic tradition in *Seder Olam Rabbah 20* places the prophet in the reign of Manasseh (about 688-642 B.C.). Karl Budde, the great German scholar on the prophets in the last century, reordered the text so that much of chap. 1 could be dated against the Assyrians; others have suggested that the book is a disguised tract against Alexander the Great and his Greek conquest between 330 and 322. Still others, even more skeptical, identify the "real" situation as the struggle of the Jews under Judas Maccabeus against the Seleucid kings of Syria in the 2nd century, B.C. At least one commentator allowed part of chap. 1 to the 7th century Habakkuk, with the rest written at the time of Cyrus the Great of Persia and his victory over the Babylonians in 539 B.C.

These last three suggestions all share belief that a widespread custom of writing prophecies under the name of famous heroes or prophets of old continued in a later age when prophecy no longer existed. The Book of Daniel has been composed in this manner, using the story and name of a legendary wise man of the past to speak to later generations. The similarities between Daniel, supposedly an exile in Babylon, who speaks to those suffering persecution in the Maccabean period (167-164 B.C.) through his prophecies and apocalytpic visions, and the Habakkuk figure who brings porridge to the imprisoned hero in *Bel and the Dragon* (Dan 14), has led some scholars to ask if our Book of Habakkuk is not modeled on the legendary figure and also written in prophetic and apocalyptic language for the post-exilic period. They usually cite the inconsistent nature of the text and the supposedly "advanced" nature of the theology which questions whether a good God can also allow evil. They also compare it to the so-called "late" Pss 37 or 73, which reveal wisdom reflections that they believe only developed in the post-exilic period about the same time as the Book of Qoheleth (Ecclesiastes).

None of these arguments can carry much weight today. Recent research into Wisdom literature has shown that much of its thinking on the problem of good and evil has roots well back into the pre-exilic period of Israel's history. In fact, the nearest parallels come from Egyptian and Mesopotamian writings that can be dated before the existence of the Israelite nation. At the same time, investigation of the genre of apocalyptic, so characteristic of the Book of Daniel and other late books including the New Testament Gospels and Book of Revelation, has forced biblical scholars to abandon the belief that cosmic language belongs primarily to a late way of eschatological thinking. Modern study can trace the roots of much of the divine warrior vocabulary and cosmic description to the earliest poetry of Israel, formed in the tribal period and heavily indebted to the Ugaritic and Canaanite style of the late second millennium B.C. From this base, changes in such images as the Day of the Lord or Yahweh the Warrior continue to develop through the prophetic books before and after the exile. In this development, the language found in Habakkuk, esp. in chap. 3, belongs to the pre-apocalyptic stages found in Ezek 38-39 and Isa 24-27, rather than to the later visionary genre of Daniel, Revelation and such apocryphal works as I Enoch and IV Ezra.

One of the great helps in dealing with the text of Habakkuk has been the discovery of the first known commentary on the prophet among the famous scrolls in Qumran. It is what scholars call a *pesher*, a running comment on each verse that applies the original message to a new situation many centuries later. Since Qumran was the center of a sect of Judaism called the Essenes, in the century before Christ, the authors of this *pesher* reinterpreted all of the threats and prophecies directed against the "Chaldeans" to apply to the "Kittim," a code name for the Roman empire; and applied all the oracles against Judah to the ruling priestly and pharisaical leaders of the religious establishment in Jerusalem. This Qumran commentary is not complete, but it does provide enough information so that we know that the Essenes read almost the identical text as we possess today, even if their interpretation of it might differ greatly. The greatest surprise was that it did not include chap. 3, the psalm of Habakkuk. Scholars who had held that this psalm was a very late work, added on by editors to increase the apocalyptic thrust in the book, were pleased at this confirmation of their position. However, the answer may not be that simple. We don't know why the writers of the Qumran *pesher* did not include this psalm. Possibly they were not acquainted with it, but this seems highly unlikely in view of its appearance in the even earlier Greek translation, the Septuagint. More likely, they specially excluded it because it was not strictly prophecy at all, but a liturgical song. For this reason, it did not lend itself to their hidden predictions of the future. Another possibility is that it did not agree with their ideas about the Messiah, and so was left out.

4. Cultic Prophecy and Habakkuk

The express liturgical overtones of chap. 3 and its unusual combination of prophecy and psalmody have long led commentators to explore the possibility that Habakkuk, like Nahum, represents the words of an official "cult prophet." Unlike an Isaiah, Amos or Jeremiah, who showed a great deal of independence from any official institutions of priesthood or royal court, these cultic prophets played a regular role in the religious services of the temple. They are mentioned only rarely in our Bibles, almost always as passing references in the prophetic books (Amos 7:14-15; Jer 8:1, 10; 13:13; 14:13-14; 23:11, 15; 28:1), but never in the official lists of temple personnel gathered by the Book of Chronicles (1 Chron 23-27) or elsewhere (Num 3-4). If knowledge of the cult prophet depended only on explicit mention in one or another text, we could not even be sure they existed at all, for in the final edition of the Pentateuch and Prophetic Books after the exile, only priestly and levitical jobs are defined. Temple prophecy had either died out as an acceptable means of finding God's will for the community, or more probably, it had been suppressed as unreliable. Thus for the post-exilic Israel, there was no reason or interest in preserving information about such roles. This became all the more true as Israel began to cherish and preserve the oracles and lives of the prophets who stood apart from the official temple establishment and had challenged them.

Still modern scholarship generally accepts the existence of such cultic prophets, partly because they played a part in all other Ancient Near Eastern religions of the time, and partly because of hints within the Scriptures themselves, especially in the Psalms. The so-called "prophetic psalms" (*e.g.,* Pss 14, 15, 81) convey many of the themes and concerns of our major prophetic books, and seem to have been used or pronounced in the liturgical services. Other psalms which open with laments and petitions to God for healing and salvation suddenly change to thanksgiving for blessings received. An example is Ps 22 where the break comes after v. 21. Commentators commonly believe that a prophet (or a priest) delivered an oracle of blessing at this point assuring the petitioner that God would heal him or her. Other clues appear in prophetic books such as Second Isaiah (Isa 40-55), where the style of the oracles imitates that of liturgical hymns found among those in the Book of Psalms.

Further comparisons to prophetic personnel in the religious rites of Babylon and Assyria provide a clearer picture of how such cult prophets may have functioned in Israel. Israel's liturgy for major feasts such as the New Year, or Feast of Booths, which fell in the Autumn months of September and October would involve actions and processions in which the high point was God's manifestation of his glory and presence. How this "theophany" or divine appearance took place can only be guessed at, but one possible means was an unveiling of the Ark of the Covenant after processing around the temple grounds. In any case, many of our psalms were composed for the procession of the people, the unveiling of the Ark, or as a response to "seeing" God's awesome presence (*cf.*, Pss 15; 24; 29; 93; 96-98; 146; 148). At some point in the liturgy, prophetic personnel would be called on to deliver a word of the Lord expressing the hoped-for blessing or promise of salvation, victory, fertility of the fields, healing, or whatever was needed. Possibly the prophet composed the poem in advance and recited it on cue; more likely he (or she) uttered it under charismatic inspiration. Whether the moment of revelation was a fixed point in the liturgical sequence or came upon the prophet unexpectedly during the course of the ceremonies cannot be determined.

This portrait has been built up through clues gathered from many scattered biblical texts and from the models taken from pagan neighbors. It must be considered only an educated guess at this point, but it does make sense out of many puzzling aspects of prophetic and psalm structures. And it certainly helps to make sense out of Habakkuk. If we envision the whole of the book as parts of a liturgical action, then the lack of any mention of historical kings or individuals, the mix of dialogues and hymns, the repetitious list of "woes," the interweaving of national events and cosmic theophanies can all find a place. We do not need to suppose that this collection of three chapters makes up the rubrics for a single celebration on one New Year's feast in the middle of the Babylonian crisis. Rather it may be more of the genre of a "Best of Habakkuk," in which an editor has put together the landmark pronouncements of the prophet which can best serve as lessons and reflections for future generations both in liturgy and in private use. See the introductory remarks to chap. 3 for more details about the liturgical aspects of individual verses.

5. Major Themes

Another way to approach the problem of the unity of the book begins with the search for major themes that tie the three chapters together. Most notable of these is the prophet's questioning of how God will answer the problem of the wicked. It takes many forms: in 1:2-4, it is a rhetorical cry of anguish; in 1:5-11, an oracle announcing that God uses pagan nations as instruments of his justice; in 1:12-17, another lament on why the wicked prosper and why pagan nations whom God uses turn into oppressors; in 2:1-5, the prophet's call for an answer and God's response; in 2:6-20, the lessons of God's justice spelled out; in 3:1-19, a psalm of trust in the face of adversity. Habakkuk's message is clear: the Lord is *always faithful* to the just and acts on their behalf; they in response must be *patient* and *trust* entirely and solely in him. He explores the interlocked human doubts about divine justice, the silence of God, the apparent success of evildoers, the value of faithful observance of God's commandments.

Another facet of Habakkuk's prophecy deals with the ability to live with uncertainty. Trust in God is possible even if we do not always understand how the divine plan will work out. In this regard, the book draws on many themes found in the wisdom literature and stands closest to Pss 37; 49; 73 and 119, the traditional Wisdom Psalms. The right to question must be coupled with a dignified and patient trust. Unlike Nahum, who expects God to act soon, Habakkuk counsels against anguished impatience. His realistic understanding of suffering and evil in the world opposes any false hopes and optimism. The person who cannot relay quietly on God as a support tries to impose his or her own all-too-human demands and vengeful feelings on the divine will. Even as the people rejoice that opponents are getting theirs, they complain bitterly about tragedy that befalls them. This attitude shares the same arrogance condemned by Habakkuk, an attitude that cannot stand alongside the call to trust which God gives the prophet to proclaim. God does not act in haste, for as Ps 90:4 says, "a thousand years are as yesterday in his sight." But as the woes of 2:6-20 point out, evil sows the seeds of its own destruction. Evil may endure much longer than a Nahum foresaw, but at no time could it triumph over God's control of history.

The confidence in God's plan, so strongly a part of the message of Isaiah (Isa 7:4-7; 10:5-15; 30:15) and Jeremiah (26:3; 32:19; 49:20; 51:12; 51:29) stands out also in Habakkuk. The entire book and its wrestling with the power of evil and arrogant force carries the underlying conviction that God has an iron control over the outcome of history and alone exercises the universal rule over all nations near and far. This intense faith reaches its peak in the hymn of chap. 3 in which the victory of God over both internal evil and foreign oppression is described in cosmic language that involves the whole of creation and all its visible and invisible powers.

Finally, we may also note in Habakkuk a strong interest in the wrong use of national power. He must struggle with the divine word that announces Babylon to be a divinely appointed means of punishing his own people's sin, and yet watch while they use violence and oppression and terror for the honor and glory of themselves and their pagan gods. Babylon's greatest sin involves *hubris*, perfectly expressed in 1:16 in which they offer divine worship to their own weapons, the symbols of their own might and excellence. The prophet's book answers all who, like the Babylonians, justify their crimes of violence and greed in the name of their own important positions or rights. Even in our own age, individual and political crimes of terror, intrusion of privacy, and random violence seem to go unpunished much more often than not. Habakkuk counsels trust among the victims and those who "hunger and thirst for justice" that there is a power working against individuals and nations seeking evil ends by force—the God of the covenant, the God of Israel, the God who promises that the just person by fidelity will live (2:4).

Paul and the Letter to the Hebrews may have applied the message of Habakkuk only to their new proclamation of faith in Christ, but they did so by capturing the heart of his prophetic word—that nothing but faith in God as savior gives meaning to the uncertain questions and threatening powers of death and evil in this life. But Judaism itself has also appreciated this truth. In the Babylonian Talmud, Rabbi Simlai stated that Habakkuk had based all 613 commandments of the Torah (Pentateuch) on the single statement of 2:4: "The just shall live by faith" (Makkoth 24a).

HABAKKUK 1:1 – 2:5a
A CRY FOR DIVINE JUSTICE

THE FIRST PART of Habakkuk can be subdivided into four units, 1:2-4, 5-11, 12-17 and 2:1-5a, headed by the label for the whole book in 1:1. The four sections follow a distinct pattern of lament-oracle-lament-oracle in a kind of dialogue between the prophet and God. Each lament follows a set pattern which opens with a rhetorical question challenging God's action, followed by a second question of "why?", and then by a description of the terrible effects that are going to result. This last segment is introduced by a "therefore . . . (such and such is happening)."

This four-part series makes up what many scholars call a "prophetic liturgy." One must envision a service in which the congregation (or the prophet) expresses aloud the people's prayer, and the prophet responds with an oracle of consolation and hope. Scholars who tend toward a strongly liturgical interpretation for much of the Bible, such as Sigmund Mowinckel, consider all of 1:2—2:5a to be composed for a given occasion; those that stress form-critical analysis, such as Gerhard von Rad or Walther Zimmerli, view the four segments as independent pieces that were combined by editors. Nevertheless, 1:2-4 and 1:12-17, the two laments, show a strong similarity in themes, contrasting the just with the wicked, and using the same terminology for evil and iniquity. If they do not come from the same situation, they certainly have been chosen because of their parallel ideas.

On the other hand, the first oracle in 1:5-11 seems to deal more with the question of the foreign nation than with the punishment of a sinful Judah, and has sometimes been considered a late intrusion into an originally unified lament made up of 1:2-4 and 1:12-13 at least. These critics consider the continuation of the lament in 1:14-17 to come from the same secondary source as 1:5-11 because it deals with the pride of the foreign power. Thus opinion on the structure of chap. 1 has been sharply divided. Some claim two separate sources have been interwoven: (A) 1:2-4, 12-13a, 2:1-4, and (B) 1:5-11, 14-17. Others are disturbed by the apparent mixing of judgment against Judah with oracles against Babylon in the first chapter, and rearrange the material so that 1:2-4, 12-13 stand together, followed by 2:1-4 and 1:5-11. By putting this last unit at the end it stands next to the woes in 2:6-20 and keeps all the oracles mentioning a foreign power gathered in one place, and at the same time preserves a traditional order with the judgments against Israel in first position. These judgment oracles reach a climax in the great vision of the prophet in his watchtower in 2:1-5.

All of this minute discussion can best be put aside since the rhetorical power of the present arrangement is far more persuasive than the conflicting and uncertain guesses about a hypothetical original ordering of the material. 1:2-17 brings in the anguished concern of the prophet about the wickedness and deserved punishment of Judah along with his dismay at the arrogant ungodliness of the conquering Babylonians whom God is using. The answer to both questions comes in 2:1-5a.

1   The oracle of God which Habakkuk the prophet saw.

The first verse of the book forms a small label which tells us only that the prophet's name was Habakkuk and that he "saw" this oracle. The ecstatic and visionary nature

of the prophetic experience lies behind the frequent combination of "word" and "vision" in opening lines of
prophecy. Good examples can be found in Num 24:1-4,
15-16, Amos 1:1 and Isa 2:1. The special meaning of the
word *massa'*, "oracle," is discussed in the comments on
Nah 1:1, but the most unusual feature of this label is the use
of a title, *nabi'*, "prophet." Only the post-exilic prophets
Haggai and Zechariah are also called, "so-and-so, the
prophet." It may indicate that Habakkuk held an official
position, even possibly among the professional cultic
prophets of the temple; but we cannot be sure.

The name Habakkuk comes from the intensive form of
the verb "to embrace." It does not occur again in the
Hebrew Bible and we have no history of Habakkuk's
ministry, but Jewish tradition has identified Habakkuk
with the son of the Shunamite woman in 2 Kgs 4:16-17
because a form of the verb "embrace" occurs in the story
of his conception. This has been developed for Jewish piety
in the medieval mystical writings of the *Zohar* (1:7, 2:44-45).
But the tradition has no basis in recorded fact, and it is even
possible that the name comes from an Assyrian noun for
some kind of fragrant herb rather than from Hebrew at all.

> 2O LORD, how long shall I cry for help,
>   and thou wilt not hear?
> Or cry to thee "Violence!"
>   and thou wilt not save?
> 3Why dost thou make me see wrongs
>   and look upon trouble?
> Destruction and violence are before me;
>   strife and contention arise.
> 4So the law is slacked
>   and justice never goes forth.
> For the wicked surround the righteous,
>   so justice goes forth perverted.

The first small unit in 1:2-4 follows the classic psalm
lament format. The initial "how long, O Lord" occurs
regularly in the Psalter (Pss 13:1; 22:1; 74:10; 79:5; 88:1;

89:46; 94:3; etc.), and the list of evils that follows has all the richness of psalm expression: violence, iniquity, strife, contention, injustice. The piling up of nouns both intensifies and touches each listener's own experience. One word alone, *ḥamas*, "violence," runs like a theme melody through chaps. 1-2. It recurs in vv. 2, 3, 9 of chap. 1 and in 2:8, 17. The poignant cry of the prophet that God does not seem to hear or see evil, or fight for the just against the wicked, reminds us of the laments in Jeremiah's "Confessions" (Jer 11:18—12:6; 15:10-18; 17:14-18; 18:18-23; 20:7-18). In good psalm tradition, both Jeremiah and Habakkuk express the depths of disaster, not to revile God for his inaction or lack of care but to show the utter helplessness and weakness of the one who laments. The prophet expects God to take decisive action, but many times the form of divine action will be harsh oppression by a foreign conqueror. The prophet must prepare the people psychologically to accept such drastic punishment as the will of a just and merciful God.

The chaotic situation of evil contrasts sharply with the right order of law and judgment (vv. 3-4). One needs to read Psalm 119 to understand the deep love of God's covenant law (*torah*) that lies behind the grief of the prophet. One has but to look, to see the violence against the divine law. The prophet calls for a covenant lawsuit, a trial in the heavenly court in which God will declare the violent and unjust guilty and will execute his final punishment upon them.

> [5]Look among the nations, and see;
>   wonder and be astounded.
> For I am doing a work in your days
>   that you would not believe if told.
> [6]For lo, I am rousing the Chaldeans,
>   that bitter and hasty nation,
> who march through the breadth of the earth,
>   to seize habitations not their own.

God's answer comes to Habakkuk's cry in vv. 5-11. This passage has several problems including the exact meaning of some references, especially "the nations" in v. 5 and the "Chaldeans" in v. 6. One must take a stand on these texts because it matters greatly whether the prophet envisions the Babylonian conquest in 598-87 or some other period in history. The Hebrew word for "nations" looks very much like the word for "wrongdoers" in v. 13. If indeed a copyist made a mistake, then by changing "nations" to "wrong-doers" in v. 5 the entire passage will be directed to Judah as a warning rather than to the foreign nations as witnesses of God's power. Older scholars sometimes thought that this book was a pseudo-prophecy of Habakkuk really directed to the Greek invasion of Alexander the Great, and made a second change to read "Kittim" for "Chaldean" in v. 6. They interpreted Kittim as the Greeks since the word meant "islanders" or "coastdwellers." Later on, the Qumran *pesher* commentary understood the Kittim to be the Romans and also used Habakkuk to speak about them, but we know that the Qumran scribes had "Chaldeans" in their text even as they were re-applying it to the Roman Kittim.

Because of the overall setting of the book in the period from 609 to 586, it is preferable to maintain both "nations" and "Chaldeans" as the RSV has done. The oracle opens with a call for the nations to see and be in awe at what God will do. The other exilic prophets, Ezekiel and Second Isaiah, often refer to God's saving deeds as "wonders," miraculous and awesome signs of God's power that will convert unbelievers and unfaithful Israelites alike. For Israel, the narration of the many times that God acted on their behalf was an important part of worship. Alone among ancient peoples Israel had a keen sense of the historical nature of their existence as a nation. Once they had been nothing but a collection of disparate tribes with little in common but this oppression, very much like those remembered in the old tribal blessings of Gen 49. Then suddenly God did things for them: in Egypt, in the Sinai desert, in the wilderness of Kadesh Barnea, in Transjordan, in the conquest of Joshua. Their faith never forgot that the proclamation of God's merciful wonders past and present stood at the heart of their national life.

Habakkuk now announces that God's commissioning of the Babylonians stands in this tradition. The prophets often interpreted the aggressive invasions of foreign powers as not only allowed by God but as even "raised up" (Amos 6:14; Isa 10:5; Jer 5:15) or "sent" (Jer 49:37; Ezek 5:16; Joel 2:25; Hos 8:14) by him to be "instruments" of his punishment (Isa 10:5-15; 41:2-3; 42:24; 44:28; 45:1-6; Jer 5:14-19; 27:6-7; etc.). God employs them for his own purposes despite their pagan beliefs.

Prophetic rhetoric generally uses colorful and fearsome terms to describe the enemy forces (*cf.*, Deut 28:49-53; Isa 5:26-30; Jer 5:15-17; 6:22-23; etc.), and Habakkuk proves no exception. The Babylonians inspire dread by their appearance and by their reputation for ferocity; they need to take advice from no one, for their armies prove swifter than the famed Arabian wolf or an eagle swooping down on its victim (v. 8). The imagery gives the impression that the Babylonian cavalry were famed for their speed in responding to emergency flare-ups. Their king, Nebuchadnezzar, considers the petty leaders of other states with mocking scorn; his siege ramps can overwhelm any of their fortified cities. Like the wind is the royal "spirit." When the king changes his mind, he moves on where he wills. In his power, he is guilty of confusing his strength with that of a god, and considers himself possessed of divine authority. Success has made him drunk with pride.

> ¹⁴For thou makest men like the fish of the sea,
>   like crawling things that have no ruler.
> ¹⁵He brings all of them up with a hook,
>   he drags them out with his net,
> he gathers them in his seine;
>   so he rejoices and exults.

16Therefore he sacrifices to his net
   and burns incense to his seine;
for by them he lives in luxury,
   and his food is rich.
17Is he then to keep on emptying his net,
   and mercilessly slaying nations for ever?

The most natural explanation of vv. 12-17 sees them as a
later reflection on the actual course of events begun by the
Babylonian rise to power. Perhaps five or ten years have
passed since 609 or so when Habakkuk began to preach.
These verses form a second lament delivered not long before
the first siege of Jerusalem in 598, or even just shortly
after it. The prophet has Babylon firmly in mind as the
wicked power who swallows up the just in vv. 12-13. The
passage has been skillfully drawn to contrast the two
opponents. On the one hand Babylon, appointed as a rod of
judgment, committing treachery and injustice at will, and
using his weapons to pull nations apart and leaving them
leaderless. On the other Yahweh, a "rock" (Deut 32:4, 18,
30, 31; 2 Sam 23:3; Pss 18:2, 31; 95:1), the "holy" one (Isa
1:4, 5:16; 6:3), "eternal" (Pss 90:2; 93:2; Deut 33:27) and a
god who will not live with evil (Ps 5:4-5). This confrontation
should have been no contest at all except that God seems
to keep silence and let Babylon continue its evil ways under
its pretense of giving "correction" and establishing "judgment" in Israel. The prophet is deeply troubled by God's
apparent acceptance of a pagan evil far worse than the sins
Judah had committed in the first place. It brings back all
of the searching questions about God's justice when a
punisher exceeds his role and becomes worse than the
sinner.

Verses 14-17 describe Babylon like some fisherman who
sweeps up everything and anything into his nets or onto
his baithooks. People become no better than animals or
even insects to him, and he delights in his total power over
the helpless creatures snared in his control. The challenge

to divine authority comes out once more in the reference to fishes and creeping things, created by God on the fifth day (Gen 1:20-22), and now claimed by a new master of creation, Babylon. Even the image of the fisherman over nations makes a mockery of divine power, for the traditional imagery portrays God himself as the fisherman (Ezek 29:1-3; 32:1-3; Jer 16:16). The *hubris* reaches its climax when the Babylonians offer divine worship to their own weapons of war, the symbols of their own self-importance. Herodotus once described the Scythians offering sacrifice to a sword (*History* IV:62), and Alexander the Great dedicated the siege engine which had conquered the city of Tyre in its chief temple (Arrian, *Anabasis* II, 24, 6); so Habakkuk may have a touch of mockery at such pagan tendencies to confuse the tool with the maker and controller of the tool. Second Isaiah heaped similar scorn on pagan idol makers (Isa 44:9-20).

> **2** I will take my stand to watch,
>   and station myself on the tower,
> and look forth to see what he will say to me,
>   and what I will answer concerning my complaint.
> ³And the LORD answered me:
>   "Write the vision;
>   make it plain upon tablets,
>   so he may run who reads it.
> ³For still the vision awaits its time;
>   it hastens to the end—it will not lie.
> If it seem slow, wait for it;
>   it will surely come, it will not delay.
> ⁴Behold, he whose soul is not upright in him shall fail,
>   but the righteous shall live by his faith.
> ⁵Moreover, wine is treacherous;
>   the arrogant man shall not abide.
> His greed is as wide as Sheol;
>   like death he has never enough.

The final unit in this section describes the divine response to Habakkuk's plea. The involved preparation for the coming of the divine word found in 2:1-5 replaces the expected song of confidence and sure divine answer that lament psalms call for. Instead, a prophetic word is needed to break the divine silence. Habakkuk assumes the role of watchman to await God's message. The position was an important one for ancient cities. A useful description of how such watchmen stood alert for the coming of a messenger with good news occurs in 2 Kgs 9:17-20. The prophets picked up on this common scene in times of danger and described their own missions partly as messengers and partly as watchmen ready to call a warning or see in advance the coming divine actions. The classic examples of this prophetic consciousness are found in the Call Narratives of the prophets Jeremiah (1:11-17) and Ezekiel (3:16-21; 33:7-9). Its use reveals that the prophet did not just *bring* a message from God to the people; he believed that he must also *convince* a stubborn and heedless audience to listen and put the word into action.

Habakkuk did not have to wait long. The message comes as a vision which can be written down in plain words for all to read and understand, even if they happen to be running by in haste! But v. 3 prepares us that this divine response to Habakkuk's lament may not be fulfilled immediately. The prophet is to speak the word now, but the complete vision, that is, its fulfillment, has its own time, and will come when God determines. RSV's choice of "it hastens to the end," seems to contradict this need to wait for its delayed arrival. A better rendering of that line comes from translating the verb slightly differently: "it *witnesses* to the end." The "end" in prophetic thought has eschatological overtones, it will be a decisive future event that reveals God's judgment on a people or situation, and begins a new era or stage in the nation's history. Ezekiel employs it dramatically in his judgment oracles of chap. 7, and it becomes a favorite apocalyptic expression in the Book of Daniel (8:19; 11:13, 27, 35; 12:4-13).

Habakkuk assures the hearer that this will not be another false oracle like so many before (note the anger in prophetic condemnations of "lying oracles" in Mic 2:11; Hos 7:13; 12:1; Zeph 3:13 and especially in Ezek 13:6-19; 21:34; 22:28). Its visible effects may be slow, even much slower than hoped for, but when God does fulfill his word, it will be far greater than anyone ever dreamed of. The Qumran *pesher* on 2:3 notes that God may delay his fulfillment beyond any of the expectations of the prophets, but the "men of truth," those who rejoice in obeying the Law, never grow weary as they wait. Ps 116:10-11 echoes the message of this passage: "I kept my faith even when I said 'I am greatly afflicted,' and in my anguish spoke, 'All men lie!'"

Verses 4-5a state the message succinctly and sharply. Once again, RSV tends to weaken the clear contrast between the wicked and the just. By saying that a "soul is not upright" and that it "shall fail," the translators create a far too weak antithesis. The verb "fail" means rather "to be puffed up, arrogant," and the whole expression comes closer to the version in the NAB: "The rash man has no integrity." It would have been better to translate v. 4 generally as a contrasting couplet:

> Surely the arrogant person has no uprightness,
> But the just by steadfast fidelity will live.

The contrast may be between good and bad Israelites, but far more likely it refers to Babylon as the "puffed up" conqueror claiming divine status and acting against an Israel that places its trust solely in Yahweh its God. The "just" or "righteous" person stands opposite the "wicked" of 1:4, 13. The Hebrew concept of "fidelity" stresses the permanence and steady quality of loyalty. It can be used of marriage love in Hos 2:20, or of steady hands in Exod 17:12, or of trustworthy bankers in 2 Kgs 12:16.

In a footnote RSV points out that the next two lines which form the first half of v. 5 are obscure. The image of wine (*yayin*) after such a crucial statement about fidelity and life has always seemed out of place to commentators. Some have suggested we read similar-sounding Hebrew words that could make better sense, such as the word for "Greeks" (*yawen*), but that presupposes the text speaks to the invasion of Alexander the Great, which just does not make any sense of the rest of the book. A more likely possibility understands the word for "wealth" or "success" (*'on*) which places v. 5a as a comment and a parallel to the "puffed up" person of the preceding couplet. The new verse complements the thought of 4a and continues the contrast with 4b. Where the just will live because of fidelity, the arrogant and puffed up, fed by their success, will not abide. It makes a little rhetorical device much loved by Hebrew writers, a "sandwich," where the first and third verses enclose a middle verse with the opposite thought: (A) the arrogant lack all integrity / (B) but the just find life by being faithful / (C) these proud lose life because of their self-success.

The whole message of Habakkuk's prophecies is summed up in this special vision of vv. 4-5a. It was written or spoken in the crisis of Israel's apostasy and Babylon's cruel tyranny, but it now becomes a timeless word for all generations of believers in the power and promise of the covenant. God does not want political or international "success," he will not act simply to give political or immediate "benefits"; he asks for fidelity in patience, and he gives in turn his promise faithfully kept to those who wait patiently: life.

HABAKKUK 2:5b-20

CRITICS HAVE LONG BEEN DIVIDED over the place
of the five woe oracles in 2:5b-20. Many commentaries at
the beginning of the 20th century treated them as later
additions referring to some Judean tyrant of the post-
exilic period. Others saw them addressed to any number
of foreign powers: Assyria, Babylon, Egypt, Greece,
Seleucid Syria, or even the wild Scythian hordes. The
general imagery suggests nation against nation, and all
share a similar theme of vengeance against an oppressor
nation personified in various ways. This single overview
controls the first four woes and only the last one (vv. 18-19)
seems to stand apart as an aside on the nature of idol
worship. Their closest parallel lies in Jer 22:13-17 which
might date from about the same period if these do come
from the hand of Habakkuk. Possibly the prophet already
knew the words of Jeremiah.

The literary genre of Woe Oracles imitates the funeral
lamentation of professional mourning women. While
examples like David's lament over Saul in 2 Sam 1 gives
an idea of the deep expression of grief that funeral songs
can convey (*cf.*, also 1 Kgs 13:30), these others are mock
laments which carry a great deal of actual joy at the fate of
the victims. Masterful examples occur also in Ezek 26, 27,
31 and 32 against Tyre and Egypt, in Isa 14 against Babylon,
and to a lesser extent in Num 21:29; 24:23, and Amos 5:16.

The "mourning" masks a song of triumph that rejoices because vengeance has been taken. However, the form can also have a second use, namely to warn people to watch their step. Some scholars believe that they actually serve as the words of wisdom teachers who use many concrete and colorful examples to help the young learn to avoid danger. Even if this is so, in Habakkuk, they have now been applied to Babylon as confirmation of the preceding oracle in 2:4-5a.

Each woe has a threefold structure in which (1) the "woe to . . ." introduces the description of the evil act; (2) the richly deserved consequences are announced; and (3) the reason for divine retribution is given in a clause begun by the word "for . . . ." Some expand the description of the evil or the scope of the punishment more than others.

The section can be divided into (1) an introduction in vv. 5b-6a; (2) five woes in 6b-8, 9-11, 12-14, 15-17, 18-19, and (3) a conclusion in v. 20.

Habakkuk 2:5b-20
Judgment on the Nations

He gathers for himself all nations,
    and collects as his own all peoples."
6Shall not all these take up their taunt against him, in scoffing derision of him, and say,
"Woe to him who heaps up what is not his own—
    for how long?—
    and loads himself with pledges!"
7Will not your debtors suddenly arise,
    and those awake who will make you tremble?
    Then you will be booty for them.
8Because you have plundered many nations,
    all the remnant of the peoples shall plunder you,
for the blood of men and violence to the earth,
    to cities and all who dwell therein.

Many commentaries include v. 5b with the message of vv. 4-5a. But with only a slight re-reading of the Hebrew opening word, it can be joined to v. 6a to serve as the introduction for the following five sets of woes. In the Hebrew text, the phrase begins with the relative pronoun "whose," as though it continues the analysis of the arrogant nation. Accepting this reading, the RSV offers a fine interpretation. However, when looked at from another angle, the Hebrew word also spells the name "Assyria," and may initiate a taunt song directed against the nation in its time of collapse, similar to the Book of Nahum. That would date these verses originally to early in Habakkuk's career, probably around 612 B.C., although they have been reused here sometime later to apply the same message to the Babylonians. Thus either Habakkuk or his editors may be responsible for their insertion at this point. The passage borrows from Canaanite mythical language about the god Mot, who is described in the Ugaritic epic of Baal with "one lip stretched up to heaven, the other down to the nether-world" into which the god Baal must descend like a delicious tidbit of food, to be swallowed alive. Israelite poets liked the image, and variations on Death's appetite and wide-open mouth can be found in Isa 5:14, Prov 1:12, and Ps 141:7. The medieval representations of Christ's descent into Hell often show a monstrous mouth; and it has become part of our modern imagery, especially through Tennyson's *Charge of the Light Brigade*: "Into the jaws of Death, into the mouth of Hell rode the six hundred."

Death's appetite cannot be satisfied, nor can the craving for empire by the Babylonians and Assyrians. The oppressed nations and peoples take up their taunt against the tyrant in derision. Literally they take up their "proverb" and their "riddle." In Hebrew, the two words connote more than a clever saying or funny puzzle; they also signify a mocking chant whose verses capture the enduring truth, "evil does not pay," which the violent nation or person has forgotten. It promises that they will become the living example of that truth, a "proverb" so to speak, for future generations. The same two expressions recur in Mic 2:4; Jer 24:9; Ezek 17:2; 18:2, 3; 24:3; Isa 14:4; Deut 28:37 and Ps 44:15 with the same note of mockery.

The first woe in 6b-8 plays on the unjust money lender who suddenly must face the wrath of his victims when they suddenly rise up and demand all their payments be returned. The rapacious Babylon will itself be plundered, just as Assyria was when the Babylonians overran Nineveh in 612! Blood calls out for blood!

The second woe in vv. 9-11 pictures the greedy man who cheats and steals and tries to spirit it away to a safe place or respectable business, perhaps like the Mafia investing their payoffs in resort hotels or insurance companies. Isa 14:13 and Ezek 17 depict the eagle as a symbol of pride. Other prophets occasionally employ the image of an eagle escaping to its nest for security. In these cases, the bird stands for a foreign nation who cannot escape the divine vengeance by its flight (Isa 10:14; 16:2; Jer 49:16; Obad 4; and Num 24:21). So, too, Babylon's shameful greed in destroying nations to build up its dynasty and the glory of its royal house will prove its downfall when the very peoples who make up this glorious edifice rebel and rip apart the empire. The crime demands capital punishment in divine justice because it lacks all spirit of repentance (*cf.*, Prov 8:36: "The one who sins against me, forfeits his life; all who hate me love death!"). The Lord alone can maintain the national structures or let them fall into ruins (*cf.*, Ps 127:1-2; Lam 2:8 and esp. Jer 51:58).

The third woe shows strong similarities to a number of other prophetic texts. Building a city on blood and iniquity resembles Mic 3:10; tiring oneself out only to see it burned and come to nothing resembles Jer 51:58; and the earth filled with knowledge of the Lord as waters fill the sea nearly duplicates Isa 11:9. Many commentators use this fact to discount the originality of vv. 12-14. Like so much of prophetic language, however, originality is not a highly-valued quality. The inspiration for this woe, and for much of Habakkuk's thought, probably comes from Isaiah, one of the most original of all Israelite prophets. The mention of Lord of Hosts and the Glory of the Lord summons up the vocabulary of the temple and the Holy War, both characteristic of Isaiah (see esp. Isa 6), and later of Jeremiah, who regularly titles God the "Lord of hosts" (*yhwh Sebaoth* in Jer 2:19; 9:6; 11:17; 15:16; 19:11; 25;8, etc.). The glory of the great capital cities will be destroyed and all will come to know the power and awesome vindication of Israel's God who defends those maltreated and enslaved by overbearing rulers. The building metaphor continues the thought of the previous woe, in vv. 9-11.

> ¹⁵Woe to him who makes his neighbours drink
> of the cup of his wrath, and makes them drunk,
> to gaze on their shame!
> ¹⁶You will be sated with contempt instead of glory.
>
> Drink, yourself, and stagger!
> The cup in the LORD'S right hand will
> come around to you,
> and shame will come upon your glory!
> ¹⁷The violence done to Lebanon will overwhelm you;
> the destruction of the beasts will terrify you,
> for the blood of men and violence to the earth,
> to cities and all who dwell therein.

The fourth woe in vv. 15-17 adds more charges against Babylon. Prophets frequently use the metaphor of a cup of wrath to express divine punishment upon evil nations. The poisonous and bitter drink makes the recipient drunk, lose all control, be reduced to a pitiable mockery of his or her arrogant self. It creates a vivid contrast between the proud and self-controlled person and someone reduced to utter degradation and shame. See Isa 51:17-23; Jer 49:12-13; 51:7-8; Obad 15-16; Lam 4:21; Pss 11:6; 75:9, and above all the extended description of Jer 25:15-29. Closely tied to the drunkenness is the motif of nakedness and shame. The final indignity comes in being stripped naked like a prostitute found guilty or a man exposed to the laughter of all around him (compare the important incidents in Gen 9:20-27 and 19:32-38). Twice in v. 16 alone, the prophet sets Babylon's hoped-for "glory" over against the "shame" that it will actually receive. The reasons given for this punishment to Babylon derive from its cruelty to the Phoenician cities while conquering them. The invading armies leveled the forests and destroyed all the cattle (*cf.*, Isa 14:8). "May the same happen to you!" the prophet declares.

Verse 17 ends with the same refrain as in v. 8, "for the blood of men and violence to the earth, to cities and to all who dwell therein." Blood spilled cries out for vengeance (Ezek 24:7-8; Gen 37:26; Isa 26:21; Job 16:18; Hos 1:4; 2 Sam 16:8; 2 Kgs 9:7). Perhaps in this phrase, we have left only a part of an original refrain that would have followed each of the woes. But even as it is, the repetition indicates that cruelty and violence form Habakkuk's basic charge against Babylon.

The fifth woe occurs in vv. 18-19 but seems to be out of order in such a way that v. 19 should precede v. 18, so that it too can open with the "Woe to..." The motif of the vanity of pagan idols occurs also in Second Isaiah (Isa 40:1-20; 42:17; 44:9-20; 45:20; 46:7) and in Ezek 15:1-8 and Jer 10:3-9. It reflects a new insight for Israel gained during the time of exile as prisoners in Babylon. In that case, these verses have been added to Habakkuk to round out and complete the full list of crimes which Babylon has committed, and may come from the hands of Habakkuk's editors some twenty years or so after the prophet's own oracles. The idols teach lies, they cannot give revelation, they offer the exact opposite of the vision of Habakkuk announced in 2:3, a word that will not lie. By this antithesis, vv. 18-19 link the whole series of woes to the central message in 2:1-5a. RSV translates the famed Hebrew word *ruaḥ* as "breath" in the last line, but an ancient Israelite would have recognized the stronger overtones of Gen 1:2 and Ezek 37:14 in which the *ruaḥ* means the divine spirit, the creative and life-*giving* force.

The whole series now ends in v. 20 with a liturgical formula found also in Zeph 1:7 and Zech 2:17. It suggests a temple setting for the prophetic liturgy in which the proclamation of the oracles was followed by a call to worship in awe-filled silence. The "holy temple" (Mic 1:2; Jon 2:5, 8; Pss 11:4; 5:8; 79:1 and 138:2) mirrors on earth the true heavenly temple where the divine assembly worshipped before the glory of God (Pss 89:5-6; 82:1, and especially 11:4, "The Lord is in his holy temple, the Lord's throne is in heaven").

HABAKKUK 3:1-19

THE PSALM OF HABAKKUK

CHAPTER 3 OPENS with its own introductory label and sets off the poem before and after with musical instructions. It has a simple but elegant structure in four parts, arranged in a chiastic pattern of A:B: :B:A. It begins in v. 2 with a prayer that God remember his mercies of the past in order to act today. In this it resembles some of the older hymns of Israel: Jgs 5; Deut 33; Ps 77:17-20. And it closes in vv. 16-19 with a prayer accepting whatever God will do, but confident that he will indeed act on the psalmist's behalf. The middle of the psalm has two equal parts which give praise for the two chief aspects of divine power: God's saving love in the Exodus and history of Israel (vv. 3-7), and his lordship over all creation (vv. 8-15).

Most commentators have been impressed with the archaic elements of this chapter. The poem employs the same cosmic language found in very early Israelite poetry such as Ps 18 or Exod 15. The triple climactic parallelism, vv. 2, 8, 11, resembles the style of Ugaritic poems of the 13th century more than that of classical Hebrew psalms. The mythical imagery, too, has roots back into Canaanite literature and liturgy. And yet the whole fits nicely into the plan of the whole book. For example, the message about God's coming in glory gives an answer to the prayer of

Habakkuk in chap. 1, "How long, O Lord . . ." (vv. 2, 12) and provides the theophany expected by the call to awed silence in 2:20. The summary in vv. 17-18 jumps back over the psalm to echo the demand for trust expressed by the oracle in 2:4-5. Because of this integration with chaps. 1 and 2, it appears best to consider all of chap. 3 to come from the hand of Habakkuk himself. The prophet reworked very old material into a response to the divine word he had received.

The general introduction above discusses at some length the liturgical character of the Book of Habakkuk. As we consider the psalm of chap. 3 in detail, it may be good to list briefly the more important cult aspects that tie this psalm to the rest of the book:

a) The prophet is titled a *nabi'* in 1:1, which apparently refers to a professional office. In Dan 14, he is further called a Levite.

b) The language of chaps. 1 and 2 mixes hymnic and prophetic vocabulary as much as does the explicit cultic hymn in chap. 3.

c) The format of a prophetic liturgy, with a lament followed by an oracle, is well known and fits Habakkuk as much as it does many of the psalms in the Psalter.

d) The psalm in chap. 3 shows strong prophetic influences, including detailed visionary experience of theophany, intercessory role, the mix of hearing and seeing, the ecstatic characteristics of a visionary in v. 16 (*cf.* Isa 21:3-4; Jer 23:9).

e) The use of the liturgical summons in 2:20 ties chap. 3 to what has gone before.

f) Chapter 3 does not relate divine acts of the past, but describes them liturgically as timeless events which are actually effective now (vv. 6, 7, 14, 16).

g) The shift from third person narrative to second person direct address in v. 8 typifies the liturgical telescoping of past, present and future.

h) The whole book has a dramatic quality which goes beyond a collection of past oracles, and resembles cult recitals.

i) The descriptive events in chap. 3 do not conform to the actual historical traditions of Israel found in Ps 77:17-20 or the Pentateuch, but consciously connect them to mythical (liturgical) language about God.

According to John Eaton the New Year's festival in the Fall offers the best setting for Habakkuk. The king and the people would gather to celebrate Yahweh's kingship over the world and to pray for salvation. This salvation concretely means (a) prayer for deliverance from foreign oppressors, and (b) fertility and rain for the year ahead. These two categories correspond neatly to the remembering of God's work in history (vv. 3-7) and of his dominion over the cosmic powers (vv. 8-15). At the same time, the festival fell in the Autumn change of seasons in which the hot winds of the desert alternated with the first rainstorms from the Mediterranean Sea. Verses 3-7 can represent the hot sirocco winds as symbols of God's approach in judgment from the East, and vv. 8-15 his opposite arrival as lord of fertility in the rainclouds of the West. They form the heart of the Fall New Year's feast. The battle between the two stormfronts represents the moment when chaos seems to be at its strongest. God comes then to save and deliver. In the face of withering desert heat at the end of a long dry summer the rains arrive with a bang—thunder and lightning and wind—to make possible the planting of the new crops. Psalm 144 reflects the same pattern and may also belong to the New Year's liturgy.

3 A prayer of Habakkuk the prophet,
   according to Shigionoth.
2O LORD, I have heard the report of thee,
   and thy work, O LORD, do I fear.

In the midst of the years renew it;
  in the midst of the years make it known;
  in wrath remember mercy.
3God came from Teman,
  and the Holy One from Mount Paran.
His glory covered the heavens,
  and the earth was full of his praise.

Selah

4His brightness was like the light,
  rays flashed from his hand;
  and there he veiled his power.
5Before him went pestilence,
  and plague followed close behind.
6He stood and measured the earth;
  he looked and shook the nations;
then the eternal mountains were scattered,
  the everlasting hills sank low.
  His ways were as of old.
7I saw the tents of Cushan in affliction;
the curtains of the land of Midian did tremble.

The *shigionoth* remains a mystery word. It may be a musical instrument, a special type of melody, or a class of lament psalms. Some scholars have looked to a Babylonian word, *shegu*, which means a "lament," for its meaning. But little lamentation can be found in this poem, rather it soars in praise of the Lord who marches forth to victory.

Verse 2 sets the stage for the dramatic recital of God's power by offering a prayer that God may do again what the prophet has heard so often about his saving deeds in the past. The report of God's work always inspires deep awe in the Israelite community and among nations (*cf.*, Num 14:15; Deut 2:25; Isa 66:19; Nah 3:19 and Ps 44:1-2). God will *remember*, that is *renew* his mercy in the midst of the years. The "midst of the years" may well refer to the moment of change from the old year to the new in the cultic celebration of New Year's.

The divine appearance, or theophany, takes the form of God as warrior marching to battle. It opens with an archaic title for "god," *'eloah* instead of *'elohim*, and conjures up for us echoes of the Sinai desert even though it never mentions it by name. God comes from Teman and from Paran, both mountainous areas to the South toward Sinai and often associated with the Midianites and Edomites. Other early poetry about the divine warrior also picture the victorious procession from the southern deserts near Sinai: Deut 33:2; Jgs 5:4; Ps 68:16-17. His brightness and glory radiate from him. If the author imagines the desert sandstorms of the sirocco in his vision, he describes here the heat lightning and the diffused glow as the sand hides the sun. The storm gods of the Canaanites are usually depicted with the thunderbolt and lightning shaft as weapons in their hands. Job 36:32 says that God covers his hand with the lightning as he sends it forth. And Babylonian statues of the gods sometimes have rays projecting from them as signs of their glory.

The two companions, plague and pestilence, are the products of disaster, whether the prolonged sandstorm or warfare. Like all warrior gods, Yahweh must have his attendants in battle, just as Ares, the Greek god of war, had "Fear and Terror," and Marduk had attendants of wind and storm to accompany him against the fearsome monster Tiamat in the Creation story of the *Enuma Elish*. *Resheph*, the noun for "plague" in Hebrew, was a god in Canaanite myth and often associated with Baal the storm god. These helpers are personifications of the tragic results of war, and the Israelite use of them with Yahweh comes from a conviction that God permits war as punishment for infidelity and evil.

Another aspect of God's coming is the shaking of the earth. Verse 6 seems to speak of God "measuring" the earth. This image may signify God's "rule," if we are permitted a pun, but many commentators believe that the verb actually means "to convulse" and is exactly parallel to the second

line of the verse, so that four expressions of terror follow
in a row: God convulses the earth, shakes the nations,
splits the mountains, and brings low the hills as he goes on
his eternal path. The immediacy of the language suggests
that this manifestation is cultic, acted out now in liturgy,
not centuries ago. The description then closes with a
reference back to the land of the south. Cushan is probably
a poetic variant for Midian (see the possible reference in
Num 12:1 where Cush and Midian are the same). It recreates the timeless sense of theophany back at the desert
tents around the foot of the Sinai mountains. Midian
typified the enemies that Israel had to overcome in their
exodus wanderings (Num 25 and 31; Jgs 6-8).

> [8]Was thy wrath against the rivers, O LORD?
>   Was thy anger against the rivers,
>   or thy indignation against the sea,
>   when thou didst ride upon thy horses,
>   upon thy chariot of victory?
> [9]Thou didst strip the sheath from thy bow,
>   and put the arrows to the string.
>   *Selah*
>   Thou didst cleave the earth with rivers.

The thought changes abruptly in v. 8 away from the
desert to the rivers and water, symbols of the watery chaos
which the gods had to conquer before the world could be
ordered and subjected to divine goodness and security.
The mythological plot of a battle between the king of the
gods, whether *Marduk* in Babylon or *Baal* in Ugarit, and
the god of the sea, whether *Tiamat* in Babylon or *Yamm* in
Ugarit, formed the central event of pagan creation faith.
Israelite poets often borrowed aspects of this myth to show
Yahweh's superiority to the pagan gods and to prove he
did not need to fight another divine being to gain mastery
over the world. This becomes very clear in Habakkuk where
he certainly alludes to the battle (as does Gen 1:2), although

victory is assured. The mention of the bared bow recalls a famed Babylonian portrait of Marduk standing over the dragon with his bow in his hand (*ANEP* #523) and the chariot recalls the title of Baal and Yahweh both as "Rider on the backs of the Clouds" (see Ps 68:4, 33). "The Deep" in both Gen 1:2 and Hab 3:10 is the Hebrew equivalent of the chaos goddess *Tiamat*; even the name comes from the same root: *tehom*. Ps 77:17-20 has almost the identical language as vv. 10-11, and Ps 74:12-17 resembles vv. 9 and 13 closely. Many of the same phrases and metaphors can be found in other hymns of praise of God's victory in battle (Exod 15; Jgs 5; Deut 33; Pss 18 and 68). These stem from very ancient liturgical traditions that bring together the forces of nature—the lightning, storms, volcanic fire, thunder, wind, flooding torrents—and the personal intervention of divine beings who use these frightful manifestations of natural power as their weapons. From what we know of pagan cult, we can be sure that Israel has borrowed almost all of these expressions from the Canaanites. Of course, Israel did not believe that God had to do battle in nature to gain control over chaos or to maintain his own position as God, but they found the language useful to show that Yahweh was greater than the other gods. Thus they were able to refute pagan claims on their own grounds. The warlike vocabulary also provided an excellent framework to proclaim Yahweh as a god who acted in history to defend Israel, to protect Israel, to bestow land and position on Israel. Because of this, even in Hab 3:8-15 the imagery moves from the cosmic level in 8-12 to the benefits that God gave to Israel in vv. 13-14: salvation for your people and your anointed king and the destruction of the enemy and its army. It then returns to the cosmic defeat of the sea in v. 15, which recalls the metaphors in Ps 77:20; Deut 33:26-27 and Isa 43:16-17. Most of all, however, it recalls to the ears of faith the greatest of Yahweh's acts of salvation, the passage through the Red Sea narrated in Exod 14-15. In that hour the divine warrior decisively destroyed

the arrogant power of the pharaoh, the man who claimed
to be a god. It makes a fitting conclusion to a hymn which
expresses confidence that God will soon do the same to the
pride of a new tyrant nation, Babylon.

> [16]I hear, and my body trembles,
>   my lips quiver at the sound;
> rottenness enters into my bones,
>   my steps totter beneath me.
>
> I will quietly wait for the day of trouble
>   to come upon people who invade us.
>
> [17]Though the fig tree do not blossom,
>   nor fruit be on the vines,
> the produce of the olive fail
>   and the fields yield no food,
> the flock be cut off from the fold
>   and there be no herd in the stalls,
> [18]yet I will rejoice in the LORD,
>   I will joy in the God of my salvation,
> [19]GOD, the Lord, is my strength;
>   he makes my feet like hinds' feet,
>   he makes me tread upon my high places.
>
> To the choirmaster: with stringed instruments.

The final small unit in vv. 16-20 gives the people's response to the cultic proclamation of God's victory. The
prophet speaks on behalf of all believers when he offers
this prayer of confident trust. It opens with a traditional
description of the trembling fear that enters the body of a
person who receives tragic news or faces the coming of the
divine warrior. Other classic passages occur in Jer 6:22-23;
Isa 13:7-8; Ezek 21:11-12 (and see the further discussion at
Nah 2:10). But in this case, the prophet trembles not for
himself or for Israel, but for the pagan conqueror who does
not even know the power of the god of Israel. RSV's "rottenness enters into my bones" confuses the sense, and *rakab*,

the word for "rottenness" probably comes from still another Hebrew verb meaning "to shake" or "to tremble." The whole body reacts: the frame shakes, lips quiver, bones tremble, feet totter.

Verses 17-19 then state the words of trust. Even though all of nature fail completely, all the signs of divine blessing and bounty—the fig trees, the grape vines, the olive and the barley, the sheep and goats and cattle—still the prophet will sing the praise of Yahweh as giver of blessing! Habakkuk alludes to the cosmic powers in struggle, he even hints that the pagan belief that chaos was a divine power to be reckoned with may appear to be right. Yet he will still give faith only to Yahweh. To understand the profound courage of this answer, we must remember the close connection between success in farming and the divine blessing in Israelite thought. The Psalms are filled with such praise in God's goodness: "According to your loving kindness remember me, for your goodness' sake, O Lord!" (Ps 25:7); "Have mercy on me, O God, in your steadfast love, according to your abundant goodness, blot out all my sins" (Ps 51:1); "I will proclaim your name, O Lord, for it is good" (Ps 54:6); "Give thanks to the Lord, for he is good" (Ps 118:29).

The prophet's trusting words reflect his acceptance of the oracle of 2:4-5. Indeed, they express in a concise and unexcelled manner the meaning of the phrase "A just man shall live by fidelity." To help capture the spirit of Habakkuk in this, read for yourself Isa 54:1-10, another deeply moving hymn of confidence in the divine warrior. It, too, recalls the tents of the desert experience and the promise of God to give the people land; it calls on Israel to trust and not to fear; it proclaims God's love will endure as that of a husband for his wife, a love of everlasting compassion. It declares, in words very much like those of Habakkuk, that God will never let his steadfast love depart from Israel. Isa 54 expresses the promise, Hab 3:17-19 the total trust in that promise.

Verses 18 and 19 create a tightly knit union of joy and victory. Note how the author speaks of rejoicing in the *Lord* and taking joy in *God*, and then locks them together in reverse order, crying out that *God*, the *Lord* is my strength! Israelite prayers of trust generally bubble with a spirit of rejoicing that makes them unique in the ancient world: see Pss 5:11; 13:5-6; 16:11; 32:11; 33:1; 35:9; 47:1; 67:4 and many others. But just as characteristically, they look to victory and success from the strength that God gives his faithful people: Pss 18:46-48; 29:11; 68:35; 89:17-18. The hope that Israel will tread on its enemies and rule from the heights comes from the older divine warrior hymns in Deut 32:13; 33:29 and Ps 18:34. Just like the sure-footed mountain antelopes, Israel will be confident and right at home in its victory.

Modern readers may find themselves uncomfortable with the warlike spirit in the descriptive language in Habakkuk. But we must remember that the heart of the message of *salvation* stresses the expectation that God always acts in new ways because he is eternally faithful to us. What meant the most for Habakkuk in his time of constant military siege and threat of war was Yahweh's fidelity towards those who believed in him. God had fought for his people before, he would defend them again. But already the prophet understood that fidelity meant more than gaining victory over Babylon. He explores a deeper faith that trusts even when there is defeat and collapse of all the external structures of success. If Habakkuk could come to this insight in his day, how much the more does his message challenge us to understand a God who asks trust for the twentieth century in ways that go beyond the bankrupt solutions of war, political one-ups-manship, and selfish national goals. Both personally and socially, this book demands of its readers enough trust to seek God's new directions in our day. If we want to live, we must discover how to promote and to celebrate God's steadfast love through a just way of life. The just shall live by their fidelity, but they must have enough faith to live justly.

The Book of Zephaniah

THE BOOK OF ZEPHANIAH

INTRODUCTION

1. The Historical Background of the Book

THE OPENING LABEL tells us that Zephaniah preached his message in the days of Josiah. Since Josiah reigned from 640 until 609 B.C., and instituted one of the major reforms of Israelite religion in the middle of his rule (622 B.C.), it is desirable to know more exactly when Zephaniah was active. Scholars have long sought indications from within this short book about the circumstances under which the prophet worked, but the results have been uncertain. The book has only three chapters, and really a single theme, the Day of the Lord, so that traces of changing events cannot be isolated very easily. Some authors have been so doubtful that any period within the lifetime of Josiah fits the context of Zephaniah's message that they have discounted the label altogether and opted for a date in the reign of his son Jehoiakim, between 609 and 598.

In order to take seriously the claim of the book that it does come from Josiah's days, other scholars conclude that its stern tone of condemnation and warning best fits the time just before the great reform. The prophet gives more than ample evidence of the inroads of pagan religious practices in chap. 1. Could such a condemnation be leveled after Josiah had made tremendous efforts to remedy these very evils? But if it is that early, then what nation does the prophet envision who will come as a scourge to punish Judah? Since Babylon was just emerging into freedom at this moment, and Assyria was growing weaker rather than stronger under the attacks of the Medes, no known power in the area fits the needed description.

Many therefore propose an invasion of the Scythians, a wild horde of raiding warriors from southern Russia. Herodotus reports such an attack in his *History* (I:1-3-105) during the decade from 630 to 620. However, this Scythian raid has no independent confirmation, and has left no other trace on the records or literary memory of the Near East. Early commentaries discussed this possibility at great length and generally opted in its favor, but today few wish to stake their reputations on a great Scythian wave that disrupted the Mediterranean world of the time (see further remarks on the Scythians and the "foe from the north" in Jeremiah at Jer 4:5—6:30 in the preceding volume of this series).

If not the Scythians, then might the enemy simply be unknown, but expected to arise from the far corners of the world? Isa 13:5 calls up a distant nation against Babylon, while Ezek 38-39 names the distant northern power as Magog. The possibility of a traditional vocabulary of the far-distant scourge should not be ruled out in Zephaniah.

If, on the other hand, we wish to avoid the difficulty of finding a world power in the 620's, we can push the date of Zephaniah's ministry down closer to the time of Josiah's death in 609. This would provide the proper threat in the growing power of Babylon which ended the Assyrian empire in a series of bloody sieges of their major strongholds between 614 and 610. Moreover, the Books of Nahum and Jeremiah (chaps. 4, 6, 8) also make use of Babylon as a terrible scourge of God. But then we must still face the question of why the prophet judged his own nation so harshly while Josiah was working so hard for reform. Perhaps the reform touched only the institutions and did not win over the people from their private practices.

Jeremiah, too, makes little mention of the Josianic reform, and may have understood his prophetic task in those early years as a warning voice against still prevalent evils. Periods of renewal often stimulate even greater condemnations and sterner judgments against evil as the momentum of reform increases. We need only think of the great revival movements in the United States during the 19th century.

But several notable critics in recent years have abandoned any attempt to locate Zephaniah during the lifetime of Josiah. They point to the mention of a "remnant of Baal" in 1:4, the oracle against Cush in 2:12, and the prophecy against Ammon in 2:8 as evidence of events that occurred during Jehoiakim's years. The few devotees of Baal would be a post-reform remnant that escaped Josiah's purge, while Cush used as a name for Egypt reflects Israel's dismay at the deportation of Jehoahaz in 609, and anger at Ammon stems from their support of the Babylonian attack of 598. These commentators also point to the prediction of Assyria's fall in 2:13-15 as a *vaticinium ex eventu*—that is, the prophet composed it after the fall had already taken place! Some would detect echoes of deuteronomic language in 1:13, 17; 2:2, 7, and identify the prophet himself with "Zephaniah, the second priest," in 2 Kgs 25:18 (Jer 52:24), who was put to death by the Babylonians in 587. Indeed, it may even be the same Zephaniah who dealt with Jeremiah in 597 (Jer 29:29-32).

Most of this "evidence" for a later date has been strained terribly. By themselves, the pieces of evidence could never stand alone, and their combination doesn't give much better support. The deuteronomic language, for example, is so vague that it raises the opposite doubt, *i.e.*, why does the Book of Zephaniah not have more deuteronomic influence than it does?

All in all, despite the problems raised above, a date in the time of Josiah still appears convincing, although it could fall on either side of the reform of 622. This would make Zephaniah a contemporary of the early Jeremiah, and an important figure in his own right. If Zephaniah preached close to 626, then he may well be the first prophetic voice heard since the death of Isaiah sometime after 700 B.C. The reign of king Manasseh, although condemned by the deuteronomic thinkers (2 Kgs 21:10-15; 23:26-27), left no prophetic record of opposition. But the first chapter of Zephaniah gives us a valuable glimpse into just how far pagan cults and religious syncretism had gained a hold on Judah in the 7th century. The words of the prophet seem directed mostly to the upper class of Jerusalem, yet have no direct condemnation of oppression of the poor. Zephaniah himself may have been an aristocrat, or even a member of the royal family (see comments on 1:1). The setting of his work was Jerusalem (*cf.*, the geographical references in 1:4, 10).

2. *The Composition of the Book*

The present Book of Zephaniah can be divided into three major divisions corresponding to the plan laid down in Ezekiel some years later, in which oracles of judgment (1:1—2:3) are followed by condemnation of the foreign nations (2:4-15), and by a promise of restoration and hope mixed with judgment (3:1-20). Isaiah and (in the Greek version) Jeremiah also roughly reflect this structure. Theologically it provides a framework in which the divine word can move from threat to completion of its threat, and still claim the power eventually to save and to direct the destinies of nations. If prophetic oracles offered only judgment and destruction by foreign powers, the discouraged and defeated worshippers of Yahweh would turn to the stronger gods of these pagan nations for succor. Instead, the same Yahweh who must punish his people also promises to control the pretensions of foreign deities and will in turn bring them to judgment so that his justice will be worldwide. When all understand his dominion over world events, then will the stage be set to trust his promise of rebuilding Israel.

This threefold structure in Zephaniah is the result of careful editing, which has juxtaposed the separate units side by side even if they were spoken over a considerable number of years. Studies on Zephaniah have spent the largest amount of energy on trying to identify which verses came from Zephaniah and which are the products of later editors and traditionalists. This has led to widely different conclusions. Some, such as Charles Taylor, Jr. in the *Interpreter's Bible*, allow only a few core passages to Zephaniah, and see the rest as largely the product of an ongoing tradition. He accepts 1:7, 10, 11, 13a, 14-16; 2:1, 2a, 4-6, 7b, 12-14 as authentic, and maybe 3:1-7. The criterion for such radical surgery on the text involves vocabulary similarities to other books of the Old Testament, especially usages close to the language of Ezekiel or Second Isaiah, both of whom come after the time of Zephaniah. Most of the examples are single words, not even phrases or sections, and these isolated parallels do not mean much unless a close parallel in theological purpose and specific application to the exile can be pointed out. But none can with any clarity, and thus it is better to conclude that similarities in wording come from the common stock of expressions and popular vocabulary of the period as a whole. In fact, there are as many similarities to Jeremiah as there are to the later prophets, and chap. 3, often universally denied to Zephaniah, has the closest connections of all with the thought-world of Jeremiah!

In terms of an overall message, Zephaniah stands closest to the 8th century prophets Micah and Isaiah. The renewal of Zion, the call for trust in God, the condemnation of *hubris*, the notice of a remnant with which God will work, the mention of "Daughter of Zion," Sodom and Gomorrah, the unfaithful city, and the rebellious city, as well as the resonances of cult language, would be at home in Isaiah. Zephaniah may have been a cult prophet himself. The close connection among the three chapters favors that the entire message was delivered over a relatively short period of time, and possibly even in one Spring or Fall festival period.

Theodor Gaster (*Myth, Legend and Custom in the Old Testament*, p. 679) has suggested that the use of the verb to "sweep away" in 1:2-3 reflects the feast of Ingathering in the Fall. The words sound alike (*'asep/'esop* and *'asip*), and the setting would be perfect. The people had gathered to rejoice and give thanks for the harvest (Exod 23:16), but the prophet uses the occasion to denounce the pagan practices that they have introduced into its celebration. By a play on words, he turns the feast of confidence in Yahweh into a moment of impending judgment.

Research in recent years has focussed a good deal of attention on the phenomenon of cult prophecy in Israel, and the verdict, while still not firm, generally favors its important place in Israelite worship, and a much closer link between our writing prophets and the cult than many critics used to accept. See the introductions to Nahum and Habakkuk for a more detailed discussion of this possibility for our three minor prophets. Of them all, Zephaniah is the least likely to be a strictly cultic functionary.

Many commentaries point to the apocalyptic imagery in Zephaniah and see reasons to cut out any passage with cosmic overtones as a later development. Examples include 1:2-3 on creation, 3:8-9 on the world assembly, 3:11-13 on the humble remnant, and above all, 1:7 with its eschatological slaughter. Here, however, the strong eschatological language serves to intensify the historical expectations of the prophet in the near future, and does not approach the extravagant lengths of later books, nor does it look to a paradisial situation in another world. It is rather a baroque development of the *Day of the Lord* motif which became itself a source for later apocalyptic developments. Believers in the first centuries of the Christian era did, however, cherish Zephaniah's eschatological emphasis, for Clement of Alexandria (3rd century, A.D.) cites in his *Stromata* V:11 an *Apocalypse of Zephaniah* current at the time.

As a result of these considerations, we can reasonably maintain that nearly all of the book comes from the prophet Zephaniah, with the usual understanding that individual lines here and there reflect a developing tradition and interpretation which the editors have included in the final edition. Quite likely, too, the final entire unit in 3:14-20 is such a reflective interpretation.

3. The Structure of the Book

Zephaniah can be outlined according to the following scheme as a single prophetic drama about the *Day of the Lord* that moves through three acts with several scenes to each act:

I. The Coming Day of Judgment (1:1—2:3)
   A. Label (1:1)
   B. The indictment of idolatry (1:2-6)
   C. The punishment (1:7-13)
   D. The Announcement of the Coming Day (1:14-18)
   E. Call to repentance (2:1-3)

II. The Judgment Day for the Nations (2:4-15)
   A. Against the Philistines (2:4-7)
   B. Against Moab and Ammon (2:8-11)
   C. Against Cush/Ethiopia (2:12)
   D. Against Assyria (2:13-15)

III. Call to Jerusalem to Repent and be Restored (3:1-20)
   A. The Condemnation of Jerusalem (3:1-5)
   B. Israel converts at the Judgment of Nations (3:6-8)
   C. The Promise of Salvation (3:9-13)
   D. Rejoicing in God's Deliverance (3:14-20)

ZEPHANIAH 1:1—3:20

THE COMING DAY OF JUDGMENT
1:1—2:3

1 The word of the LORD which came to Zephaniah the son of Cushi, son of Gedaliah, son of Amariah, son of Hezekiah, in the days of Josiah the son of Amon, king of Judah.

2"I will utterly sweep away everything
  from the face of the earth," says the LORD.
3"I will sweep away man and beast;
  I will sweep away the birds of the air
  and the fish of the sea.
I will overthrow the wicked;
  I will cut off mankind
  from the face of the earth," says the LORD.
4"I will stretch out my hand against Judah,
  and against all the inhabitants of Jerusalem;
and I will cut off from this place the remnant of Baal
  and the name of the idolatrous priests;
5those who bow down on the roofs to the host of the
  heavens;
those who bow down and swear to the LORD
  and yet swear by Milcom;
6those who have turned back from following the LORD,
  who do not seek the LORD or inquire of him."

The Book of Zephaniah opens with an unusual heading that traces the ancestry of the prophet back four generations to one Hezekiah. Most prophetic books list only the prophet's father (Isa 1:1; Jer 1:1; Ezek 1:3; Hos 1:1), so that we expect special emphasis of Zephaniah's heritage. Almost certainly the Hezekiah can be no other than the king who ruled Judah from 715 to 688 and lived during the career of Isaiah (2 Kgs 18-20; 2 Chron 29-32). This would make Zephaniah a second cousin of king Josiah and would help explain his direct concern with the practices of the wealthy and merchant classes in his oracles. Some have identified the prophet with the Zephaniah who was assistant High Priest in 2 Kgs 25:18, and whom Nebuchadnezzar executed after the taking of Jerusalem in 587. But that must remain a guess. The name signifies in Hebrew, "God has hidden" or "God has protected," and is a common name type.

The first prophetic oracle in vv. 2-6 opens with a world-wide vision of judgment. The language in vv. 2-3, in particular, reflects the picture of creation in Gen 1-11. But here the order of God's creation has been reversed. God wipes off man and beast from the face of the earth despite his promise in Gen 8:21; he clears away the birds and beasts and fish despite his giving them over to Adam and Eve to rule in Gen 1:26; and finally he cuts apart the relation of humans to the land from which they came, despite the bond proclaimed in Gen 2:7 and 3:17-19. The verb, "sweep away" or "remove," *'asap*, is exactly the same word that Gen 8:21 uses to say God will never again destroy the world, so that the reference could not be clearer. Thus the prophet announces at the very beginning that God's judgment will be the equivalent of a new flood, and a negation of all the ordered expectations on which the peoples rely. There is no call to "return," no sense of possible escape.

Verses 4-6 then apply this cosmic warning to Judah and Jerusalem because of the rampant idolatry among the people. The list of false practices is long. Some still worship the Canaanite god Baal, some 200 years after Elijah's great confrontation in 1 Kgs 18. Others worship astral gods and goddesses, a cult very typical of the Babylonian and Assyrian cultures (see Jer 8:2; 19:13 and 32:29; Ezek 8:16; Deut 4:19). Some honor Milcom, the god of the Ammonites (*cf.*, Jer 49:1-6; 1 Kgs 11:5), always spoken of with loathing by the prophets. Still others simply reject Yahweh, the God of Israel, whether by conscious decision or plain neglect. The Book of Proverbs condemns those practical atheists (Prov 14:1) as do many of the Psalms (53:8; 80:18).

Two particular aspects of false worship can be noted in this passage. First, there are well-organized sects of Baal worship with their own priests freely operating in Judah. These "priests" are not called by the same Hebrew name as Yahweh's priests, but *kemarim*, which seems to imply false cults wherever it is used in the Old Testament (2 Kgs 23:5; Hos 10:5). Even though the text speaks of a "remnant" of Baal, the meaning must lie close to that of Isa 14:22, which also speaks of cutting off from Babylon both a name and a remnant, *i.e.*, exterminating every trace. God will leave no idolators in the land. The second aspect is the double loyalty by which Israelites play off both Yahweh and Baal in order to get the best of both worlds. This practice succumbed to the polytheistic mentality of the Ancient Near East in which one placated evil spirits to keep them friendly and honored all major sources of divine aid to win their favor. It effectively denied a true faith in the sovereignty of Yahweh over all peoples and all creation. Ezek 23:37-39 describes the same double loyalty to Yahweh and Milcom, as does the condemnation of the false prophets in Jer 23:13-14.

Verses 7-13 go on to describe a great slaughter of God's enemies under the image of a sacrificial feast. Israel, like many of its neighbors, was well familiar with the religious practice of the Communion Sacrifice, in which the victim was killed, dressed, offered to God and divided with part going to Yahweh alone, part to the priests, and the rest to be eaten by the family of the person who made the offering (Lev 7). But now the invited guests to this sacrifice will not be God's people but their enemies who shall eat up Israel. Commentators often point to this passage as an example of late apocalyptic imagery. Yet Zephaniah in the following verses limits the sacrifice to the guilty, a group combining both foreign devotees of foreign gods and the wealthy who are self-satisfied and do not recognize any duty to God in thanksgiving, devotion, or sense of guilt. Thus this is a limited sacrifice, and not a great worldwide judgment. A comparison with similar imagery in Isa 34:6; Jer 46:10 and Ezek 39:17 will show how restrained Zephaniah really is.

The scene opens with a liturgical call for silence. This must reflect temple practice at the moment of worship (*cf.*, Hab 2:20; Zech 2:13). The list of those to be sacrificed includes royal officials (princes and the sons of the king), those who wear foreign dress (either the wealthy who paid high prices for their luxury or the priests of the foreign cults with their vestments), and those that jump over the threshold (a reference to some religious practice which saw the threshold as particularly numinous because boundaries of sacred places had special significance; *cf.*, 1 Sam 5:5). The list ends with those who do violence and fraud in their master's house. If we see the four classes of people in chiastic fashion, then the doers of violence are the royal officials that frame both ends of the list, while the two middle groups are the idolators. This fits well with the traditional condemnations by prophets against legalized oppression (Isa 1:23; 3:14-15; Jer 23:1-4; Ezek 22:25-29; Hos 7:3-4).

Verses 10-13 give a short tour of Jerusalem, naming a variety of locations and quarters within the city not entirely known to us today. The Fish Gate would be in the north wall if we guess correctly from Neh 3:1-3 and 12:39. The "mortar" is an area, perhaps of extensive brickwork, otherwise unknown. Possibly all the places refer to the merchant's area of the city which is probably located in the hilly northern section of the city. However, the word for "traders" in the RSV can also mean "Canaanites" and point to a quarter for foreigners in Jerusalem. In this case, the references to Baal worship may include not only true Israelites but the public and open practice of Canaanite rites by Phoenician merchants.

The punishment for these evils shall come on the Day of the Lord. It will be a day in which nothing shall escape

Yahweh's eyes (v. 12), and in which all who are self-satisfied
and unaware of the Lord's coming will be found out (*cf.*,
Jer 48:11, where Moab also acts like settled wine). The fate
of them all will be destruction even as they are confidently
expecting things to go on just as they have always been.
Verse 13 borrows its conclusion from Amos 5:11 or from a
body of shared tradition containing prophetic curses
(*cf.*, Mic 6:15 and Isa 65:21).

> [14]The great day of the LORD is near,
>   near and hastening fast;
> the sound of the day of the LORD is bitter,
>   the mighty man cries aloud there.
> [15]A day of wrath is that day,
>   a day of distress and anguish,
> a day of ruin and devastation,
>   a day of darkness and gloom,
> a day of clouds and thick darkness,
> [16]a day of trumpet blast and battle cry
>   against the fortified cities
>   and against the lofty battlements.

Verses 14-18 conclude this threat with a magnificent
poem on the coming Day of the Lord. The contrast between
a day of light and a day of darkness is first brought out in
Amos 5:18-20. The tradition of a day in which God defends
Israel against its enemies has been turned into a day of
judgment against God's own people. Isa 2:6-22 develops
the idea further, as does Ezekiel 7 at a still later date.
Zephaniah stands in this tradition. See more extended
comments on Nahum and Habakkuk for the combination
of the divine warrior and Holy War motifs with the Day of
the Lord. All of the elements are present in Zephaniah as
well. There are few original contributions in this picture.
The need for total destruction because of the people's sins,
the day of terror, wrath and distress, the darkness and

clouds, and the hope for a future time of relief for a remnant come to the prophet from tradition. Zephaniah's particular interest in the universal scope of God's judgment, however, extends beyond the predictions of the prophets before him. And some of his images are particularly popular in the preaching of his contemporaries. As in Jeremiah, the wrath of Yahweh as a fire is a popular image (*cf.*, Jer 4:4; 15:14; 21:12; etc.). People will collapse in total help-lessness like the blind (Isa 59:10; Deut 28:29). Thus the blindness of their ways is matched by the utter darkness of their end. All their wealth will be useless to them (Ezek 7:19).

Verses 14-18 resemble the thinking of Ezek 7 very closely. The suddenness of the day, the desperate attempts of the people to buy their way out, the fiery wrath of Yahweh, and the sounding trumpets all play a role in Ezekiel's descrip-tion. There is no reason why the later prophet could not have known the themes from prophetic tradition (*cf.*, Isa 13:9; Amos 2:2; 3:6; Jer 4:19; Joel 1:15; 2:1-2), but their association in one passage suggests he may have been familiar with Zephaniah's portrait of the terrible Day. The famed Latin hymn for Masses of the Dead, the *Dies Irae, Dies Illa*, begins with the opening words of v. 15.

The first three verses of chap. 2 also belong with this poem, although many older commentators took them as the introduction to the oracle against the Philistines in vv. 4-7. They have many problems because some lines seem to be repetitive, and the stress on the "meek and humble" has often been associated with a postexilic development in Jewish piety at the time of Daniel and the *Hasidim*, the "pious" ones, who were the forerunners of the Pharisees. However, most of the biblical references to the humble fall into passages that are not necessarily so late, such as Amos 8:4; Isa 11:4; Pss 76:10; 147:6; 149:4. This is par-ticularly so, since recent research has revealed that many more of the Psalms should be dated earlier than was common in the past.

The major themes in 2:1-3 can easily be identified with pre-exilic thought. The "commands" (*mishpat*) are frequent in Deuteronomy (Deut 4:5, 8, 12, 14; 5:1; 7:11) and Jeremiah (5:1; 7:5; 9:23; 21:12); while the "humility" in v. 3 (*anawah*) is found in several older proverbs (Prov 15:33; 18:12; 22:4) and two of the pre-exilic Psalms (45:5 and 18:36), and in no late work at all! Moreover, the theme of seeking the Lord is unique to Zephaniah. He uses it in 1:6 and 2:3 in a way that can be only remotely paralleled in the general prophetic tradition (Amos 8:12; Hos 5:6; Isa 51:1; Zech 8:21-22; cf., Pss 105:3; 27:6). The meek and humble are those who obey the commands of the Lord and seek to do justice (*sedek*) and to trust in Yahweh. The anger of God which runs like a theme melody through this section will not touch them.

JUDGMENT DAY FOR THE NATIONS
2:4-15

⁴For Gaza shall be deserted,
    and Ashkelon shall become a desolation;
Ashdod's people shall be driven out at noon,
    and Ekron shall be uprooted.

⁵Woe to you inhabitants of the seacoast,
    you nation of the Cherethites!
The word of the LORD is against you,
    O Canaan, land of the Philistines;
    and I will destroy you till no inhabitant is left.
⁶And you, O seacoast, shall be pastures,
    meadows for shepherds
    and folds for flocks.
⁷The seacoast shall become the possession
    of the remnant of the house of Judah,
    on which they shall pasture,
and in the houses of Ashkelon
    they shall lie down at evening.
For the LORD their God will be mindful of them
    and restore their fortunes.

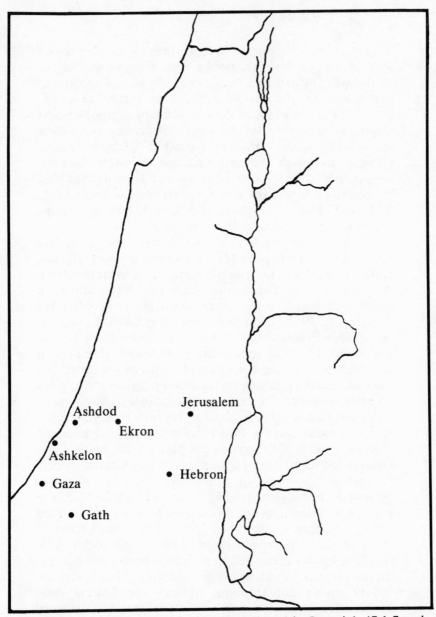

The Philistine League of Five Cities mentioned in Jeremiah 47:1-7 and Zephaniah 2:4-7.

The Oracles against Foreign Nations in Zephaniah list the four peoples at the points of the compass: Philistines to the west, Moab and Ammon to the east, Cush to the south, and Assyria to the north. They symbolize all the nations of the world and thus no attempt at completeness should be expected. For the most part, these verses follow the famed "Qinah" rhythm typical of Hebrew funeral laments, in which the first half line is longer than the second half (a 3 + 2 meter). The use of a lament to indicate judgment on a foreign nation occurs also in Ezekiel (*cf.*, 27:1-14; 28:11-19; 32:1-16; 32:17-32), so that we can assume it was a popular form at this time.

The Philistine oracle in vv. 4-7 names four of the five cities of their Pentapolis (*i.e.*, a five-city league). All had suffered attack and destruction many times in the past from Assyrian or Egyptian armies, and had frequently been allied with Judah in resistance to foreign powers (see Isa 20; 2 Kgs 18-19; 2 Chron 26:6; Jer 47:1-7). Gath, the missing city, had been totally destroyed by the Judean king Uzziah about 760 B.C., and apparently never rebuilt. The present text has many difficult words and points of grammar, but the technique of punning still comes through in the original Hebrew, although English cannot duplicate it. In v. 4, both Gaza and Ekron are subjects of a play on words. In v. 5, the name "*Canaan*" for the Philistines suggests being humbled (*'anah*); in v. 6, RSV misses the play on the name Crete (*Karet*) and its becoming a meadow (*korot*) when it renders "Crete" as "pastures." In other passages, Crete was considered the homeland of the Philistines (1 Sam 30:14; 2 Sam 8:18), and sometimes the Philistines were simply labelled among the Canaanites (Josh 13:3f). The overall effect of these verses is to deprive them of their right to the land, until the upshot is reached in v. 7; their homes will become Judah's homes. And it will come suddenly. The expression, "to be driven out at noon," reflects the Ancient Near Eastern language of the royal victory against a national enemy. Examples date from Sumerian times down to the 9th century of kings' boasting that they overthrew the foe or destroyed his city in a single day. The famed stele of Mesha of Moab, for example, records: "And Chemosh said to me, 'Go, take Nebo from Israel.' So I went by night and fought against it from the break of dawn until noon, taking it and slaying all . . ."

The use of a list of enemy cities that will be overcome is also employed by Ezekiel in 30:13-19 and stems from a long tradition of national victory hymns in the Ancient Near East. Pharaoh Merneptah recorded his triumphant campaign in Palestine about 1230 B.C. with just such a list: "The princes are prostrate, saying, Peace! Not one raises his head among the Nine Bows. Desolation is for Thehenu; Hatti is pacified; plundered is Canaan with every evil; carried off is Ashkelon; seized upon is Gezer; Yanoam is made as that which does not exist; Israel is laid waste, his seed is not; Hurru is become a widow for Egypt!" (ANET 378).

The final line in v. 7 may be an editorial comment reflecting the hope that Judah shall come back from exile and not remain homeless as will Philistia. The verb, "be mindful," reverses the fate of Judah in 1:8, where the same verb, *paqad*, means "to punish." It also mirrors the concluding promise in the last verse of the book, 3:20, when God will restore the fortunes of Judah.

> 8"I have heard the taunts of Moab
> and the revilings of the Ammonites,
> how they have taunted my people
> and made boasts against their territory.
> 9Therefore, as I live," says the LORD of hosts,
> the God of Israel,
> "Moab shall become like Sodom,
> and the Ammonites like Gomorrah,
> a land possessed by nettles and salt pits,
> and a waste for ever.
> The remnant of my people shall plunder them,
> and the survivors of my nation
> shall possess them."

¹⁰This shall be their lot in return for their pride,
  because they scoffed and boasted
  against the people of the LORD of hosts.

The oracle against Moab and Ammon is often considered
a post-exilic addition that reflects the animosity of Judah
towards its neighbors who began moving into its land or
helping its enemies during the Exile. Ezek 25:1-7, 8-11,
would be an example of such thinking. As it stands, the
word against Moab and Ammon divides into a first person
oracle in vv. 8-9 and a comment in vv. 10-11. Much of the
material parallels other prophetic words against these
two nations, especially the charges of pride and haughty
insolence toward Judah. Because attacks on Yahweh's
people mean attacks on Yahweh, the prophetic invective
uses strong language (*cf.*, Jer 48:29; Isa 16:6; Ezek 21:33).
    The divine oath, "as I live," in v. 9 resembles similar
beginnings of judgment oracles in the later prophet Ezekiel
(13 times in all), and the remnant of the people also sounds
like it presupposes an initial exile from Judah. When
combined with the mention of Sodom and Gomorrah,
which many scholars assume to refer to the written Pentateuch account in Gen 19:24-28 (probably post-exilic in
date), it gives good reason to wonder how this line could
have been uttered by Zephaniah. To further complicate
this authenticity problem, v. 11 sounds like Second Isaiah
near the end of the Exile (*cf.*, Isa 41:1, 5; 42:10; 49:1; 51:5),
when he envisions all the nations coming to worship
Yahweh. Quite possibly, a core oracle of Zephaniah has
been expanded in light of the fates of Judah and the small
neighboring nations during the exilic period. The original
ran from v. 8 through the first half of v. 9. The part beginning with the remnant in v. 9b up to v. 11 serves as a
commentary. Given that Jer 49:18 also uses Sodom and
Gomorrah as curses against Edom, and Isa 1:9 against

Israel, there is no reason to doubt that the two cities were well known symbols of evil even before the written text of Genesis was finished, and thus belong to the original words of Zephaniah.

Since v. 12 addresses the people of Ethiopia in such a fragmentary way, we must assume that the editors took some small word and placed it here in order to achieve the fourfold geographical balance needed for the organization of Zephaniah's material. Hebrew *cush* may refer to the Ethiopian family of pharaohs who ruled as the 25th Dynasty from 715 to 663. Thus the Ethiopians represent a symbol for that archenemy of Israel, Egypt.

In vv. 13-15, the last of the four oracles directs mocking irony toward the greatest city of the time, Nineveh, capital of Assyria. The particular charge of pride stands very close to the language of Nahum. The *hubris* of foreign capital cities represents the epitome of evil because it opposes the lordship of Israel's God over all lands. It becomes a special motif in the prophetic books: see Isa 14, 47; Jer 50:18 and 29; Ezek 17:32; 32:1-16. The accompanying curse of being a wasteland, uninhabited except by wild animals, is popular in the Oracles against Nations (*cf.*, Isa 13:21; 18:6; Jer 49:33). All the magnificent buildings which have symbolized her power and her luxury now stand as empty as her proud boasting. Even the huge amounts of precious cedar stand naked before wind and sun and rain.

Different translations will offer a variety of names for the animals in v. 14. Accurate knowledge of ancient species of wild animals has always suffered from the paucity of references in discovered texts and from the lack of any real description of shape, size, or habits by which to identify the names very precisely. At least we know those listed are all denizens of uninhabited places. The curse closes with a traditional hissing and an unusual shaking of the fist (see Jer 19:8; 49:17; 50:13; Ezek 27:36; Lam 2:15; Nah 3:19).

THE CALL TO JERUSALEM TO REPENT AND BE RESTORED
3:1-20

3   Woe to her that is rebellious and defiled,
    the oppressing city!
²She listens to no voice,
    she accepts no correction.
She does not trust in the LORD,
    she does not draw near to her God.

³Her officials within her
    are roaring lions;
her judges are evening wolves
    that leave nothing till the morning.
⁴Her prophets are wanton,
    faithless men;
her priests profane what is sacred,
    they do violence to the law.
⁵The LORD within her is righteous,
    he does no wrong;
every morning he shows forth his justice,
    each dawn he does not fail;
    but the unjust knows no shame.

Chapter 3 opens with a series of judgments and threats in vv. 1-5 worthy of the great Jeremiah himself. Note how Jerusalem refuses correction in v. 2 (Jer 7:23-24; 11:4, 7; 22:21), how her judges are wolves (Jer 5:26), her priests and prophets fail in their duties (Jer 2:8; 6:13), and how the wicked have no shame (Jer 3:3). But similar charges are also found in other prophetic books, for example, Ezek 22:25-29. In contrast to this evil performed at every level in Jerusalem, God remains faithful. Even when the leaders prey on their own people like lions and wolves, no one thinks of turning to Yahweh. They trust in what they can get for themselves, but forget to trust in God. This short passage gives further sharpness to the basic message of chap. 1. The

idolatry and rampant worship of pagan deities both stem
from, and leads to, a selfish injustice and wicked greed that
betrays the fundamental character of Yahweh in the
covenant: his justice or righteousness. Verse 5 calls God
"the righteous one," who gives "justice" every morning
with the same reliance and assurance that one places on the
sun's rising. The combination of justice and righteousness
comes down to Zephaniah from the Isaian tradition where
the two words are a repeated topic sentence for that great
prophet's message (*cf.*, Isa 1:21, 29; 5:7; 16; 9;7, etc.) It is
taken up again by the Second Isaiah in the end of the exilic
period (Isa 41:10; 42:21; 45:19, 21—all of which call Yahweh
the Righteous One). Zephaniah as a Jerusalem prophet
through and through stands in that tradition.

The description of utter devastation in vv. 6-8 should be
understood as a general threat that does not refer to a
specific Scythian or Assyrian raid. A depopulated city with
jagged brick towers sticking up from the ruins was a
familiar sight everywhere: the Assyrians had left more than
one Judean city destroyed in 701. And we must remember
that the past tenses may not be intended to refer to the past,
but serve as "prophetic perfects," a future prediction stated
as though it had already happened: "I have cut off nations
. . . (in giving sentence against them, although not yet
executed)." The use of such a definitive sentence high-
lights the judicial character of the scene. The divine judgment against other nations should have been a lesson for
Judah, yet it did not seem to take hold, but rather incited
Judah to worse sins. The theology of a divine sentencing
against one nation that will bring other guilty parties to
reform themselves becomes a very careful point in Ezekiel's
interpretation of the fall of the state as well. In Ezek 16
and 23, he recalls the fate of Samaria and the northern
kingdom as a lesson to Judah. The failure to pay attention
to the lesson makes the guilt of the second party worse.
The primary charge in both Zephaniah and Ezekiel centers
on the rejection of proper worship and obedience to

Yahweh. Likewise, "Fear of the Lord" plays a significant part in the Book of Proverbs and its attempts to define true wisdom (see Prov 1:8, 33; 8:13; Job 28:28). It corresponds to the demands for obedience and "knowing the Lord" in the prophets (see Isa 11:2-3).

Israel's lack of knowledge is revealed in the eagerness with which they do evil (literally, "they rise early in the morning to corrupt" in v. 7; *cf.*, Jer 7:13; 11:7; 24:4; 25:3; 26:5; etc.). Their wicked deeds indeed condemn them, and we expect punishment, but suddenly v. 8 reverses what should follow and promises a change, although not without an outpouring of God's just anger. The anger theme has been frequent in the pre-exilic prophets (Hos 5:1; 11:9; Jer 4:8, 26; 25:37; etc.), and the gathering of the nations for judgment is certainly implied by Jer 25:15-29 where each nation must be handed the cup of wrath to drink. The legal proceedings now include the Lord himself giving witness against evil (*cf.*, Mic 1:2; Jer 29:23 and Mal 3:5).

Some of the particular expressions here are more common in the later Old Testament writings; *e.g.*, the assembling of nations (Joel 4:2 and Zech 14:2; Ezek 38-39), but the basic theme of the just waiting for the Lord's vindication is rooted in the thought of Isaiah (Isa 8:17), and became part of the liturgical prayer of the Psalms (Pss 33:20; 37:7; *cf.*, Hab 2:3). So there is no overwhelming reason to assume that most of this material has been added at a later date. This holds true also for the next five verses, 9-13, which have close parallels to the oracles of hope and consolation found in Second Isaiah, Zechariah and Joel. Most such words are rooted in parts of the message of Isaiah, and seem to have been accepted into the cultic prophecy of Israel during the century following his death. This would make Zephaniah one of the earliest witnesses to this national hope of restoration after oppression and humiliation as the people experienced it especially under the Assyrians. At its best the character of this prophecy stressed, as does Zephaniah, the need for reform and return

to Yahweh; at its worst, in those prophets confronted by
Jeremiah, the false optimism that God will save even the
worst members of Israel regardless of their inner attitude.

> 8"Therefore wait for me," says the LORD,
>   "for the day when I arise as a witness.
> For my decision is to gather nations,
>   to assemble kingdoms,
> to pour out upon them my indignation,
>   all the heat of my anger;
> for in the fire of my jealous wrath
>   all the earth shall be consumed.
>
> 9"Yea, at that time I will change the
>   speech of the peoples
>   to a pure speech,
> that all of them may call on the
>   name of the LORD
>   and serve him with one accord.
> 10From beyond the rivers of Ethiopia
>   my suppliants, the daughter of my dispersed ones,
>   shall bring my offering.

The dream of the prophet that a day will come when
God will purify the tongues of nations shows the importance
placed on praise and public confession of Yahweh. The
silent believer, or the believer who scoffed, fell far short
of the ideal of the pious Israelite. The Psalms open regularly
with a call to praise Yahweh (see 29:1; 33:1-2; 117:1; 135:2;
145:1; 148:1; 150:1-6); Psalm 8, especially, calls on Israel to
praise God's name over all the earth for what he has done
for humanity. Glorifying the divine name becomes a sign
in the post-exilic community of God's day of salvation
(Isa 41:25; Joel 3:5; Zech 13:9), when all nations shall
serve him (Zech 14:16-19). In those days they will bring
their gifts to the Lord (Isa 45:14; 66:20; Zech 8:23). However, even in the pre-exilic period, the prophetic concern

with right speech in the service of God stands out. Isaiah could not become a prophet until his lips were purified (Isa 6:5-7), and the hymns of Isaiah praise the divine name (Isa 12:3). Some passages are almost idyllic in their hopes for all nations to serve God together (Isa 2:2-4; 11:9; 19:23-25). Zephaniah's language bridges between the cultic hymns of Isaiah and the highly developed eschatology of salvation found in writings after the return from exile.

In v. 10, the mention of Ethiopia brings to mind the earlier judgment of 2:12. But here the remote lands of Africa symbolize the farthest corners of the world. Even from there, God shall call peoples. See the similar vision in Isa 19:16-22. In this passage, Zephaniah recalls the universalism of Amos 9:7, "Are you not like the Ethiopians to me, O people of Israel, says the Lord." A salvation for all nations is opened up as a real possibility in God's long-range planning, even if Zephaniah now passes quickly on to other ideas.

> [11]"On that day you shall not be put to shame
>   because of the deeds by which you have rebelled
>   against me;
> for then I will remove from your midst
>   your proudly exultant ones,
> and you shall no longer be haughty
>   in my holy mountain.
> [12]For I will leave in the midst of you
>   a people humble and lowly.
> They shall seek refuge in the name of the LORD,
> [13]those who are left in Israel;
>   they shall do no wrong
>   and utter no lies,
> nor shall there be found in their mouth
>   a deceitful tongue.
> For they shall pasture and lie down,
>   and none shall make them afraid."

Verses 11-13 describe that "day." The evil deeds of v. 7 will be reversed, the pride and self-satisfaction of v. 2 will be rooted out, and even those who refuse all help or correction in v. 7 will seek refuge in the Lord's name. The passage begins with a promise that they shall not bear the shame that their sins deserve. This refers to the humiliation of defeat and exile, with all its indignities, seen as divine punishment. Instead of receiving further chastisement for their evil deeds, God will root out only the evil ones from their midst. Verse 3 above suggests that these "proud" are mostly leaders, but we should not assume that the prophet had only the officials, judges, prophets, and priests in mind. Amos 6:13 speaks of soldiers filled with self-importance, and Isa 3:16 accuses the women of Jerusalem of haughtiness, and Jeremiah addresses the pride of the whole nation in 13:17.

The haughty and proud whom God puts down on his "Day of the Lord" included both foreigner and Israelite who did not give praise and exaltaton to Yahweh. Isa 2:11-17 is the fundamental statement of this view. From it, Zephaniah draws a new message. God will not only spare the poor and lowly who have no such pride, but he shall purify and protect them besides. They shall not tell lies (recall the constant anger of Jeremiah against servants of "the Lie"; Ezekiel, too, warns against perverse prophets who lie—13:6, 7, 8, 9, 19; 21:34; 22:28). They shall not commit wickedness or depravity, an accusation often brought by the prophets: Jer 2:5; Ezek 3:20; 18:24, 26; Mic 3:10; Hos 10:9, 13. Instead, they shall have security from all danger. The expression "none shall make them afraid," perhaps originated in the blessings that accompanied covenant ceremonies (cf., Lev 26:6 and Deut 28:26), but it rapidly became a standard word of promise in the prophets: Isa 17:2; Jer 7:33; 30:10; 46:27; Ezek 34:28; 39:26; Mic 4:4; 7:14; Nah 2:12, and even in Job 11:19. One of the covenant blessings most sought was the "rest" that

God alone could give his people: Pss 23:2; 95:11; 125:5; Isa 11:10; 28:12.

God will establish only those who are humble and lowly. Since the most common root word for the poor in Hebrew is *'anah,* these humble ones are often referred to as the *'anawim,* a plural form. Note that Zephaniah contrasts the proud of both Israel and foreign nations with the humble who seek refuge and a hiding place in God (2:3 and 10, 3:2 and 12). The basic concept in this prophet therefore centers on trusting Yahweh. In an early poem such as the Song of Hannah in 1 Sam 2, the poor and the lowly are those who suffer want. God specially protects them. Further development within Israelite religious thought applies this special protection to those who seek God. We should trace this understanding through the prayer of the temple. The Psalms carry out the dialogue between the lowly believer who presents himself or herself before God and the divine response. God does not forget the *anawim* (Pss 9:13; 10:12), he teaches them and listens to them (Pss 25:9; 10:17), he protects them (Pss 18:28; 34:7; 35:10; 72:4), he gives them bounty (Ps 68:11) and victory (Ps 149:4), he fills them with joy (Pss 22:27; 34:3), and guarantees justice (Pss 72:2; 140:13).

> [14]Sing aloud, O daughter of Zion;
>   shout, O Israel!
> Rejoice and exult with all your heart,
>   O daughter of Jerusalem!
> [15]The LORD has taken away the judgments against you,
>   he has cast out your enemies.
> The King of Israel, the LORD, is in your midst;
>   you shall fear evil no more.
> [16]On that day it shall be said to Jerusalem:
> "Do not fear, O Zion;
>   let not your hands grow weak.
> [17]The LORD your God is in your midst,
>   a warrior who gives victory;

> he will rejoice over you with gladness,
>   he will renew you in his love;
> he will exult over you with loud singing
> ¹⁸as on a day of festival.

Verses 14-20 look forward to a day when that peace and happiness will be present because God truly rules as king and can be found in their midst. It fulfills a dream like that of Ezekiel some years later, that the name of Jerusalem will be "The Lord is here" (Ezek 48:35—the final verse of the book!). Thie entire section has been almost universally discounted as a late addition, and certainly the general tone of rejoicing and peaceful restoration finds many echoes in Isa 49:13; 54:1, while the hope for Yahweh to be king occurs in Isa 41:21; 44:6, and Zech 9:9. The expression, "fear not," recurs regularly in Second Isaiah as a word of hope: Isa 40:9; 41:10, 13, 14; 43:1, 5; 44:2; 54:4, 14; and also Isa 57:11, Joel 2:21 (all exilic or later writings). Additional support for a late date can be added if one assumes the royal Pss 96 and 98 are quite late, for they follow this same theme, as does another passage that scholars often date in the post-exilic period, Mic 4:1-8.

Working against this, however, is the comparison of the total message of Micah with Zephaniah. In many ways, Micah has stronger condemnations and predictions of destruction than does Zephaniah, and also a more extensive vision of the restoration of the people. If we refuse to simply dismiss all of Micah's words of hope as late additions, we can see that the two books actually share much in common. Micah promises rest from the enemies, a remnant in peace, security from all fear and a demand for justice among the chosen people (Mic 4:1-7; 5:2-8; 6:8; 7:8-20).

A second factor that raises doubts whether the themes of vv. 14-20 should be considered late is the resonance of this passage with the preceding topics within Zephaniah. The concluding verse sums up the promise of 2:7, and the three-fold title of Jerusalem in 3:14 (daughter of Zion, Israel, daughter of Jerusalem) reverses the threefold condemnation in 3:1 (the rebellious, the defiled, the oppressing city). Many expressions, too, can be traced more to Isaiah and Jeremiah than to post-exilic writings. Note the "reproach" in v. 18, which is a favorite of Jeremiah (6:10; 20:8; 15:15; 24:9; 29:18; 42:18; etc.; *cf.*, Ezek 5:5, 14; 22:4; Isa 30:5). The titles, "Daughter Jerusalem, daughter Zion" are found in Isa 1:8; 10:32; 16:1; 37:22; Jer 4:31; 6:2; 6:23 and Mic 1:13; 4:8, 19, 13—far more times than among later prophets. The weak hands in v. 16 can be compared to 2 Sam 4:1; Isa 13:7; Jer 6:24; 50:43; Ezek 7:17; 21:12; and even the staple of the salvation oracle, "fear not!" derives from an early setting (Isa 7:4; 10:24; Jer 30:10, and above all in the Call Narratives of major prophets, Jer 1:8; Ezek 2:6; 3:9).

With this mixture of early and late vocabulary, one can decide either that Zeph 3:14-20 stands as the oldest witness to a true hope for a paradisial restoration, or that this passage has been composed at a later date when such hopes were more likely to be articulated. But because the language here has strong ties to the preceding chapters and really fits the exultant combination of judgment with hope that suffuses the whole book, it would be better to insist that the basic message of the divine warrior (v. 17), the kingship of Yahweh (v. 15), the call to strengthen the hands and not be afraid (v. 16), the trust in the divine warrior (v. 17), the reference to festal celebration (v. 18), and the gathering of the lame and outcast (v. 19), all belong to the original Book of Zephaniah. This affirms that important passages in earlier prophetic books, such as Mic 4 and Isa 9 and 11, must also be understood from the same tradition. All of these show strong signs of the liturgical concerns and the praise attitude of the psalms, and should be identified with cultic moments of expression in the pre-exilic period.

Arvid Kapelrud has suggested that the language best fits the pattern found in the "enthronement psalms" (Pss 47; 95; 96; 97; 98). These would be sung on the great New Year's festival celebrating God's kingship over the universe. They stress the same themes found in 3:14-20: (1) the summons to shout and rejoice addressed to "Daughter Zion"; (2) the description of the divine glory; (3) the worship of the foreign gods and their devotees; (4) the sound of the trumpet.

A post-exilic addition has been included, however, in the final verse, to update the message with the mention of the return from exile and the promise of universal renown, and the echo of the restored fortunes. Originally, Zephaniah had Assyria in mind as God's agent of punishment, and used this concluding poem to reassure Judah that if they rooted out evil, and returned to God, they could foresee restoration of all the covenant blessings. It is the oracle of healing, so to speak, that follows the moral preaching in chaps. 1 and 3. While it may be going too far to claim that Zephaniah was a cultic prophet, we can see in the organization of this one prophet and in the development of his thought, some evidence that the same person could be both an independent prophet and capable of speaking in the cultic assembly.

Although short, the Book of Zephaniah witnesses a fine balance between moral sensitivity to evil with radical demands for reform, and a sense of office as healer and consoler. We should not be surprised at this. How else could we envision people of the stature of Jeremiah, Isaiah, or Zephaniah who blaze with anger at the evil done to the poor and helpless. Compassion and healing are their middle names.

The Book of Nahum

THE BOOK OF NAHUM
INTRODUCTION

1. Date and Origin of the Book

ALTHOUGH A SHORT BOOK, Nahum is one of the most dramatic texts in the Old Testament. From the opening lines straight through to the last verse, the intense feelings of the prophet sizzle and flame up like fat dripping on a charcoal fire. The present three chapters actually contain several distinct poems of prophecy, but they blend together in a passionate outburst against the evil of Nineveh, the capital city of Assyria in the seventh century, B.C. Many commentators have described the prophecies of Nahum as an orgy of hatred; and declared them to be deficient in theology, thus the least valuable part of the Hebrew canon of Scripture. Certainly they will not provide the ordinary stuff of Christian or Jewish prayer, but they do offer not only a valuable insight into the struggles of Israel to preserve faith in Yahweh against the might and power of the Assyrian religious threat, but also a distinctive hymn of a prophet to the glory and universal kingship of the God of Israel. The book deserves a careful reading since it reveals much about the intertwined roles of prophecy, politics, and liturgy (worship) in the times of the kings of Israel and Judah.

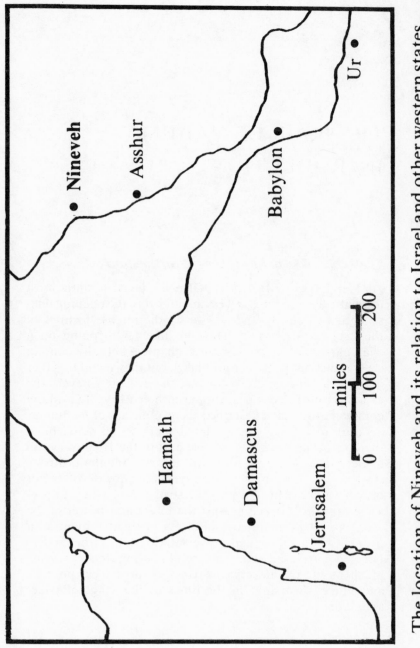

The location of Nineveh and its relation to Israel and other western states.

Clear references in the book itself provide us with reasonable certitude about the date of Nahum's life. The label at the beginning does not give us any help, but the city of Nineveh is named in both 2:8 and 3:7 as the object of God's wrath and the victim about to fall to its enemies. Since we know that the combined Medes and Babylonians took the city in 612 B.C., we can assume that Nahum's prophecies date to a moment very close to that event. They have too much vigor and freshness to be far removed in time from the siege itself. Whether the prophet composed his descriptions immediately after the news of the conquest reached him in Jerusalem or just before it, cannot be known for sure. If he did write his prophecies after the loss of Nineveh, they served as a prediction that the whole empire of Assyria now neared its final end. Arguments are sometimes advanced that the style is so breathless and excited that it could not have been written afterwards; they do not have much value since we know so little of this Hebrew poet's gifts other than the few verses of his book. The descriptions are among the best in Hebrew literature, and tell us a great deal about ancient battle practice; but they use very ordinary cursing language found elsewhere in the prophets, especially in Jeremiah (compare the war scenes in Jer 6:22-26; 46:3-9; 50:21-30). Indeed, Jer 51 has many scenes similar to the overall imagery of Nahum. On the other hand, while the images create a very specific and detailed picture, the general consequences of the fall of Nineveh remain vague and apparently not yet foreseen. No mention of Babylon's newly-won power appears in the oracles, so that a date before the actual destruction of Nineveh remains the more probable choice.

Verse 3:8 makes reference to the fall of the Egyptian capital city of Thebes before the armies of Ashurbanipal in 663 B.C. This sets the earliest possible time for Nahum's preaching sometime after this event. Older critics sometimes suggested a date for his ministry close to that victory, often proposing 652 B.C., on the occasion of the revolt of

Ashurbanipal's brother, Shamash-shum-ukin, who was serving as governor of Babylon. This civil war created major disturbances within the Assyrian government, pitting brother against brother, and it took Ashurbanipal several years to finally win back control of the Babylonian territory. However, no record of any assault on Nineveh exists from this rebellion, and so it must remain a most unlikely guess. Just as doubtful is the theory of a Scythian invasion, based on a report of Herodotus the Greek historian some two hundred years later. It would have occurred about 627 or so, but none of Nahum's reports fits the tactics of a raiding party of these fierce barbarians (see the comments on this in reference to Jeremiah's preaching in Jer 4:5—6:3 in the previous volume of this commentary). More recently A. S. van der Woude has described the Book of Nahum as a letter written by a prophet who was among the exiles from the Northern Kingdom of Israel which were deported to Assyria in 722 when Sargon completed the destruction of Samaria. He notes the Assyrian vocabulary, the lack of interest in Jerusalem and Zion, the possible firsthand knowledge of the city of Nineveh, and similarities to other exilic writings among the prophetic books, notably Isa 52. An important point in his argument centers on the use of the phrase, "The book of the vision," rather than just "the vision of Nahum," which is the more common prophetic expression. This "book" in Hebrew can also refer to a letter, and would explain why Nahum can be so bold as to attack Assyria while it still held power enough to silence him; he wrote only a letter to be read privately by friends and Judean leaders in Jerusalem! However, none of van der Woude's points has much strength. General similarities to exilic writings and references to Assyrian words and customs only show that the language and culture of the Ancient Near East shared much in common and that communications were good between nations, especially between conqueror and subject peoples. The lack of any certain knowledge of a surviving or flourishing Judaism from among those sent into exile in 722, and the silence of the book itself about Nahum's exilic status, make the author's case very weak and quite speculative. Actually his strongest argument is one that he does not give, namely that the town of Nahum's origin, Elkosh, has sometimes been identified with a place near Nineveh itself. See the comments below on 1:1. Van der Woude instead accepts a location in Galilee for Elkosh.

2. The Assyrian Danger

The historical situation which led to Nahum's preaching can be sketched briefly. After the death of Ashurbanipal, the last strong king of Assyria, about 632 (or 628-627, if his son co-ruled with him for four years), the Assyrian empire began to crumble rapidly. Year after year, the armies of the Medes and the Babylonians mounted attacks on various outposts and cities until only the heartland remained. In 614, the ancient city of Asshur fell and all the small subject nations to the West could see the end was near. Nahum would not have had to witness or even to know for sure that a siege of Nineveh itself had begun to rejoice in the thought that such was coming. Josiah, king of Judah, had already acted as if free from Assyrian control since his first reforms in 627 or so; this was seen most blatantly in his takeover of the old Northern Kingdom of Israel which was at that time a full Assyrian province (2 Kgs 23:15, 19; 2 Chron 34:33). No wonder then that Nahum's triumphant cry of joy at the coming fall of Nineveh would have fallen on welcoming ears.

Nineveh itself represented a symbol of all that was evil about the Assyrians who had so long oppressed the people of Israel and Judah. Nahum's contemporary, Zephaniah, also reveals the deep-seated hatred for Nineveh as a symbol of pride and oppression (Zeph 2:13-15); and long after its final disappearance, it still remained the standard example of sheer wickedness for the Book of Jonah to use against the Israelite's own hard hearts. Jonah's author tells a story of how *even* Nineveh could convert back to God! The outlook of the prophet Nahum is strictly that of a citizen of Judah, writing to proclaim the final vindication of Yahweh, God of Israel, against his pagan enemies.

3. Plan of the Book

As it stands today, the Book of Nahum presents one long and sustained prophetic poem against Nineveh. Almost all scholars have seen, however, at least two separate original pieces that have been joined together. These roughly correspond with chaps. 1 and 2-3. Since 1880, commentators generally refer to the acrostic or alphabetic poem in vv. 1-10 of chap. 1 as an independent unit, and either consider the following seven verses (1:11—2:2 in the RSV and many other translations) as additions to this poem or as a separate small unit. Thus the whole of chapter one serves as a kind of preface to the remainder of the book. It does not mention anything specific about Assyria, but rather sets the stage by glorifying the majesty, power and justice of Yahweh. The material in chaps. 2 and 3, on the other hand, is directed straight at the hated Nineveh, and is often treated as a single prophetic piece. At the very least they must be taken together, although it seems best to distingiush two parallel movements, one in chap. 2 and the other in chap 3. In the following treatment, the book will be divided into three parts:

1) 1:1 to 1:15 (RSV; 1:1 to 2:1 to Hebrew), a hymn to Yahweh.

2) 2:1 to 2:13 (2:2 to 2:14 in Hebrew), description of the siege.

3) 3:1 to 3:19, theological reflections on Nineveh's fall.

4. Oracles Against Enemies

Even with these divisions, the Book of Nahum does not resemble the typical prophecies found in Isaiah or Jeremiah, Amos or Hosea, which are directed towards Israel itself. It belongs instead to the special genre of Oracles against Foreign Nations that can also be found gathered in Isa 13-23; Jer 46-51 and Ezek 25-32. All of these avoid charging the pagan nations with violations of the divine covenant, and so lack many of the specific themes of justice and fidelity characteristic of the charges against Israel. They rather stress that the political aggressions and oppressions of foreign peoples are a terrible sin of pride and snubbing of Yahweh's divine rule over the world. Israel's God has determined the place for each nation and given each its land and rightful independence, and has especially favored the Chosen People with its possession of Canaan. For other nations to covet the Promised Land directly challenges the right of God's universal kingship.

Unlike oracles delivered against the Israelites, the enemy presumably never heard the words of Nahum. Thus these words did not function to turn the hearts of a people back to God, or even to scare them, but did serve to bolster the hopes and confidence of Israel that God was on their side, did hear their prayers, and was about to act on their behalf. This helps to explain why such oracles as Nahum's seem to be more hymns and prayers than threats or moral exhortations. The theories of the origins of oracles against other nations have filled many pages of learned journals over the decades, but a general consensus has emerged that they include both the curses hurled at an enemy before battle and a liturgical ceremony. War between nations was war between the gods of those nations; from earliest times, the will and support of the national god had to be sought before marching to battle. In desperate situations, the war was a holy war to defend the god, and the Bible seems to know of such traditions connected with Israel's own conquest (compare the ancient poems in Exod 15 and Jgs 5, and the Book of Joshua). The beginning of such a war required solemn cultic ritual, and so would include prayer, sacrifice, prophecy of victory, ritualistic cursing of enemy, and praise of the might of Yahweh. Interesting examples occur in the stories of Balaam in Num

23-24, and in the wars of Ahab in 1 Kgs 22. Careful reading of the Psalms also reveals many themes of the Holy War celebrated in cultic praise: the triumph of Zion in Pss 46; 48 and 76; God's protection of the king in battle and fighting the king's wars as God's wars in Pss 2; 20; 21; 91 and 110; God's just rule over all nations because he is creator and lord in Pss 93; 95; 96; 99.

5. Nahum and The Cult

Nahum shows elements of all these motifs and has often been called a cultic prophet. Such cultic prophets often appear in a poor light in the oracles of our major writing prophets such as Amos 7 or Jer 23. Nevertheless prophets attached to shrines with functions of giving oracles and direction from God seem to be accepted as normal and legitimate even in these passages (*cf.*, Amos 7:14; Jer 23:28), and play a clear role in 1 Kgs 22 and Num 12:6. Several Psalms also display a structure and wording that indicate a place for a prophetic oracle of support or healing given to the one who petitions God, thus Pss 81:11-17, 95:8-11, 50:7-15, among others. The combination of oracular forms, praise hymns and sustained poetry can still be best explained by assuming some cultic setting, that is, *officially* delivered words, whether in the royal court or in the temple. The long and vivid descriptions of the battle derive from the ancient belief in the power of the spoken word to accomplish what is uttered. Words unleash power which either brings it about or must be channelled or blocked by counter-force. It borders on a superstitious belief, but also shows the weight given to the spoken word; and if a god, or one speaking in the name of a god, says something, the more seriously it must be taken (*cf.*, Isa 55:10-11).

On the positive side of cult prophecy, the Book of Nahum reveals the intense concern with Yahweh's universal kingship over all peoples, an intense hatred of injustice and oppression, a deep trust in the divine providence that rights all wrongs, and a beautiful faith in the goodness of God as creator and provider. If it lacks mention of the covenant, of fidelity to God, or of many of the everyday hopes and evils of the human heart, we should suspend judgment on the onesideness of Nahum the man. We possess only one small oracle given on one particular occasion. Possibly he spoke eloquently at other times on other issues, perhaps not. In any case, this segment was saved, almost surely because of the beauty of the poetry and the relevance of a prophecy that sets the contrast between the evil symbol of godlessness and the trustworthy vindication by a just God so starkly before us. Israelite faith would never have proclaimed that Nahum contained the fullness of their faith, but they would cherish the message that the book does bring readers and listeners even in later ages.

CHAPTER ONE

MOST SCHOLARS who have worked with the first chapter of Nahum divide the material between vv. 1-10 and 11-15 because of the conviction that the original Hebrew text starts as an acrostic poem, i.e. each line begins with a successive letter of the alphabet starting from the first letter *aleph*. This has not been a modern critical discovery by university professors but stems from Jewish tradition itself which marks out in large print the significant letters of the alphabet. However, we cannot be sure that this tradition is soundly rooted in the text since many letters in the series are out of order and others are missing altogether. It may well be more an act of later Jewish piety than an original intention of the authors. But it intrigues many because it seems to carry the alphabet down to the letter *nun*, which begins the word "Nineveh," and then to stop there, refusing to write the "n" in its place. Working from this possibility, commentators usually try to explain the disorder in the text by proposing later editorial revisions and additions that have crept in. They set themselves to reorganizing the verses into a possible original order. Very few of these attempts have won any supporters beyond their proposers, which should lead us to be cautious about playing with the text. This is especially true since we can make very good sense out of it as it stands, and whether this goes back to Nahum himself or to his editors, it comprises the only certain and forceful text that we can work with, and therefore should be kept intact.

Building on the belief that someone added verses to the acrostic poem, commentaries at the turn of the century often searched for even further additions. Many reject the acrostic itself, others suspect the oracle of doom against Nineveh in vv. 12-13, and some the oracle of salvation in v. 15. Here, too, no consensus has been reached, and many of these suggested revisions are based on a belief that a true prophetic statement must be very tightly organized and logical, and that repetition or shift of focus always reveals the hands of later readers who saw new possibilities in the text and built new thoughts into it. By far the greater part of these proposals fail to respect the rhetorical vigor and force of the passages they deal with.

At the same time, older scholars did not know enough about the cultic and liturgical aspects of Israel's worship and so did not appreciate many of the forms associated closely with cult. The language about the divine warrior, so prominent in chapter one, and of the rejoicing at his coming, resembles the hymns and psalms that are tied to the New Year's festival celebrations in the ancient world, and which almost certainly were used also by Israel. We are hampered in understanding this feast fully because the Bible lacks any one place where it is described in detail. The literature today on the nature of this New Year's celebration links it to the festival of Succoth in the Fall. Scholars have brought together enormous amounts of biblical and other Ancient Near Eastern texts in order to gain a good sense of its main points, most of which centered on the kingship of Yahweh as God and his covenant with Israel. One must reckon seriously with the possibility that Nahum was composed for a New Year's festival, possibly even the New Year of 612 B.C.!

1   An oracle concerning Nineveh. The book of the vision
of Nahum of Elkosh.

The Book of Nahum opens with a standard label, but it
is more complete than usual. The word for "oracle" in line 1,
massa', derives from the Hebrew verb "to lift up (the voice)"
and occurs most often with oracles directed against foreign
nations. It contrasts with the common expression used by
prophets who direct their words mostly to Israel and
Judah, "The word of the Lord came to . . ." It may possibly
be a liturgical formula.

The addition of the expression, "The book of the vision,"
is unique among prophetic writings. A "book" here can
mean either a short inscription or a letter, or a full length
scroll. Presumably it helps explain what this "oracle" is,
but the passage of time has made it difficult to know what
the editors had in mind. At the very least it tells us that
what follows is the copying down of a vision of Nahum.
But it may mean more than that and actually imply a letter
or scroll sent by Nahum himself. The word "vision" seems
to belong to the *massa'*, "oracle." Hab 1:1; Isa 13:1; Lam
2:14 all indicate that prophets *saw* this type of oracle
against nations. Once again this could well indicate a
liturgical setting in which the utterance of a prophecy
took place in a trance. A. S. van der Woude, "The Book of
Nahum: A Letter Written in Exile," has suggested that
indeed Nahum was a *letter* sent by a prophet living in exile
in Assyria to Israelites and Judeans back in Palestine sometime in the period from 700-650 B.C. The letter form would
help to explain certain passages that we shall see below,
but remains too hypothetical and not appreciative enough
of the liturgical-prophetic aspects of the book.

Nahum comes from Elkosh. If we knew where Elkosh
was located, it would help identify the author as either a
Judean, or a northern Israelite, or an Assyrian resident.
Unfortunately, town-sites related to the name Elkosh have
been found in all three areas. St. Jerome favored a Galilee

location, Elcesi; modern Iraqis claim Al Qush near Mosul, and most modern scholars favor Beit Jibrin, some twenty miles SW of Jerusalem. The prophet himself bears a good Hebrew name meaning "Comforted." It does not occur again in the Bible, but comes from the same root as Nehemiah, "Yahweh comforts," the governor of Jerusalem in the 5th century, B.C., and as Menachem, "Comforter," a common name in modern Israel. When all is weighed, however, we cannot learn much about the prophet's place of writing from the label.

> 2The LORD is a jealous God and avenging,
>> the LORD is avenging and wrathful;
> the LORD takes vengeance on his adversaries
>> and keeps wrath for his enemies.
> 3The LORD is slow to anger and of great might,
>> and the LORD will by no means clear the guilty.
>
> His way is in whirlwind and storm,
>> and the clouds are the dust of his feet.
> 4He rebukes the sea and makes it dry,
>> he dries up all the rivers;
> Bashan and Carmel wither,
>> the bloom of Lebanon fades,
> 5The mountains quake before him,
>> the hills melt;
> the earth is laid waste before him,
>> the world and all that dwell therein.

Verses 2 and 3a form a short litany of praise to open the book. It is marked by the repetition characteristic of early Israelite poetry and of the Canaanite poetry found at Ugarit. The triple use of the avenging Lord can be compared to Ps 29:1, "Ascribe to the Lord, O heavenly beings, ascribe to the Lord glory and strength, ascribe to the Lord the glory of his name." Other such passages include Pss 29:4-5; 93:3-4; 96:7-8. The Hebrew text opens with the dramatic words: "a jealous god," and then follows with the proper name "Yahweh" five times to emphasize the majesty and awe of the divine presence. "Jealous" has the sense of zeal—Yahweh is active and concerned for Israel. In all, the poet lists six qualities of God: zealous, avenging, wrathful, slow to anger, mighty in power, and requiting justice against the wicked. To a modern reader, this may seem to make God an angry deity. But it must be remembered that many of these words are the language of the theophany, the majestic awesomeness of God's appearing, and stress the divine reign over all peoples, especially in guarding justice in the world. Thus the prophet calls Yahweh both "lord of wrath" (where RSV has "wrathful") and "slow to anger," and sees no problem because God surely controls the fury of the natural elements as instruments against evildoers among the nations, and yet does not let them loose arbitrarily or upon a whim. The words are the words of divine power, but the echo is the echo of the covenant on Mount Sinai when v. 3 quotes God's own words from Exod 34:6-7. There is no need to presume that this verse was added later. In fact, when we compare Ps 103:9-10 to this passage, we discover that later thought generally tried to soften the hard saying that God would not clear the guilty, by praising him for not holding our sins against us. The whole passage with its poetry and its strict correlation of the God of universal majesty with the God of Israel's covenant suggests a cultic psalm. See such psalms as 86:15, and 145:8 and Joel 2:13. But it contains prophetic warning as well. Twice Jeremiah uses the same expression that God by no means clears the guilty (30:11; 46:28).

Verses 3b through 8 go on to detail the theme of the march of the divine warrior against his enemies. This was already treated in the comments on Habakkuk 3, and it needs only a few remarks here on the particular coloring that Nahum gives to the motif. The divine appearance is often described as coming in the storm and whirlwind in the Old Testament. Compare such passages as Isa 29:6; 66:15; Zech 9:14; Job 38:1. This does not refer to the rainstorms that come in from the Mediterranean but to the desert sandstorms from the East and Southeast, the dreaded sirocco that comes in the Fall. The powerful winds and driving sand make an excellent metaphor for a divine theophany. The reference to the clouds as the dust of God's feet pictures Yahweh riding his chariot or walking on the clouds above the storm. The divine step raises the whirlwinds of dust and sand just as an earthly hiker might trail dust on a backroad of Judea. A similar image appears in Ps 18:10, but for the possibility of the journey made in a chariot, see Isa 66:15 and especially, Ps 68:4, "Lift up a song to him who rides upon the clouds." The same language was used of the pagan gods. The Babylonian Creation epic describes Marduk "riding the storm" against the monster Tiamat, and the Ugaritic epic of the storm god Baal gives the god the title "Rider upon the clouds." Isa 14 applies the same title in derision upon the king of Babylon who thinks himself a god (v. 14).

The mention of Bashan, Carmel and Lebanon together in v. 4 has been used by some to prove that this poem of Nahum came from the northern kingdom area or even from Lebanon itself rather than from the South. Theodor Gaster in his *Myth, Legend and Custom in the Old Testament*, 662, even guesses that chap. 1 was adapted from a hymn to Baal, the storm god of the Canaanites. A look at Ps 68:15-17, which extols Zion as Mount Bashan, the fertile mountain of the northern Israel area that stands across the Jordan River, or the description of Zion as the mountain of the North in Ps 48:2-3, make this guess quite unnecessary. However, any comparison between the Ugaritic epic of Baal's fight against his enemies and this passage would show that Nahum certainly had in mind the traditional language of the storm god to describe Yahweh's own victory. Baal fights Prince Sea/Judge River, the mountains quake when he thunders, he brings the flood. Allusions to all of these can be found in vv. 4, 6 and 8. Nahum is not the only OT writer who refers to Yahweh's battle against the chaotic monster Sea, which corresponds to the battle between Marduk, king of the gods, and Tiamat, the chaotic sea, at the beginning of the Babylonian creation story. See also Ps 74:13-14; Isa 50:2; 51:9-10.

For the idea of mountains quaking when Yahweh speaks, see Joel 4:16, and for their melting before his coming, see Mic 1:4; Pss 46:7; 97:5. The idea of anger as a fire that shatters rocks recurs in the poem of Deut 32:22 and Ps 69:24, as well as Zeph 3:8 (see above for the comments on that passage). As always the anger of God really signifies a *righteous* anger against human evil (*cf.*, Hab 3:12; Isa 10:5, 15 and Ps 78:48).

The key verse follows these horrific descriptions in vv. 7-8. The first words can be translated with the emphasis given by the RSV, namely: the Lord is Good!—and the rest made into a description of God's justice in which he gives mercy to those who trust but punishes the evil doers. Or else the same line can be rendered with as much passion: "The Lord is *better than* a fortress on the day of trouble." The biblical books frequently give positive assurances. God is a fortress (Pss 27:1; 31:4; 37:39; 52:7), and is a refuge (Pss 11:1; 16:1; 36:7; 91:4). When negative, the prophets often threaten Israel itself that God could make a full end of them (*cf.*, Jer 4:27; 5:18; 30:11; Ezek 11:13; 20:17; Zeph 1:18; although Jeremiah puts it as his hope that God will *not* make a full end). If the flood brings out the power of the great mythical battle of creation, then the darkness at the end of v. 9 can only refer to the pit of Sheol as it does in Job 17:13; Ps 88; Qoh 11:8.

At v. 9, the attention shifts—it no longer focuses on the cosmic action of God but zeroes in on Nineveh. The RSV has not made very good sense out of vv. 9-10, and they should rather be read in the light of many new linguistic findings as follows:

> Why do you plot against the Lord?
> He will make a full end [of his foes].
> His enemies shall not rise up twice [against him].

> Indeed, even as tangled thorns and those drunk with
>   drink,
> They shall be consumed like exceedingly dry stubble.

The imagery is the picture of the farmer setting fire to the chaff and dried up tumbleweed at the end of the harvest season. After a Near Eastern summer, the twigs and hay are so dry that they nearly explode in flame when lit.

> ¹¹Did one not come out from you,
>   who plotted evil against the LORD,
>   and counseled villany?
> ¹²Thus says the LORD,
> "Though they be strong and many,
>   they will be cut off and pass away.
> Though I have afflicted you,
>   I will afflict you no more.
> ¹³And now I will break his yoke from off you
>   and will burst your bonds asunder."

The remaining verses in chap. 1 (11-15 in the RSV) have created difficulties for all commentators. They seem to be an alternating dialogue in which the prophet addresses Nineveh in v. 11, Jerusalem in vv. 12-13, Nineveh again in v. 14 and Jerusalem in v. 15. The quick movement back and forth gives emphasis to the belief of the Israelites that destruction for God's enemies means salvation to themselves. The scene opens with reference to the king and his policies of conquest. No particular king need be in mind, for the Assyrian ruler represented the designs of the whole people. A similar setting occurs in Isa 10:5-15, in which Isaiah foresees God punishing the king of Assyria for his attacks on Israel and Judah. The last part of v. 11 might better be translated literally: "and who counselled Belial." The word probably stems from the verb *bl'*, "to swallow," and refers to the God of death who swallows down his victims (see the commentary on Jer 23:9-40 in this series). He stands for evil, and in late Judaism represented Satan, prince of evil; a meaning used by St. Paul in 2 Cor 6:15.

CHAPTER TWO

CHAPTER 2 describes a great attack against Nineveh by a
powerful enemy who is never named. Part of its artistic
effects comes from the author's assumed viewpoint within
the besieged city. We do not march with the victorious
army of Babylon as it approaches and sets up its weapons
and breaks through the walls, but rather look on in horror
from within as the enemy suddenly appears before the city.
Confusion and fear reign; "courage!" is the all important
cry of the moment; soldiers rush everywhere. But quickly
pandemonium becomes defeat, hope utterly collapses, and
we watch helplessly as the enemy destroys all that the city
held precious. Then once more the scene shifts, this time to a
reflection on what we have just witnessed. God's judgment
sounds through the now still and silent ruins of a once
mighty city: Assyria, the lion who always ripped open
victims for itself, has become the prey for others.

The Bible offers few rival passages for colorful information about war comparable to this chapter. We might turn
first to the next chapter in Nahum itself, and then to Ezek 26
which describes in similar detail a Babylonian attack on the
Phoenician city of Tyre; or to Isaiah 20, on the siege of
Babylon by its enemies; or to Jer 50 and 51, another series
of impassioned battle scenes against Babylon. Almost all of
the extended passages about battle come from prophetic
books such as these and reflect the political experience of

Israel in the 8th to the 6th centuries under the constant pressure of Assyrian and Babylonian armies. The prophetic poetry carries so much force because it stemmed from firsthand experience.

In light of the shifting focus of chap. 2, we can divide the following comments into three parts:

1) 2:1-5   The Enemy attack on the city

2) 2:6-10   The collapse and defeat of the city

3) 2:11-13   The reflection on the meaning of defeat

> **2** The shatterer has come up against you.
>   Man the ramparts;
>   watch the road;
>   gird your loins;
>   collect all your strength.
>
> ²(For the LORD is restoring the majesty of Jacob
>   as the majesty of Israel,
>   for plunderers have stripped them
>   and ruined their branches.)
>
> ³The shield of his mighty men is red,
>   his soldiers are clothed in scarlet.
>   The chariots flash like flame
>   when mustered in array;
>   the chargers prance.
> ⁴The chariots rage in the streets,
>   they rush to and fro through the squares;
>   they gleam like torches,
>   they dart like lightning.
> ⁵The officers are summoned,
>   they stumble as they go,
>   they hasten to the wall,
>   the mantlet is set up.

The scene opens with the enemy at the walls of the city. RSV calls him the "shatterer," while other scholars argue that the Hebrew word signifies a "scatterer." Philology does not answer the question clearly. In light of v. 8 where Nineveh is like waters that run out, or of vv. 11-12, where the lion drags away his prey, "scattering" may well be the main image of the passage. But it can also be taken as a picture of the battering down of the walls, particularly since Jer 51:20 has a very similar expression that clearly suggests that besieging armies were considered as hammers: "You [Cyrus the Persian] are my hammer and weapon of war, with you I break nations in pieces, with you I destroy kingdoms." Moreover, the threat of total destruction carries more dread than does a threat of exile. Thus we should accept the RSV reading here. Verse 1 continues with four dramatic imperatives, what Hebrew calls the Infinitive Absolute form, that underscore the need for *immediate* action. They must prepare for the enemy to appear at any moment. Above all, they rely on the watchman to give a final warning when the armies come into sight. Compare the importance of the watchman in Isa 21:6 and Jer 48:19 for the defense of the city, and how this was taken over into the theological reflection of the prophets and psalmists, and applied to the moral sphere, either in terms of God as watchman over Israel in Ps 127:1 or as the prophet as watchman in Ezek 3:16-21 and 33:7-9 and elsewhere. The further commands to gird up one's loins and collect all one's strength both refer to gaining courage to face the impending battle.

This initial battle preparation sketch is followed in v. 2 by the insertion of a prayer which originated within the Israelite liturgical assembly, and expresses the people's trust that their god will bring about this hoped for defeat of their oppressor. "Jacob" and "Israel" generally both refer to the older northern kingdom centered in Samaria; but in writings after the Fall of that kingdom in 722, "Jacob" can be used of Judah, as it is in Isa 43:1; 44:1; 46:3; etc. The verse expresses hope that the entire Israelite nation,

North and South, will once again be restored. Most translations have also kept the metaphor of stripping fruit trees of their fruit and their valuable branches in the second part of the verse, but since both verbs, "to strip" and "to ruin," are used at other times for military attacks (*cf.*, Isa 24:1, 3 and Ezek 26:4), the Hebrew-speaking listener would have understood a battle image such as "plunderers have plundered them and destroyed their soldiers."

Verses 3-5 describe the enemy's approach, but the text has several difficult words in it and most translations, including the RSV, sound confused when they place the racing chariots in v. 4 next to the stumbling officers in v. 5. In any case, the references are entirely to the approaching enemy and their breakthrough into the city. The descriptive technique of the poet adds to the dislocation by painting the chariots' charging through the city before mentioning the foot soldiers scaling the outer walls. The soldiers dressed in scarlet remind us of a passage in Herodotus which explained how the troops of Xerxes, the Persian king, painted their bodies red in battle. Ezekiel's description of the Assyrian army in Ezek 23:6-7, specially notes that they dress in purple. The poet may even be alluding to the ferocity of the army of Medes that is coming against Nineveh by hinting that they are bloodstained with victory. The Hebrew phrase in v. 3 which RSV renders as "the chargers prance" certainly must mean something more like "their spears shake in the air" since the noun means "cypress wood" and not horses. And the uncertain word for "flame" in the preceding half line probably means "trappings" or "coverings" as we now recognize from its use in Ugaritic passages. So the whole of v. 3 should read:

> The shield(s) of his mighty men are red,
> his soldiers are clothed in scarlet,
> the trappings of his chariots are like fire
> on the day of their mustering,
> and the spears shake.

Destruction in the squares and streets of an ancient city is also mentioned in Amos 5:16. The impression created is one of haste and mad rushing about. This might explain the awkward opening of v. 5 in which the officers must be "summoned" and "stumble" in their haste to get to the attack. The context clearly does not imply that they stumble out of failure or fear, so the sense must be more that they trip over each other in their work, or they use a ducking and charging tactic to avoid the arrows and stones of the defenders on the walls. Their mission is to set up the protective shield over the heads of the soldiers who undermine the walls. This device resembles the well-known Roman *testudo*, literally a "tortoise shell" protection, made up of the interlocked shields of soldiers or of wooden sheds that could be placed against the wall of the city so that the sappers could operate safely.

> [6]The river gates are opened,
>   the palace is in dismay;
> [7]its mistress is stripped, she is carried off,
>   her maidens lamenting,
> moaning like doves,
>   and beating their breasts.

The second movement of the poem in vv. 6-10 now describes the despair of the city as defeat becomes evident. The enemy manages to open the sluice gates in the canals or aqueducts that supply the city and its surrounding fields with water from the Tigris. Possibly the purpose was to flood the city and help undermine whatever mud-brick walls were left; but the open gates may just as well have diverted water away from the city and thus forced its surrender from lack of drinking water and risk of disease from unsanitary conditions. We just cannot be sure.

Verse 7 is even more difficult. The mistress stripped and carried off sounds to a modern reader like a reference to the queen, but it may be a veiled way of referring to the statue of the patron goddess of the city, Ishtar. Some scholars would read the Hebrew differently so that the first line of v. 7 says, "The Beauty is sent into exile and carried off," in which "Beauty" stands for the special ornaments that decorate the cult statue of the goddess of sexual attraction and love. The idea has enough merit to be taken seriously, particularly since many good parallels exist both in the Bible and in Sumerian-Babylonian documents. Isa 46:1-2 describes the Persians carrying off the gods of Babylon from the sacked city. Even more forceful are the accounts of gods and goddesses carried off from their captured temples by barbarian invaders in the important Sumerian text, "A Lamentation over the Destruction of Sumer and Ur" (ANET 611-619). Some samples include: (1) "At Zabalam a devastating hand was placed on the holy *giguna*, Inanna was carried off from Erech, was brought to enemy territory"; (2) "Mother Bau wept bitter tears in her house Krukug, 'Oh my destroyed city, destroyed house,' bitterly she cried"; (3) "Gaesh was poured out like milk by the enemy, they destroy it utterly, its (well-) made statutes fair of form, they shatter" (ANET 614-615). The Assyrian king, Tiglath Pileser III, recorded that he had presented the gods of those countries he conquered "to the temple of Ninlil, the greatly beloved wife of Ashur, my lord, to Anu, Adad, the Assyrian Ishtar, the temples of my city Ashur and the goddesses of my country" (M. Cogan, *Imperialism and Religion: Assyria, Judah and Israel in the Eighth and Seventh Centuries, B.C.E.*, p. 27). Later, Ashurbanipal claims that "I had the gods, as many as I had captured through the help of Ashur and Ishtar my lords, take the road to Damascus" (Cogan, p. 26).

If the mistress is indeed a goddess, then the handmaidens who moan like doves refer to the priestesses of the temple of Ishtar. The scene is a lamentation over a divinely decreed destruction, a literary form common in the ancient world. Besides the resemblance to the "Lamentation over Sumer" above, another "Lamentation to Ishtar" (ANET 383-85) specifically refers to the women "mourning like doves."

The author picks up a new image in v. 8, comparing the ruined city to a broken pool of water or a cistern which cannot hold water no matter how often one fixes it. The people who survive the arrows and spears of the attacking army, and who manage to escape capture, run for their lives into the countryside. No shouts to "stand firm, stand firm," as the text literally says, can stem the flight. With no more than what they wear on their backs, the people abandon their glorious capital. Verse 9 shows us the enemy at leisure gathering the valuables that made Nineveh the richest city in the ancient world—the treasure appears endless. In this, Nahum seems to echo the phrase of Isaiah about the heedless wealth of Judah, "Their land is filled with silver and gold, and there is no end to their treasures; their land is filled with horses, and there is no end to their chariots" (Isa 2:7). The Book of Daniel describes a victory of the Second Century Greek kings of Egypt, the Ptolemies, over their northern rivals, the Seleucids of Antioch, in a similar vein: "He shall also carry off to Egypt their gods with their molten images and with their precious vessels of silver and of gold . . ." (Dan 11:8). Note, too, the famous list of king Jehu of Israel's tribute to king Shalmaneser III of Assyria found on the "Black Obelisk" in the Assyrian capital, now kept in the British Museum. It indicates the wealth that flowed into the Assyrian capital from subject states:

> The tribute of Jehu, son of Omri; I received from him silver, gold, a golden saplu-bowl, a golden vase with pointed bottom, golden tumblers, golden buckets, tin, a staff for a king, and wooden *puruḫtu* [uncertain object] (ANET 281).

The second scene closes in v. 10 with a stereotyped reaction to bad news. Almost always the setting is one of battle and impending defeat. Thus in Isa 13:7-8, the poet says of the Babylonians facing their enemies that "all hands will be feeble, and every man's heart will melt, and they will be dismayed. Pangs and agony will seize them; they will be in anguish like a woman in travail, they will look aghast at one another; their faces will be aflame." Jeremiah 6:24 reads, "We have the report of it, our hands fall helpless, anguish has taken hold of us, pain as of a woman in travail."

As with several other lines in vv. 5-10, alliteration is very strong here in order to create the sense of speed and breathlessness. Note the beginning of v. 10, *buqah umebuqah umebulla qah*, "desolation and slaughter and ruin." Verse 5 has strong "k" sound alliteration, and v. 8 strong "m" repetition. The full effect of the poetry only comes through of course to the reader of the original Hebrew.

> [11]Where is the lions' den,
>   the cave of the young lions,
> where the lion brought his prey,
>   where his cubs were, with none to disturb?
> [12]The lion tore enough for his whelps
>   and strangled prey for his lionesses;
> he filled his caves with prey
>   and his dens with torn flesh.

The third scene in chap. 2 shifts from the description of the victory of Medes and Babylonians over Nineveh to a metaphorical lament over the defeat of the city. Here Nineveh and the fierce Assyrian armies appear as a lion who hunted prey throughout the Near East and brought the victims as torn and strangled food for the appetites of the Ninevites. RSV's choice of "cave" for the dwelling place of the lion seems somewhat strange, since lions do not usually live in caves, but on the open veldt, or grasslands, where their favorite prey live, grazing animals such as antelope. In fact, the word for "cave" here can just as easily be read to mean "pasture," and that would be by far the more natural understanding. The emphasis placed on the torn flesh of the victims in v. 12, where the word appears three times ("prey" and "torn flesh" translate the same

Hebrew root), may reflect the Hebrew prophet's disgust at the Assyrian policy, initiated by Tiglath Pileser III in 745 B.C., of sending captured populations into exile far from their homelands and resettling the old area with captives from still other battles. Thus the Assyrian policy was to rip flesh from bone.

Verse 13 gathers the entire chapter into an oracle of judgment from the God of Israel against Assyria. The title "Lord of hosts" underlines the firm belief of Israel that only their God Yahweh commands the heavenly armies that fight against Nineveh. The victorious forces of Cyaxares of Media and Nabopolassar of Babylon, who lead the sack of the city, are only instruments used by the Lord (*cf.*, a similar view in Isa 10:5-15). The divine results will be total destruction: the Assyrian war machine destroyed, their young men slain, their subject peoples all freed, and their empire completely broken so that their messengers can never again appear with commands to other nations.

CHAPTER THREE

CHAPTER 3 does not break the intense spirit created in the oracle of destruction in chap. 2. It serves as a second stanza in a single poem, repeating the basic theme in new words and even more terrifying images than before. The explicit description of great cruelty that runs through this chapter raises for many readers the question about Israel's god as a god of mercy. If we had no other biblical book than Nahum, it would be easy to believe that the Lord who had saved Israel demanded absolute obedience under threat of dire punishment, and that Israel itself understood its god to be ruthless against any who opposed the divine will. Once again, however, we must not forget that ancient peoples always made a direct connection between human actions or human cruelty and the will of the god whom they worshipped. In many ways, the language of the prophecies of doom throughout the Old Testament only reflect the cruel historical realities acted out by one nation against another again and again for the sake of conquest and expansion. The references to a god's will or to divine military leadership stand as metaphors for national policies. The close identification of a god with a specific people or tribe led victorious armies to claim success in the name of Asshur of Assyria, or of Marduk of Babylon, or, all too often, of Yahweh of Israel, with little or no reflection on

the moral or ethical questions raised by the wars themselves. But this does not mean that Israel simply viewed
Yahweh as one God pitted against those of another nation.
The lasting contribution of Israelite faith lay in her constant
conviction that no other gods had power to act on a world-
wide scale; only one God created and controlled all nations
and all history, and that God directed even the conquering
armies of foreign enemies, using them as tools of punishment for Israel's sins. Such an insight appears clearly in
the oracles of Isaiah (esp. chaps. 10:5-15 and 14:24-27),
the prologue of Amos (chaps. 1:1—2:4), and in the story of
the capture of the ark of the covenant in 1 Sam 5-6.
Naturally this insight stands out most sharply in the later
writings of the prophets, in books such as Ezekiel and
Second Isaiah (see Ezek 29-32 and 39:21-29; Isa 43:8-13;
44:6-8), and much less clearly in the earliest traditions,
such as the first commandment of the decalogue (Exod
20:2-3). There the command to worship only Yahweh can be
interpreted in *henotheistic* terms (*i.e.*, loyalty to one god
out of many possible ones). But at no time do the texts
lose sight of the universal lordship of Israel's God, even
in such early poems as Jgs 5 and Ps 18.

Thus we must understand that Nahum's perspective
begins from the strongest possible conviction that God
allowed and indeed directed the terrible destruction of
Nineveh, not out of caprice or cruelty, but out of divine
justice; to repay their evil and to show mercy and love for the
small nations who were victims of Assyrian barbarity,
especially for Israel, the chosen one.

This chapter can be divided into three major sections
which carry the action forward:

    1) vv. 1-4 the description of the siege of Nineveh;
    2) vv. 5-17 the judgment upon the city for its evil;
    3) vv. 18-19 an afterword describing the fate of Assyria
       in terms of a personal funeral lament against the
       king himself.

In turn, the long middle section, which presents the divine sentence against the city, contains a series of four specific themes: vv. 5-7, the city reviled and publicly punished like a common prostitute; vv. 8-10, the city compared to the fate of Egyptian Thebes; vv. 11-13, the weakness and helpless state of her defenses; vv. 14-17, an ironical picture of the city mustering all its resources to find them vanished in the moment of need.

> **3**   Woe to the bloody city,
>   all full of lies and booty—
>   no end to the plunder!
> ²The crack of whip, and rumble of wheel,
>   galloping horse and bounding chariot!
> ³Horsemen charging,
>   flashing sword and glittering spear,
> hosts of slain,
>   heaps of corpses,
> dead bodies without end—
>   they stumble over the bodies!
> ⁴And all for the countless harlotries of the harlot,
>   graceful and of deadly charms,
> who betrays nations with her harlotries,
>   and peoples with her charms.

Nineveh is a "bloody city," a charge laid also against Jerusalem itself by Ezekiel some years later (Ezek 22:2; 24:6, 9). When we consider how seriously the covenant law took crimes of blood, *i.e.*, of murder (Deut 21:1-9), this title symbolizes the worst kind of violence and outrage against innocent people, and signals the horrific punishment about to fall on Nineveh's head. The first verse links us to the preceding oracle about Assyria as a lion who rips up its prey, for where RSV has "no end to the plunder," we find the same word as in v. 12, "prey." Assyria demanded heavy amounts of booty from its vassal states, but even more it tore apart nations and peoples. In one campaign against

Azriau of Iuda in northern Syria, Tiglath Pileser III exiled 30,000 inhabitants to other areas from among all the towns he captured (ANET 283). Moreover, the Assyrian reputation for great cruelty, though perhaps not too much different from other nations of the time, was almost legendary, due to their own delight in telling every last detail. An annal of Shalmaneser III for his first year as king (858 B.C.) pictures a victory over a coalition of small states in southern Turkey:

> I inflicted a defeat upon them. I slew their warriors with the sword, descending upon them like Adad when he makes a rainstorm pour down. In the moat (of the town) I piled them up, I covered the wide plain with the corpses of their fighting men, I dyed the mountains with their blood like red wool. I took away from him many chariots (and) horses broken to the yoke. I erected pillars of skulls in front of the town, destroyed his (other) towns, tore down (their walls) and burnt (them) down (ANET 277).

Verses 2 and 3 create a wonderful kaleidoscope of a rushing battle scene. Until the very last line, no verb appears at all, just a series of noun images and strong adjectives. RSV captures the poetry well, but chooses only plain military terminology where the Hebrew uses cosmic terms: "thundering" wheel, "dancing" or "leaping" chariot, "lightning" spear. The mounds of slain soldiers are described by three different words in three successive lines: the slain, the corpses, the dead bodies. Nahum has captured the rapid sequence of sudden defeat and mimicked the boasts of kings like Shalmaneser about their body counts. Similar language can be found in Ezek 32:5; 35:8 and Jer 25:33 about the defeat of God's enemies.

The swift course of the battle stems from the poet's imagination rather than from any actual records. The Chronicles of King Nabopolassar of Babylon have been preserved enough to cover the first three years of his reign and then, after a gap, the tenth to twenty-first year; so that we can read his own account of the taking of Nineveh in his fourteenth year (612):

> The king of Akkad cal[led up] his army and [Cyaxar]es, the king of the Manda-hordes marched towards the king of Akkad [in] ... they met each other. The king of Akkad ... and [Cyaxar]es ... he ferried across and they marched (upstream) on the embankment of the Tigris and ... [pitched camp] against Nineveh ... From the month Simanu till the month Abu, three ba[ttles were fought, then] they made a great attack against the city. In the month Abu, [. . . the city was seized and a great defeat] he inflicted [upon the] entire [population] (ANET 304).

From Simanu to Abu is at least two full months, probably from early June to early August, and so Nineveh had held out for some time against the combined forces of Babylon and the Medes (Manda-hordes). Even after the battle, the Chronicle notes that some Assyrians escaped and made their way to a last stronghold in Harran, the city of Abraham. Thus Nahum probably wrote these lines before the actual siege of Nineveh took place.

Verse 4 ends this first scene by calling the reader back to the reason for all this carnage and slaugther, the condemnation of Nineveh as a harlot and a witch who has deceived and destroyed nations by her fatal power. Even the language suggests the image of the sorceress, who in Israelite law was subject to the death penalty if caught (Lev 20:27, "they shall be stoned with stones, their blood shall be upon them"). For where RSV has the phrase, "of deadly charms," the Hebrew really reads that she is "mistress of charms," which recalls the term for the witch of Endor in 1 Sam 28:7, "a mistress of mediums." In that case, too, the woman was afraid when king Saul appeared, for he could order her put to death (1 Sam 28:9). For an ancient

Israelite audience, the reference to being a witch would immediately bring to mind the penalty of their blood being upon them, and tie v. 4 back to the opening cry of the chapter, "Woe to the bloody city!"

> ⁵Behold, I am against you,
>   says the LORD of hosts,
>   and will lift up your skirts over your face;
> and I will let nations look on your nakedness
>   and kingdoms on your shame.
> ⁶I will throw filth at you
>   and treat you with contempt,
>   and make you a gazing-stock.
> ⁷And all who look on you will shrink
>   from you and say,
> Wasted is Nineveh; who will bemoan her?
>   whence shall I seek comforters for her?

The next scene in vv. 5-7 takes us to the seats of the city judges and pictures for us a metaphor of Nineveh as a common prostitute being dragged into the public square for punishment. The penalty seems to involve stripping the woman totally naked and then pelting her with dung and garbage as a form of totally shaming her. RSV's "lifting" of the skirts is an unnecessary softening of the image. The verb really means to "uncover," and the same punishment is described by other prophets quite clearly: Hos 2:5, 12; Jer 13:26-27; Ezek 16:37; 23:10. The custom of throwing filth on the woman occurs only here, but the word for it is sometimes used as a word of contempt for an idol (Deut 29:16; Jer 4:1; 7:30; Ezek 5:11; 11:18, 20), suggesting a detestable thing that is unclean. Thus Nahum brings together the traditional prophetic double invective against foreign gods as both idolatry and adultery. The "gazing-stock" of the RSV might also reinforce the idea of hurling dung at a convicted prostitute. At first glance the word looks like it comes from the verb "to see," thus the translation of RSV, but like English homonyms such as *sun* and *son* it may actually come from a noun meaning excrement. At least the great medieval Jewish grammarians Rashi and David Kimchi thought so. And if it does, then v. 7 opens with a pun on v. 6: "and make you like dung (*ro 'i*), and all who look upon (*ro 'i*) you will shrink from you." The metaphor suddenly ends as the prophet turns directly to his target and announces her destruction in direct address, closing with an emphatic "you," which the RSV avoids by following the Greek Septuagint translation, "her," rather than the Hebrew. The city is "wasted" (a term regularly used of the total conquest of a city; *cf.*, Isa 15:1; Jer 48:1, 18), "whence shall I seek comforters for *you*?"

The following short poem in vv. 8-10 compares Nineveh to the great capital city of Egypt, which the Assyrians themselves had destroyed and wiped out under king Asshurbanipal only a few decades earlier. Thebes, the "City of Amon," (*No-Amon* in Hebrew transcription), was 440 miles up the Nile river from modern Cairo, and was originally a stronghold of the princes who controlled "Upper Egypt," the desert reaches along the river above the Delta area that began just below Cairo. In the 11th dynasty, about 2100 B.C., its princes became the pharaohs over all of Egypt, and their local god Amon suddenly became a national deity. But it was only under the next great period of prosperity, in the so-called "New Kingdom" from 1550 until 1085, that Amon became truly the greatest god in the land, identified with the sun-god Re, and under the name Amon-Re, was worshipped as king of the gods. The great temple of Karnak, dedicated to Amon, is still the largest religious building complex ever found.

Ashurbanipal left a record of his conquest of Thebes on the Rassam cylinder, found in the ruins of Nineveh in 1878. In his second campaign, he describes the conquest and the booty taken in the following passage:

> ". . . I myself conquered this town completely. From Thebes I carried away booty, heavy and beyond counting: silver, gold, precious stones, his entire personal

possessions, linen garments with multicolored trim-
mings, fine horses, inhabitants, male and female. I pulled
two high obelisks, cast of shining zahalu bronze, the
weight of which was 2,500 talents, standing at the door
of the temple, out of their bases and took them to
Assyria" (ANET 295).

As to Nahum's colorful description of the city itself, sur-
rounded by water, as though by a double wall, we have no
information to suggest its accuracy. It seems unlikely that
moats or canals from the Nile formed barriers surrounding
the city, but it may have been so. The wall and rampart
combination occurs also in Lam 2:8 and Isa 26:1. It reflects
the ancient custom of building a high mud-brick wall with a
large sloping mound of packed earth, plastered smooth,
set in front of it as a double guard and as a block to any
attempts to move battering rams or siege engines close to
the inner walls. The Hebrew use of "sea" to describe a river
is common enough. "River" and "sea" form a poetic pair
that can be used together, and the very size of the Nile made
it more like the sea than like the small streams that Israel
knew. Isa 19:5 also refers to the Nile as a sea, and Jer 51:36
calls the Euphrates River in Babylon a sea. Commentators
frequently mention the account of a later Egyptian pharaoh,
Piankhi, who captured the town of Memphis in 721 B.C. by
sailing up to its walls while the Nile was at its annual high
flood and landing his troops on top of the ramparts. Thus
some suggest that Nahum envisions the Nile flooding up
to the city walls of Thebes.

Recent studies have also noted a number of cases in
which the verb "to sit" is applied to queens and to cities in
the biblical text with the meaning of "to be enthroned" or
"to rule." Cases include Ezek 27:3, said of Tyre, and Lam
5:19, where it is applied to the Lord, and Jer 46:19, where
it signifies Egypt as a queen. This Nahum passage makes
still another example. Thebes ruled from her stronghold
by the Nile, with all the surrounding nations of North

Africa at her service: Ethiopia, all the provinces of Egypt with its limitless population, the people of Punt (which would be the modern Somalialand along the Red Sea coast), and the tribes of Libya. In the present context, the choice of "strength" and "helpers" in the RSV for these nations listed in v. 7 misses the point. They are her "army" and her "warriors." Thebes thought she was impregnable in her power, but Assyria had crushed that myth. Now Assyria and its capital was to learn the same lesson!

The concluding verse of the story of Thebes gives a grisly account of the fate of prisoners of war in ancient times. If someone were not killed, he or she could count on either exile (see the comments above on 2:13 and 3:1) or being left homeless to wander wherever possible. Those rounded up would be separated out for differing fates. The children who were young could hardly stand any journey of hardship, so they were killed on the spot or left to starve. Isa 13:16 puts it grimly, "Their infants will be dashed in pieces before their eyes; their houses will be plundered and their wives ravished." This may also help to explain to sensitive readers of Psalm 137 why it ends with the prayer that God bash the heads of the little children of the Edomites on the rocks—it was a prayer that some enemy would seize their town and break their stranglehold on Judah's territory. As for the leaders, they would all be executed or taken back to the conquering nation's capital city. The practice of casting lots probably was the means of determining the life or death of the nobles, although some scholars suggest that the throw of the dice determined which Assyrian general got which prisoners as slaves or booty. One was very fortunate to win life as a prisoner, for the executions were horrifying. Ashurnasirpal II (883-859 B.C.) described one battle result this way: "I destroyed (them), tore down (the walls), and burned (the towns) with fire; I caught the survivors and impaled (them) on stakes in front of their towns" (ANET 276). The later king Ashurbanipal (668-628) related the execution of certain traitors in even grimmer terms: "I smashed (them) alive with the very same statues of protective deities with which they had smashed my grandfather Sennacherib . . . I fed their corpses, cut into small pieces, to dogs, pigs . . . vultures . . . and to the fish of the ocean" (ANET 288). To be chained and carried off may have been seen as a blessing given by the gods.

Verses 11-13 apply this stark message to Nineveh. If Thebes fell so easily to Assyria, so in turn the Assyrian capital will fall to Babylon. The image of a person drunk on God's wrath lies behind the mention of Nineveh being drunk and dazed in v. 11. We have seen this imagery already in Hab 2:16, "You will be sated with contempt instead of glory. Drink, yourself, and stagger! The cup in the Lord's right hand will come around to you, and shame will come upon your glory!" The most sustained use of this metaphor occurs in Jer 25:15-17, but it can be found in Obad 16 and Ezek 23:33-34 as well. The exact meaning of the second verb in v. 11, "be dazed," is less than certain. Besides the RSV's choice, other translators have offered a broad range of possible words: "be cunning," "be hidden," "be young," or "be darkened." The root of the verb probably means "grow dark," and a good guess as to its likely sense would be "grow faint," from the idea that the drunk and famine-starved will lose consciousness as their eyes grow darker and darker. It sketches the state of the people after defeat has come to at least part of the defense forces. People are trying to flee, but there are no safe refuges.

The simile in v. 12 reinforces this picture. The mighty fortresses fall to the besiegers like the earliest ripening figs whose stems are the weakest of the season. A good shake and they will drop from the tree right into the mouth of the hungry picker. This curse is followed by another, that Assyria's famed warriors will act like women in battle. This particular curse has a long history in the Near East as part of the treaties between nations. Naturally it comes from a male soldier's point of view in a time when women stayed at home and every noble prided himself on his military skill. Examples occur in Hittite soldiers' oaths

(ANET 354) and in Assyrian treaties (ANET 533), and several times among the Israelite prophets: Isa 19:16; Jer 49:22; 50:37; 51:30 and 2 Sam 3:29. The unit ends with the vision of the city and all of its outlying forts standing wide open, with the gates broken and burning, and no one to defend them. "Bars" generally refers to the metal bars used to hold the gates closed. It serves as a poetic metaphor for the gates themselves in this passage.

Verses 14-17 contain two ironic jests at the expense of Nineveh. The first urges haste in preparing the defenses against an enemy attack, and the second compares Assyria to a swarm of locusts. They are joined together by the literary device of interlocking words. A key word in the first metaphor becomes the basis for the second comparison. In this case, the locust hordes which can strip enormous fields of grain in a matter of hours becomes a figure for the death toll caused by fire and sword in the siege. This choice of the locust as an image of the attacking army leads the poet to extend the comparison to other facts about locust plagues—the rapid appearance of millions of the creatures all at the same time and the suddenness and unpredictability of their movements.

> [14]Draw water for the siege,
>   strengthen your forts;
> go into the clay,
>   tread the mortar,
>   take hold of the brick mould!
> [15]There will the fire devour you.
>   the sword will cut you off.
>   It will devour you like the locust.

Verse 14 mockingly encourages the defenders of Nineveh to get working on the two prime defensive needs of any city which found itself under attack. The people must provide enough water inside the city walls so that an enemy blockade, once it cuts off outside sources of water, would not force surrender for lack of water; and they must gather an enormous amount of bricks to be ready to rebuild sections of the walls when they threaten to collapse from enemy battering rams or from sappers who went at the walls and towers with pickaxes. Since the clay and the moisture needed for making bricks were close to the river banks, this task could not be done once the enemy had trapped them inside the city. To have a supply of bricks at hand permitted the defenders to build further defense lines at weak points, or even to use them for hurling down on the soldiers who attacked the walls. All of these aspects of the battle appear on the palace reliefs left by Assyrian kings in their cities, and we know as much about the tactics of war in ancient Assyria as about any other facet of their lives.

On the other hand, the attackers must not only surround the besieged city to prevent any one from escaping, but must mount an assault that would bring them up to the walls for long enough to either breach holes in it with battering rams and sappers, or to set fire to the main gates. Since major cities usually sat high up on mounds with the road to the gate constructed so that an enemy had to pass in narrow lines right along the walls where the defenders could shoot down on them or drop rocks and bricks on their heads, the attacking army usually had to construct a huge ramp that led up to the gates from straight out in order to get its army in for the final breakthrough. This meant lengthy sieges, often several months in all. Rarely, however, did an army persist as long as Nebuchadrezzar of Babylon did when he tried to take the island city of Tyre in Lebanon. For thirteen years he blockaded the city but could not take it because he had no naval forces strong enough to counter the fleet of Tyre and its ally Egypt. In 573 B.C., he lifted the siege in return for tribute payments.

Fire and sword are the great weapons of the successful attack—the people slain and the buildings burned to the ground. The pair of words occurs regularly in prophetic oracles of judgment (Isa 66:16; Ezek 30:8; Dan 11:33-34), and in both Ugaritic and Assyrian texts as well. Fire in particular characterizes the judgment of God against evildoers, for he is a God known to show his anger in the heat and dryness of the East Wind from the desert (see Exod 15:7). Amos 1 and 2 uses the image of fire destroying a city for each of the seven nations it condemns. Other good examples include Isa 34:9; Dan 7:10f; Amos 7:4 and Ps 18:8.

The locust simile in vv. 15-17 leads to a number of questions, even though the basic idea seems clear enough. Locust plagues have afflicted the region of North Africa and the Near East since time immemorial. Even in recent years, several major swarms have devastated large parts of the southern Sahara area from Sudan and Ethiopia across to Chad and Niger. Different species have different life cycles, but in all cases the adult locust lives only one season, eating as much plant life as it can. It lays its eggs before it dies and these grow through a larval stage that may last anywhere from three to seventeen years before emerging as new adults. Since each species has a set cycle, all the larvae emerge about the same time, and if the cycles of two or more species come together periodically, the stage is set for a major swarm. For reasons not completely understood, the locusts join together when a year brings out an extraordinary number at once and they move en masse in the millions. They can level a farm in a matter of hours, and then suddenly move on, skipping miles before alighting again. Like all insects, they are sensitive to cold and heat and cannot fly until the temperature reaches a certain level, so that at night they settle down and when the sun has warmed the day enough for them, they take off again.

The mention of "merchants," "princes," and "scribes" multiplying and then disappearing has led to a variety of explanations among commentators. Most find the three together to be an unlikely combination but that is because so many scholars take vv. 15-17 as a simile on Assyria's *army* being scattered. It may rather be her empire and its *officials*. The merchants and their caravans have free access to all the vassal states and often served as spies, the princes are really overseers in charge in Assyrian interests in subject countries (the Hebrew word root means "to guard," and surely refers to a military official of some kind), and the scribes include Assyrian officials in charge of tax and tribute collection, military musters, etc. In other words, all of these men serve the needs of keeping conquered states in line. With Nineveh's defeat, they disappear more quickly than the locust swarm. The word for scribe found in the Hebrew text is borrowed from Assyrian, and thus confirms that the job involved differed greatly from the ordinary Hebrew scribe's task of keeping local records. The repetitive nature of these few verses differs quite a bit from the tight and regular meter of the rest of Nahum and has led many experts to call them additions. But they can be defended as necessarily more passionate and rhetorical because they bring the entire prophecy to an end.

> [18]Your shepherds are asleep,
>   O king of Assyria;
>   your nobles slumber.
> Your people are scattered on the mountains
>   with none to gather them.
> [19]There is no assuaging your hurt,
>   your wound is grievous.
> All who hear the news of you
>   clap their hands over you.
> For upon whom has not come
>   your unceasing evil?

Finally vv. 18-19 serve as a summary judgment, typical of Israel's Oracles against Foreign Nations. Sleep is a euphemism for death (Isa 14:18). The leaders have been slain, the people scattered like sheep (1 Kgs 22:17; Ezek 34:7), and there can be no restoration or hope for this fatal wound (Jer 8:22; 10:19; 14:17; 15:18; 30:12; 46:11; Hos 5:13; Mic 1:9). The nations all rejoice at her fall (Ezek 25:6; Isa 55:12). RSV's "hurt" in the first line of v. 19 loses the whole point of this summary. In Hebrew, the word means "shattering," and it echoes the promise first mentioned in Nah 1:13 that God would shatter the yoke of Assyria from Israel's neck. What was promised has now been fulfilled, and the two statements on shattering make a fine inclusion at both ends of the long poem of chaps. 2 and 3, like bookends at the beginning and end of a shelf. This literary device also emphasizes the message of promise in Nahum. When all has been said about the violent destruction of Nineveh, what remains enduring is the *word* given to the prophet by the Lord that he is a God of fidelity and care who never forgets those who trust in the divine mercy and promise.

BIBLIOGRAPHY SUGGESTIONS

JEREMIAH

See the reading suggestions at the end of *Jeremiah 1-25* (volume 9 of *Old Testament Message* series). To these may be added,

Robert Carroll, *From Chaos to Covenant: Prophecy in the Book of Jeremiah* (Crossroad, 1981).

A new and very detailed study which attempts to answer some of the most difficult problems about the nature of the prose passages in Jeremiah and explore the different outlooks of the prophet, his audience and those who handed on his tradition.

William Holladay, "The Identification of the Two Scrolls of Jeremiah," *Vetus Testamentum* 30 (1980) 452-467.

Dr. Holladay identifies the contents of the two scrolls dictated by Jeremiah in chap. 36 according to whether an oracle leaves room for repentence or sees no chance of hope left.

HABAKKUK

Donald Gowan, *The Triumph of Faith in Habakkuk* (John Knox Press, 1976).

A popular treatment of the more important theological and religious themes in Habakkuk, with special interest in the phrase "The Just shall live by faith."

Kevin O'Connell, S.J., "Habakkuk—Spokesman to God," *Currents in Theology and Mission* 6 (1979) 227-231.

He places Habakkuk in the period of 607 to 587 B.C. when violence and injustice were rampant, and he begs God to intercede.

ZEPHANIAH
Arvid Kapelrud, *The Message of the Prophet Zephaniah: Morphology and Ideas* (Oslo: Universitetsforlaget, 1975).

A study of the text and its problems followed by a clear explanation of its major themes and the theology of the prophet.

NAHUM
Walter Maier, *The Book of Nahum* (Baker Book Co., 1959).

This is a conservative analysis of the book which defends the authenticity and integrity of the material, and sets a date earlier than most critics do for the life and prophecy of Nahum.

A. S. van der Woude, "Nahum—A Letter Written in Exile?" *Oudtestamentische Studien* 20 (1977) 108-126.

Identifies the author of the Book of Nahum as an exiled Israelite descended from the people of the Northern Kingdom who were deported to Assyria after 722 B.C. He is writing to the citizens of Judah before the fall of Assyria in 612 B.C.

GENERAL BOOKS ON PROPHECY IN THE LATE SEVENTH CENTURY
Norman Gottwald, *All the Kingdoms of the Earth: Israelite Prophecy and International Relations in the ancient Near East* (Harper and Row, 1964).

A thorough study of the interplay between Israel's prophets and the political problems of the eighth to sixth centuries.

Michael Cogan, *Imperialism and Religion: Assyria, Judah and Israel in the Eighth and Seventh Centuries B.C.E.* (Scholar's Press, 1974).

Cogan explains the political background of Israel's prophetic references to the Assyrians and gives many examples of Assyrian writings to show the parallels.

Richard T. Murphy, O.P., "Zephaniah, Nahum, Habakkuk," *Jerome Biblical Commentary* (Prentice-Hall, 1968) 290-299.

Good introduction and brief remarks on the individual verses of these prophets; a useful reference tool.

Ancient Near Eastern Texts Relating to the Old Testament, edited by James Pritchard (Princeton University Press, 3rd edition, 1969).

This is the standard collection of all major literary works from the Ancient Near East that throw light on biblical passages. It is an indispensable tool of the scholar, and is available in a more popular paperback edition from Princeton in two volumes, titled *The Ancient Near East*.